Youth Violence

Youth Violence

CURRENT RESEARCH AND RECENT PRACTICE INNOVATIONS

EDITED BY

JEFFREY M. JENSON

MATTHEW O. HOWARD

NASW PRESS

National Association of Social Workers
Washington, DC

Ruth W. Mayden, MSS, LSW, *President*

Josephine Nieves, MSW, PhD, *Executive Director*

Cheryl Mayberry, *Director, Member Services and Publications*
Paula L. Delo, *Executive Editor*
Steph Selice, *Senior Editor*
William Schroeder, *Staff Editor*
Anne Grant, Hyde Park Publishing, *Copy Editor*
Deborah E. Patton, *Indexer*
Donna Daniels Verdier, *Proofreader*

Cover by Metadog Design Group, Washington, DC
Typeset by Pen & Palette Unlimited, Silver Spring, Maryland
Printed and bound by Sheridan Books, Inc., Springfield, Virginia

Library of Congress Cataloging-in-Publication Data

Youth violence : current research and recent practice innovations /
    edited by Jeffrey M. Jenson, Matthew O. Howard.
        p.   cm.
    Includes bibliographical references and index.
    ISBN 0-87101-311-8 (alk. paper)
    1. Juvenile delinquency—United States.   2. Youth—Crimes against—
United States.   3. Problem youth—United States.   4. Children—Crimes
against—United States.   5. Violence in children—United States.
6. Children and violence—United States.   I. Jenson, Jeffrey M.   II.
Howard, Matthew O.
HV9104.Y6859   1999
364.36'0973—dc21   99-41182
                                                                        CIP

Contents

List of Tables and Figures

Tables

Figures

Foreword

Violence permeates American society in ways unforeseen by past generations. American children grow up listening to media descriptions of violent acts committed by citizens in their communities. Television shows and motion pictures graphically portray interpersonal acts of violence. Computer games and other forms of multimedia entertainment expose young people to realistic depictions of aggression and violence. Many children and youths witness violence in their homes, schools, and communities. Sadly, violence has become part of the fabric of American culture.

Youth violence has long been a pressing concern for the nation's mayors and for other elected officials. Recent declines in rates of inner-city violence, described in chapter 1 of this book, offer some hope for the future. Yet violence continues to plague many American cities. Equally disturbing is the spread of youth violence to the nation's suburbs and rural communities. All-too-frequent reports of children attacking classmates and teachers at school have raised youth violence to the top of our social agenda.

The tragedy at Columbine High School in Littleton, Colorado, on April 20, 1999, provided a shocking revelation that violence pervades even those suburban enclaves that thought themselves safe from such incidents. The events at Columbine have had a profound effect on neighboring Denver, on Colorado, and on the nation. Policies promoting violence prevention and handgun control are being reexamined by elected officials across the country in light of Columbine and other school shootings. Individuals and groups once divided by deep philosophical differences regarding their approaches to violence prevention are sitting at the same table to generate practical solutions to violence.

Many episodes of youth violence do not receive the media attention granted to recent tragic incidents. Nearly all American cities experienced significant increases in youth violence between the late 1980s and mid-1990s. In Denver, we witnessed significant increases in gang-related violence in the early 1990s, culminating in what was labeled the Summer of Violence in 1993. The Colorado State Legislature responded to the increase in youth violence by enacting new laws to curb gang activity and punish violent offenders. At the municipal level, we established the Mayor's Safe City Initiative, a multiagency prevention and treatment strategy designed to curb incidents of youth violence. Like other American cities, Denver invested more resources in developing positive activities and opportunities for young people. We also established a youth curfew and convened communitywide summits to involve young people in reducing violence.

In Denver, the combined efforts of law enforcement, elected officials, students, community members, social workers, teachers, and other human services professionals have led to significant reductions in levels of youth violence. However, there is much yet to accomplish. Violence continues to differentially affect African American males in our city and in all American cities. Nationwide, homicide remains the leading cause of death among young African American males and the second leading cause of death among all teenagers. These patterns should be disturbing to all Americans.

What is the next step in ameliorating youth violence? Surely we can place more police in our schools and on our streets, increase penalties for young offenders, and hold more community and policy summits. We can also direct schools and agencies to share more information about troubled youths. However, if we promote deterrence at the expense of early intervention and prevention, we will not have done enough. If we are to overcome youth violence, we need to understand its root causes and implement innovative and effective prevention and treatment approaches.

In this book, Jeffrey M. Jenson, PhD, and Matthew O. Howard, PhD, have brought together an impressive array of scholars to identify and discuss types of youth violence prevalent in American society today. This timely compilation will be useful to practitioners and policymakers interested in violence prevention and treatment. Causes of youth violence are discussed and linked to promising and effective programs. Strategies to assess the likelihood of aggression or violence in children and youths are identified. Special consideration is given to recent increases in violence among girls and to gang- and drug-related violence. Promising new community- and school-based interventions, including antibullying programs and spatial mapping strategies to reduce violence in school environments, are identified. In the last chapter, Jenson and Howard identify a number of critical practice and policy priorities necessary to reduce youth violence.

In all likelihood, we will never know all we need to know about the causes and prevention of youth violence. This book, however, is a positive step in the right direction. Practitioners, policymakers, students, and citizens should become familiar with the content in this book and apply it to their own communities. Together, we can create positive opportunities for our children and create environments free of aggression and violence.

Wellington E. Webb, Mayor
City and County of Denver
President, U.S. Conference of Mayors

Denver, Colorado
August 1999

Acknowledgments

Contributors to this book took great care in addressing the complex issue of youth violence. I thank each of them for their commitment to improving the lives of America's most vulnerable young citizens. I have been supported and influenced by many colleagues in the years leading to the publication of this book. Special thanks to J. David Hawkins and Richard F. Catalano of the University of Washington and to Mark Fraser of the University of North Carolina at Chapel Hill. Finally, thanks to Mary, Nils, and Anna, who keep the home fires burning.

Jeffrey M. Jenson, PhD

To Shanti Khinduka—a principled and visionary leader and enduring friend of social work.

Matthew O. Howard, PhD

Part I

Prevalence, Etiology, and Assessment of Youth Violence

Chapter 1

Prevalence and Patterns of Youth Violence

Jeffrey M. Jenson and
Matthew O. Howard

Violence touches the lives of nearly every American child and adolescent. Many young people in the United States grow up in familial, social, and environmental conditions in which violence and aggression are commonplace. The consequences of violence are devastating for these children. Shattered by witnessing acts of interpersonal violence during childhood, some youths withdraw from normal school and community activities in adolescence. Others perpetrate violent acts as they mature and grow older. Children fortunate enough to live outside the immediate threat of aggressive behavior often feel the effects of violence indirectly, through fear of victimization and constant concern for personal safety.

Youth violence has deep roots in American society (Eron, Gentry, & Schlegel, 1994; Reiss & Roth, 1993; Zimring, 1998). Accounts of violence committed by young persons are found in case studies of juvenile delinquents and in popular literature dating to the early 1900s (for example, Shaw, 1930). Early descriptions portrayed violent youths as wayward adolescents who were poor, mean spirited, and victims of inadequate parental support (Bremner, 1970; Mack, 1910). Individualized treatment and punishment, made possible by the creation of a separate juvenile court system in 1899, were considered by early social reformers as important elements in the rehabilitation of violent youths (Platt, 1969). The dual emphasis on treating and punishing violent youths continues to be part of the modern juvenile justice system (Jenson & Howard, 1998).

Practitioners and social scientists have learned much about violent youth behavior during the past three decades. Early studies indicated that most violent acts were committed by a small percentage of youths in a given birth cohort (West & Farrington, 1973; Wolfgang, Figlio, & Sellin, 1972). The prevalence of violent offending among children and youths has indeed been relatively stable over time (U.S. Department of Justice, 1998). Today, a small percentage of adolescents still accounts for a disproportionate share of youth violence. However, the prevalence of violent behavior among the nation's youths has risen and fallen rather sharply during the past 15 years. Increases in violent crime, most pronounced between 1985 and 1995, have been attributed to juvenile gangs (Spergel, 1995) and to a rise in crack cocaine and handgun use (Blumstein, 1995). A reduction in violence in 1996 signaled a welcome reversal of the decade-long trend of rising rates of youth aggression. Credit for the decrease in youth violence, although far from clear, has been attributed to enhanced law enforcement efforts, violence prevention programs, and healthy economic conditions (Butterfield, 1996).

The decline in youth violence has been welcome news to legislators and public policy officials searching for effective ways to prevent violent behavior. However, the disturbing nature of recent violent acts committed by young people continues to be the subject of public attention and debate. As this book goes to press, citizens in Colorado and across the nation are in a state of shock over a school shooting spree that left 14 high school students and one teacher dead in an affluent Denver suburb (Brooke, 1999). On April 20, 1999, two heavily armed adolescents entered Columbine High School in Littleton, Colorado, intent on killing students and destroying the building. The two perpetrators, 17- and 18-year-old boys enrolled in the school, were motivated by a desire for vengeance attributed to rejection they felt from popular student athletes. Negative racial attitudes expressed by the perpetrators also appeared to be a motivation for at least one of the murders. The boys' mission ended in suicide, leaving a stunned nation searching for explanations for such a horrific act.

Other upsetting accounts of aggression and homicide further illustrate the nature of American youth violence during the past decade. Stories of violent incidents can be found in every state, each report more chilling than the last.

- In 1997, two pizza deliverymen in a small New Jersey town were lured by a 17- and an 18-year-old to an abandoned house, where they were murdered in cold blood. Officials indicated that the suspects wanted to experience the "thrill" of killing someone (McFadden, 1997).

- In a span of four months in 1997, three Nevada youths were killed by rival gang members near Reno, sending shock waves through a local high school (Crowe, 1997).

- In 1998, a 13-year-old boy and his 11-year-old cousin opened fire on students in an Arkansas middle school, killing four girls and a teacher. The guns used in the crime were stolen from the home of the grandfather of one of the boys (Bragg, 1998).

- A 15-year-old Oregon youth fired a .22 caliber rifle into a crowded school cafeteria in 1998, killing one student and wounding 26 others. Police investigations led to the boy's home, where his parents were found dead. Schoolmates said the boy often talked of bombs, guns, and torturing animals (Egan, 1998).

- A shooting in West Paducah, Kentucky, in 1998 left three high school students dead and two wounded. Students were attacked while attending a morning prayer circle before school (U.S. Department of Justice, Office of Juvenile Justice and Delinquency Prevention, 1999).

It is difficult to understand such violent acts. Knowledge of the factors and societal conditions that influence young people to engage in violence is limited. Youth violence takes many forms; perpetrators often are not perceived as dangerous by parents, teachers, peers, or neighbors before their violent outbursts. This makes prediction and prevention of violent behavior challenging. Regardless of the reasons for violence, however, the effects of violence on children, youths, and society are significant.

EFFECTS OF CHILDHOOD AND YOUTH VIOLENCE

Acts of youth violence exact significant individual, social, and economic costs. Homicide is the second leading cause of death among teenagers and the leading cause of death among young African American males (Snyder & Sickmund, 1995).

American children grow up in a much more violent society than children in many other countries. Homicide rates for American youths are among the highest in the world (Zimring, 1998). U.S. firearm homicide rates for citizens ages 15 to 24 are five times the rate in Canada and 30 times the rate in Japan (U.S. Department of Justice, Office of Juvenile Justice and Delinquency Prevention, 1999). Despite recent increases in violence in many European countries, violent youth crime remains significantly higher in the United States than in Europe (Pfeiffer, 1998).

The public health and law enforcement costs associated with preventing violence and treating victims and perpetrators of violent acts are staggering. Hospital emergency treatment centers across the country reported significant increases in the number of adolescent violence victims treated in the 1990s (for example, Centers for Disease Control and Prevention, 1994). Reiss and Roth (1993) estimated that losses to victims and society average more than $50,000 per attempted or completed rape and $16,000 per assault. Responses by law enforcement add additional costs, often too complex to measure adequately.

Other adverse consequences of violence are difficult to assess. Many children in the United States report that fear of becoming a victim of violence prevents them from living a normal life (Ollendick & King, 1994). In 1997, 87 percent of high school seniors stated that they sometimes or often worried about crime and violence (Johnston, O'Malley, & Bachman, 1998). Violence was the single biggest problem in their schools, said 20 percent of 13- to 15-year-old students in a recent national poll conducted by the New York Times and CBS News (Bureau of Justice Statistics, 1998). The recent school shootings can only add to the high levels of fear expressed by school-age youths.

Violent victimization is associated with symptoms of childhood and adolescent psychological trauma (Garbarino, Dubrow, Kostelny, & Pardo, 1992); such symptoms can last for months or even years after a violent incident (for example, Pynoos et al., 1987). Furthermore, exposure to violence during childhood produces significant emotional pain, increases the risk of early involvement in aggressive behavior, and may lead to school dropout, delinquency, and drug abuse during adolescence (Dryfoos, 1998).

PURPOSE OF THE BOOK

The adverse consequences and disturbing nature of youth violence during the final decade of the twentieth century have prompted substantial changes in public policy (Butterfield, 1996; Zimring, 1998). Policy reform, motivated in part by recent trends in violence, has led to modifications in the way youths are handled, treated, and punished in the American child welfare and juvenile and criminal justice systems (Jenson & Howard, 1998). Elected officials, school personnel, psychologists, and social workers have intensified the search for effective ways to address the conditions contributing to youth violence. New approaches to preventing and treating youth violence have been developed; some have been evaluated.

The purpose of this book is to identify innovative individual, family, school, and community approaches to the prevention and treatment of youth violence. It examines recent trends in violence and factors related to the onset of violent and aggressive conduct. We hope that practitioners working with high-risk or violent youths will use the etiological and practice knowledge described here.

We begin by defining childhood and youth violence and by reviewing historical and recent trends in youth violence.

DEFINITIONS

Youth violence is defined in numerous ways. In this book, we address interpersonal violence committed by children and adolescents below the legal age of adulthood, defined by the National Academy of Sciences Panel on the Understanding and Control of Violent Behavior (Reiss & Roth, 1993) as "behavior by persons against persons that intentionally threatens, attempts, or actually, inflicts physical harm" (p. 35).

Because youth violence often involves contact with the juvenile or criminal justice systems, we also consider legal definitions of violence. The U.S. Department of Justice (1998) recognizes murder, aggravated assault, forcible rape, and robbery as violent index offenses. Children or youths who have attempted or committed these acts also fall within our definition of violent offenders.

TRENDS

There are three primary sources of information about trends in youth violence. Law enforcement data provide annual arrest rates for violent crimes by age (U.S. Department of Justice, 1998). The prevalence of self-reported youth violence has been assessed by surveys of representative samples of American youths (Elliott, Huizinga, & Morse, 1986; Johnston et al., 1998; Loeber, Farrington, & Waschbusch, 1998). Surveys of self-reported violence vary in scope, methodology, and generalizability but do include reports of violence that may be undetected by law enforcement. A third source is the National Crime Victimization Survey (NCVS), an annual assessment of crime victims conducted with approximately 50,000 individuals age 12 and older (Bureau of Justice Statistics, 1998; Perkins, 1997; Rand, 1998). Data from the NCVS provide a profile of who is most likely to be victimized by violent crime. Evidence from each of these sources is reviewed below.

Official Accounts of Youth Violence

Most crimes committed by young people in the United States are property offenses, such as theft or vandalism (Snyder, 1998; U.S. Department of Justice, 1998). Property crime arrest rates have remained relatively stable during the past three decades (Figure 1-1). Arrests for property crimes were highest in 1974, when nearly 3 percent of young people between ages 10 and 17 were arrested. Rates decreased between 1974 and 1984, then rose slowly between 1985 and 1991; they have been relatively stable since 1992. In 1997, there were approximately 2,300 arrests for every 100,000 youths in the United States (Snyder, 1998)—the lowest property arrest rate since 1984.

Figure 1-1. Juvenile Arrest Rates for Property Crimes, 1973–1997

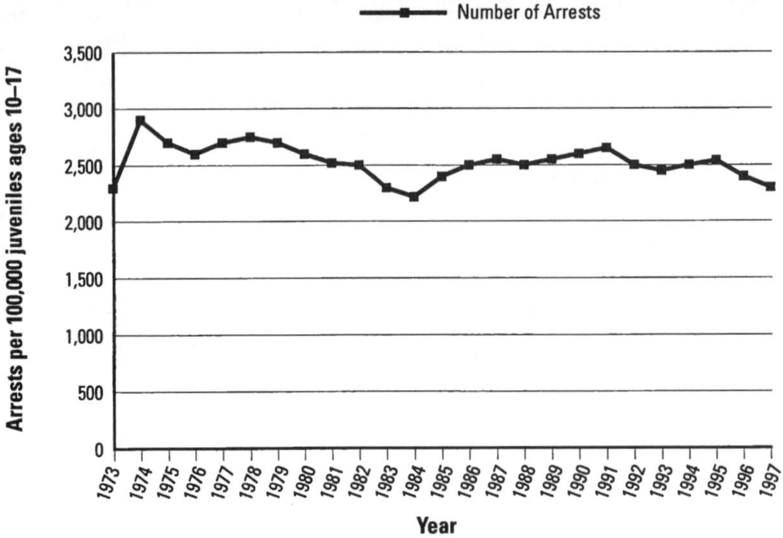

NOTE: Data are derived from Snyder, H. N. (1998, December). Juvenile arrests, 1997. *Juvenile Justice Bulletin.* Washington, DC: U.S. Department of Justice, Office of Juvenile Justice and Delinquency Prevention. Property crimes refer to the offenses of burglary, larceny-theft, motor vehicle, and arson.

Arrest rates for violent youth crime between 1973 and 1997 reveal a very different pattern. After more than a decade of stability, violent crime arrest rates increased 68 percent between 1987 and 1994 (Snyder, 1998). Fewer than 350 of every 100,000 adolescents were arrested annually for violent crimes in the United States before 1987. By 1994, the average arrest rate for violent crimes had increased 43 percent, exceeding 500 per 100,000 youths. However, after a seven-year trend of increasing rates beginning in 1988, violent crime decreased by 23 percent between 1994 and 1997 (Figure 1-2).

Trends in arrest rates between 1980 and 1997 for murder, forcible rape, robbery, and aggravated assault are shown in Figures 1-3 and 1-4. Dramatic changes are apparent for murder. In 1980, there were only six murder arrests for every 100,000 youths. Arrests for murder decreased between 1980 and 1984, but rose sharply after 1984, reaching a peak in 1993 of more than 14 of every 100,000 youths. Though murder rates declined 40 percent between 1993 and 1997, the 1997 figure remained 21 percent higher than the 1987 rate (Snyder, 1998).

Arrest rates for forcible rape by juveniles have fluctuated less than murder rates. They peaked in 1991, when more than 23 of every 100,000 youths were arrested. In 1997, when 18 of every 100,000 youths were arrested for rape, the rate was at its lowest since 1983.

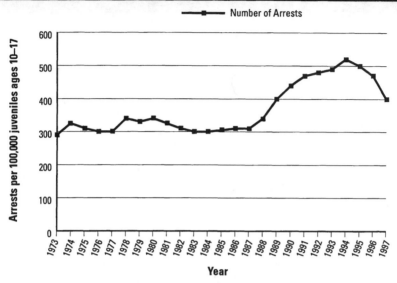

Figure 1-2. **Juvenile Arrest Rates for Violent Crimes, 1973–1997**

NOTE: Data are derived from Snyder (1998). Violent crimes are the offenses of murder, forcible rape, robbery, and aggravated assault.

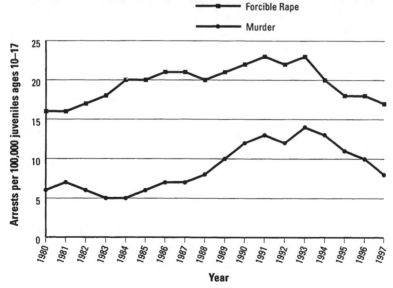

Figure 1-3. **Juvenile Arrest Rates for Murder and Forcible Rape, 1980–1997**

NOTE: Data are derived from Snyder (1998).

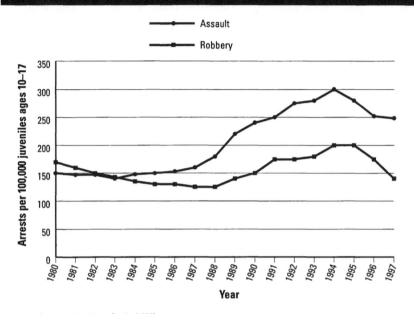

Figure 1-4. **Juvenile Arrest Rates for Aggravated Assault and Robbery, 1980–1997**

Note: Data are derived from Snyder (1998).

Aggravated assault arrest rates show a pattern similar to murder rates. Approximately 150 of every 100,000 youths were arrested for an aggravated assault in 1980. Aggravated assaults among juveniles then fell slightly between 1980 and 1983 but rose sharply after 1983 to a peak in 1994, when 300 of every 100,000 adolescents were arrested. Between 1994 and 1997 arrest rates declined 16 percent (Snyder, 1998).

Youth involvement in robbery declined from 1980 to 1988. Like arrest patterns for murder, forcible rape, and aggravated assault, robbery arrests increased significantly (60 percent) between 1988 and 1994. The juvenile robbery arrest rate then fell 30 percent between 1995 and 1997. In 1997, fewer than 150 of every 100,000 youths were arrested for robbery (Figure 1-4).

In sum, after more than a decade of stability, violent crime arrests increased significantly between 1987 and 1994. Since 1994, arrest rates for violent youth crime have fallen between 3 percent and 6 percent each year. These data provide some basis for optimism concerning youth violence at the turn of the century. Nevertheless, annual arrest rates for violent crimes in 1997 were nearly 29 percent higher than in 1987 (Snyder, 1998).

Surveys of Youth Violence

Official arrest data often underestimate the actual amount of juvenile violence, because many aggressive acts are undetected and therefore do not result in arrest (Snyder & Sickmund, 1995). Self-reported survey data allow practitioners and policymakers to analyze the prevalence of violence as reported by representative samples of American youths. Although they are appealing for these reasons, self-reported data are limited in that surveys assessing violence are seldom repeated annually. Therefore, it is often difficult to examine long-term trends in violent behavior using self-reported survey data.

One exception is the Monitoring the Future Study, an annual assessment of delinquency and drug use in a random sample of approximately 16,000 public school students (Johnston et al., 1998). In-school surveys of nationally representative samples of high school seniors have been conducted since 1975. Self-reported delinquency has been assessed since 1983.

The study assesses several violent behaviors. One item asks seniors if they had "been involved in a fight where a group of your friends were against another group." Another asks them to indicate if they had ever "used a knife or gun or some other thing to get something from a person." The percentages of students indicating that they have been involved in either of these two violent behaviors have remained relatively stable. Between 1983 and 1996, from 18 percent to 22 percent of seniors reported fighting during the previous year. Less than 5 percent of seniors used knives or guns during each of the years examined. However, self-reported fighting and use of weapons did increase slightly between 1989 and 1993, suggesting some concordance with the increase in violent juvenile arrests during this period.

The Youth Risk Behavior Survey examined the prevalence of nonfatal violent acts among students in grades 9 to 12 in 1991, 1993, 1995, and 1997. A recent report by Brener, Simon, Krug, and Lowry (1999) shows that violent youth behaviors declined between 1991 and 1997. The percentage of students participating in a physical fight during the previous year decreased from 43 percent in 1991 to 37 percent in 1997. Twenty-six percent of students carried a gun, knife, or club during the previous 30 days in 1991, compared with 18 percent in 1997. Boys were more likely than girls to engage in violence, and ninth- and 10th-grade students displayed violent behaviors at significantly higher rates than 12th-grade students. It should be noted that school-based samples miss truants and dropouts, who are at increased risk for violence.

Recent self-reported data collected by the U.S. Department of Justice Office of Juvenile Justice and Delinquency Prevention's Causes and Correlates of Juvenile Delinquency Program (Loeber & Farrington, 1998;

Thornberry, Huizinga, & Loeber, 1995) provide additional evidence about the prevalence of violent behavior among juveniles. Using data from samples of high-risk youths in Denver, Pittsburgh, and Rochester, investigators found that approximately one-third of males in each of the samples were serious offenders (Loeber & Farrington, 1998). Chronic male and female offenders constituted 14 percent to 17 percent of study samples at each site and accounted for 75 percent to 82 percent of all violent crimes (Thornberry et al., 1995). The majority of violent offenders first committed serious non-violent offenses between the ages of 7 and 14. Other self-report studies cor-roborate these findings, suggesting that a small percentage of youths are responsible for a disproportionate amount of youth violence (Cernkovich, Giordano, & Pugh, 1983; Farrington & West, 1993).

In sum, self-reported violent behavior has been relatively stable during the past two decades. Yet the number of American youths who carry weapons and display aggressive behaviors remains unacceptably high. Recent decreases in violence, although promising, have also been inconsistent across youth subgroups: Boys and youths of color continue to engage in violence at higher rates than other adolescents.

Victims of Violent Crime

Data derived from the NCVS reveal that youths are frequently the vic-tims of violent crime (Bureau of Justice Statistics, 1998; Perkins, 1997). In 1997, adolescents between ages 12 and 19 were two times more likely than adults ages 25 to 34 and three times more likely than adults ages 35 to 49 to be victims of murder, aggravated assault, forcible rape, sexual assault, and robbery (Rand, 1998). The rate of victimization for these five serious offenses ranged from 96 per 1,000 people for 16- to 19-year-olds to four per 1,000 people age 65 or older (Table 1-1). Age patterns of victims of serious violent crime have been relatively stable over time: The likelihood of being a victim of a violent crime increases during the adolescent years, peaks at about age 20, and then declines steadily (Perkins, 1997).

RACE, ETHNICITY, GENDER, AND VIOLENCE

Racial, ethnic, and gender differences in the prevalence of youth violence have been observed for much of the past century (Hawkins, Laub, & Lauritsen, 1998). Racial and ethnic comparisons have been confined primarily to vio-lent acts committed by African Americans and Caucasians, because official statistics seldom include other ethnic groups in routine data collection (Hawkins et al., 1998), although several surveys indicate that Hispanics engage in violence less often than African Americans but more often than Caucasians (Rodriguez, 1988; Valdez, Nourjah, & Nourjah, 1988).

Table 1-1. **Rates[a] of Violent Crime Victimization by Age, 1997**

Age (years)	Victimization				
	All Violent Crimes	Rape/Sexual Assault	Robbery	Aggravated Assault	Simple Assault
12–15	87.9	2.5	8.2	15.1	62.0
16–19	96.2	5.6	10.2	24.6	55.8
20–24	67.8	2.4	7.4	17.0	40.9
25–34	46.9	2.3	4.7	9.5	30.4
35–49	32.2	3.7	27.9	7.4	20.4
50–64	14.6	0.2	2.2	2.8	9.4
65 or older	4.4	0.2	0.9	0.6	2.8

NOTE: Data are from the National Crime Victimization Survey (Rand, 1998). The survey includes rape, sexual assault, robbery, and aggravated and simple assault as violent crimes.

[a] Rates represent number of victimizations per 1,000 people in the United States.

African Americans are consistently overrepresented in official accounts of violent youth crime. In 1995 they represented approximately 15 percent of the youth population (up to age 17) but accounted for nearly 50 percent of all youths arrested for violent crime. The disparity is particularly high for the most violent offenses: 61 percent of American youths arrested for homicide in 1994 were African American. In 1995 African Americans accounted for nearly 45 percent of forcible rape arrests and 42 percent of aggravated assault arrests (Snyder & Sickmund, 1995). Self-report data show a similar pattern: African Americans indicate that they participate in serious and violent offending at higher rates than Caucasians (Elliott, 1994; Elliott & Ageton, 1980; Huizinga, Loeber, & Thornberry, 1994).

Whether one considers official arrest or self-reported data, boys are more likely than girls to be aggressive or to engage in violent conduct. In 1996 girls were responsible for only 15 percent of all violent crimes and 27 percent of all property crimes committed by juveniles (Snyder, 1997). However, girls engaged in aggressive and violent behavior at much higher rates in the 1990s than ever before. Between 1987 and 1997 robbery arrests for girls increased 52 percent, and aggravated assault arrests increased 101 percent (Snyder, 1998). Arrests corresponding to the violent crime index increased twice as fast for females (130 percent) as for males (64 percent) between 1981 and 1994. Additional trends in violent behavior among girls are discussed by Cathryn Potter in chapter 5.

Describing racial, ethnic, and gender differences in rates of violence does little to explain the variation. There is no consensus among researchers as to why youths of color, particularly African Americans, participate in violent behavior more frequently than Caucasians. Blumstein (1995) offers one hypothesis to explain recent increases in violence among young African American males. He suggests that the increase in youth homicide in 1985 can be traced to the recruitment of young people, many of them African American, into the crack cocaine market. He argues that many young African Americans obtained guns to protect themselves while engaging in drug distribution activities and that over time these guns were diffused to the broader community. Blumstein suggests that parallel increases in violent crime between 1985 and 1994 not only among African American youths but also among Caucasian youths, who were not heavily recruited into crack cocaine distribution, support the diffusion hypothesis.

Other investigators (for example, Hawkins et al., 1998) criticize such explanations for relying too much on individual characteristics of adolescents to explain violent conduct. They argue that generalizations about race, ethnicity, and crime based on individual-level explanations may be inaccurate or confounded because of a failure to include community-level factors (for example, inequities in social and economic opportunities) in theoretical explanations of violence (Jankowski, 1995; Sampson & Wilson, 1995). In support of this criticism, studies have found that differences in violence between African Americans and Caucasians decrease significantly when violence rates are adjusted for factors such as geographical location or socioeconomic status (Elliott, 1994; Griffith & Bell, 1989). Greater attention to the effect of community-level factors on violence is needed to help unravel existing racial and ethnic differences in rates of violent behavior.

ORGANIZATION OF THE BOOK

Childhood and adolescence are periods of significant change and development. Lifelong attitudes, skills, and behaviors are formed as young people respond to family, social, and environmental influences that affect their lives. Interventions seeking to promote healthy development and prevent or treat aggression and violence must address such factors early. In this book, chapter authors identify effective new approaches to preventing and treating childhood aggression and youth violence and address critical influences associated with different types of youth violence.

The book is divided into three parts. The first part discusses etiological factors and strategies to assess propensity toward and involvement in violent behavior. Knowledge of the causes of youth violence and factors to consider in assessing children and youths displaying aggressive or violent behaviors are identified.

In chapter 2, Matthew Howard and Jeffrey Jenson examine a host of biological, psychological, social, and environmental factors related to violence, encouraging practitioners to become familiar with causal explanations of violence and to incorporate etiological factors into practice with aggressive children and adolescents.

Mark Macgowan identifies strategies and instruments for assessing aggressive and violent tendencies in children and youths in chapter 3. He discusses practical issues associated with the assessment process, outlining the strengths and weaknesses of different approaches. He then reviews specific instruments practitioners will find useful in working with aggressive children or violent youths, using case examples to illustrate how these instruments are applied in practice settings.

Innovative prevention and treatment strategies are explored in part 2. The chapters examine interventions in the context of victimization and gender and in the social environments of schools and communities, review programs targeting violence associated with substance abuse and gang involvement, and use case examples to help readers think about how interventions can be used to help clients. Each chapter author addresses (1) a specific type of youth violence, (2) factors associated with the violent behavior, (3) critical practice issues, and (4) promising new prevention and clinical interventions.

In chapter 4, Melissa Jonson-Reid traces the complex relationship between childhood victimization and involvement in violent conduct during adolescence. She reviews evidence indicating that many childhood victims of abuse suffer long-term effects that increase the likelihood that they will perpetrate violence later in life. Jonson-Reid calls for a new practice and research agenda focusing on how to prevent childhood victims from becoming perpetrators.

Cathryn Potter discusses violent behavior in girls in chapter 5. Noting the narrowing gap in violence rates between boys and girls, she argues for additional testing of theoretical models to explain violence in girls. Potter identifies a number of practice strategies for intervening with girls and argues for more gender-specific programs for violent girls.

In chapter 6, Ron Avi Astor, Lorelei Atalie Vargas, Ronald O'Neal Pitner, and Heather Ann Meyer review recent accounts of school violence. They outline a mapping procedure useful for tracking and predicting acts of violence in school settings and delineate innovative school-based prevention and treatment programs and strategies to promote school safety.

James Moran and Jeffrey Jenson analyze the relationship between adolescent substance abuse and violence in chapter 7. They review ways in which the relationship between substance use and violent youth crime is interpreted, noting common correlates of substance abuse and violence and innovative prevention and treatment strategies targeting both behaviors.

In chapter 8, James Herbert Williams and Richard Van Dorn discuss risk factors for serious delinquency and gang violence, recent trends in gang membership, and clinical issues associated with assessing and treating gang members. Using a case example as illustration, they review promising prevention and treatment approaches targeting at-risk youths and gang members.

What can be done to improve the efficacy of violence prevention and treatment strategies is outlined in the final part and chapter of the book. In it we offer policy recommendations addressing structural factors related to the onset and maintenance of youth violence.

REFERENCES

Blumstein, A. (1995). Violence by young people: Why the deadly nexus? *National Institute of Justice Journal, 229,* 2–9. Washington, DC: U.S. Department of Justice, National Institute of Justice.

Bragg, R. (1998, March 26). Arkansas boys held as prosecutors weigh options. *New York Times,* p. 1.

Bremner, R. H. (Ed.). (1970). *Children and youth in America: A documentary history.* Cambridge, MA: Harvard University Press.

Brener, N. D., Simon, T. R., Krug, E. G., & Lowry, R. (1999). Recent trends in violence-related behaviors among high school students in the United States. *JAMA, 282,* 440–446.

Brooke, J. (1999, April 21). Two youths in Colorado school said to gun down as many as 23 and kill themselves in a siege. *New York Times,* p. 1.

Bureau of Justice Statistics. (1998). *National Criminal Victimization Survey, 1997.* Washington, DC: Author.

Butterfield, F. (1996, May 12). States revamping youth crime laws. *New York Times,* p. 1.

Centers for Disease Control and Prevention. (1994). Homicide among 15–19 year old males: United States, 1963–1991. *JAMA, 272,* 1572.

Cernkovich, S. A., Giordano, P. C., & Pugh, M. D. (1983, November). *The chronic offender and self-report measures of chronic delinquency.* Paper presented at the annual meeting of the American Society of Criminology, Denver.

Crowe, J. (1997, March 29). Galena student is the third Reno-area youth to die in 4 months. *Reno* [NV] *Gazette-Journal,* p. 2.

Dryfoos, J. (1998). *Safe passage: Making it through adolescence in a risky society.* New York: Oxford University Press.

Egan, T. (1998, May 22). Student, 15, accused of killing 3 and of wounding 26 in Oregon. *New York Times,* p. 1.

Elliott, D. S. (1994). Serious violent offenders: Onset, developmental course, and termination—The American Society of Criminology 1993 presidential address. *Criminology, 32,* 1–21.

Elliott, D. S., & Ageton, S. (1980). Reconciling race and class differences in self-reported and official estimates of delinquency. *American Sociological Review, 45,* 95–110.

Elliott, D. S., Huizinga, D., & Morse, B. (1986). Self-reported violent offending. *Journal of Interpersonal Violence, 1,* 472–514.

Eron, L. D., Gentry, J. G., & Schlegel, P. (Eds.). (1994). *Reasons to hope: A psychological perspective on violence and youth.* Washington, DC: American Psychological Association.

Farrington, D. P., & West, D. J. (1993). Criminal, penal, and life histories of life offenders: Risk and protective factors and early identification. *Criminal Behaviour and Mental Health, 3,* 492–523.

Garbarino, J., Dubrow, N., Kostelny, K., & Pardo, C. (1992). *Children in danger: Coping with the consequences of community violence.* San Francisco: Jossey-Bass.

Griffith, E. H., & Bell, C. C. (1989). Recent trends in suicide and homicide among blacks. *JAMA, 262,* 2265–2269.

Hawkins, D. F., Laub, J. H., & Lauritsen, J. L. (1998). Race, ethnicity, and serious juvenile offending. In R. Loeber & D. P. Farrington (Eds.), *Serious & violent juvenile offenders: Risk factors and successful interventions* (pp. 30–46). Thousand Oaks, CA: Sage Publications.

Huizinga, D. H., Loeber, R., & Thornberry, T. P. (1994). *Urban delinquency and substance abuse: Initial findings.* Washington, DC: U.S. Department of Justice, Office of Juvenile Justice and Delinquency Prevention.

Jankowski, M. S. (1995). Ethnography, inequality, and crime in the low-income community. In J. Hagan & R. Peterson (Eds.), *Crime and inequality* (pp. 80–94). Stanford, CA: Stanford University Press.

Jenson, J. M., & Howard, M. O. (1998). Youth crime, public policy, and practice in the juvenile justice system: Recent trends and needed reforms. *Social Work, 43,* 324–334.

Johnston, L. D., O'Malley, P. M., & Bachman, J. G. (1998). *Drug use, drinking, and smoking: National survey results from high school, college, and young adult populations.* Washington, DC: National Institute on Drug Abuse.

Loeber, R., & Farrington, D. P. (Eds.). (1998). *Serious & violent juvenile offenders. Risk factors and successful interventions.* Thousand Oaks, CA: Sage Publications.

Loeber, R., Farrington, D. P., & Waschbusch, D. A. (1998). Serious and violent juvenile offenders. In R. Loeber & D. P. Farrington (Eds.), *Serious & violent juvenile offenders: Risk factors and successful interventions* (pp. 13–29). Thousand Oaks, CA: Sage Publications.

Mack, J. (1910). The juvenile court as a legal institution. In J. Adams (Ed.), *The child, the clinic, and the court* (pp. 290–297). New York: New Republic.

McFadden, R. D. (1997, April 24). Two youths held in New Jersey in thrill-killings of 2 pizza men. *New York Times,* p. 1.

Ollendick, T. H., & King, N. J. (1994). Fears and their level of interference in adolescents. *Behaviour Research and Therapy, 32,* 635–638.

Perkins, C. A. (1997, July). *Age patterns of victims of serious violent crimes* (Bureau of Justice Statistics Special Report). Washington, DC: U.S. Department of Justice.

Platt, A. (1969). *The child savers.* Chicago: University of Chicago Press.

Pfeiffer, C. (1998). Juvenile crime and violence in Europe. In M. Tonry (Ed.), *Crime and justice: A review of research* (pp. 255–328). Chicago: University of Chicago Press.

Pynoos, R. S., Frederick, C., Nader, K., Arroyo, E., Steinberg, A., Eth, S., Nunex, F., & Fairbanks, L. (1987). Life threat and posttraumatic stress in school-age children. *Archives of General Psychiatry, 44,* 1057–1063.

Rand, M. (1998, December). *Criminal victimization, 1997. Changes 1996–1997 with trends 1993–97* (Bureau of Justice Statistics Special Report). Washington, DC: U.S. Department of Justice.

Reiss, A. J., & Roth, J. A. (Eds.). (1993). *Understanding and preventing violence.* Washington, DC: National Academy Press.

Rodriguez, O. (1988). Hispanics and homicide in New York City. In J. F. Kraus, S. B. Sorenson, & P. D. Juarez (Eds.), *Proceedings of research conference on violence and homicide in Hispanic communities* (pp. 67–84). Los Angeles: University of California Press.

Sampson, R. J., & Wilson, W. J. (1995). Toward a theory of race, crime, and urban inequity. In J. Hagan & R. Peterson (Eds.), *Crime and inequality* (pp. 80–94). Stanford, CA: Stanford University Press.

Shaw, C. R. (1930). *The jack-roller. A delinquent boy's own story.* Chicago: University of Chicago Press.

Snyder, H. N. (1997, October). Juvenile arrests, 1996. *Juvenile Justice Bulletin.* Washington, DC: U.S. Department of Justice, Office of Juvenile Justice and Delinquency Prevention.

Snyder, H. N. (1998, December). Juvenile arrests, 1997. *Juvenile Justice Bulletin.* Washington, DC: U.S. Department of Justice, Office of Juvenile Justice and Delinquency Prevention.

Snyder, H. N., & Sickmund, M. (1995). *Juvenile offenders and victims: A national report.* Washington, DC: U.S. Department of Justice, Office of Juvenile Justice and Delinquency Prevention.

Spergel, I. A. (1995). *The youth gang problem: A community approach.* New York: Oxford University Press.

Thornberry, T. P., Huizinga, D., & Loeber, R. (1995). The prevention of serious delinquency and violence: Implications from the Program of Research on the Causes and Correlates of Delinquency. In J. C. Howell, B. Krisberg, J. D. Hawkins, & J. J. Wilson (Eds.), *Sourcebook on serious, violent, and chronic juvenile offenders* (pp. 213–237). Thousand Oaks, CA: Sage Publications.

U.S. Department of Justice. (1998). *Crime in the United States, 1997.* Washington, DC: Author.

U.S. Department of Justice, Office of Juvenile Justice and Delinquency Prevention. (1999). *Promising strategies to reduce gun violence.* Washington, DC: Author.

Valdez, R., Nourjah, B., & Nourjah, P. (1988). Homicide in southern California, 1966–1985: An examination based on vital statistics data. In J. F. Kraus, S. B. Sorenson, & P. D. Juarez (Eds.), *Proceedings of research conference on violence and homicide in Hispanic communities* (pp. 85–100). Los Angeles: University of California Press.

West, D. J., & Farrington, D. P. (1973). *Who becomes delinquent? Second report of the Cambridge study in delinquent development.* London: Heinemann.

Wolfgang, M. E., Figlio, R. M., & Sellin, T. (1972). *Delinquency in a birth cohort.* Chicago: University of Chicago Press.

Zimring, F. E. (1998). *American youth violence.* New York: Oxford University Press.

Chapter 2

Causes of Youth Violence

Matthew O. Howard and
Jeffrey M. Jenson

His name is Marvin. He's twelve years old. He lives in a Brooklyn project. He's "strapped" with a nine-millimeter. And he's out "to get a body on it." Chances are the first excuse he gets, he'll blow somebody away with the thing. Not for the sake of larceny necessarily. Not even for the sake of crime. But to buy himself some leverage. He knows, as do most of the kids in the hood his age, that if he establishes a rep for being tough, the bad guys will cut him some slack.

So he is primed to kill.

For the sake of perception.

If this scares you, take heart. There's a new governor in Albany and he has made it clear he intends to be the new sheriff in town as well. In fact, George Pataki's election relied, in great part, on his ability to establish a rep for being tough.

"As governor of New York State," said he, "I will bring back the death penalty."

Unless Pataki is a complete idiot—and even among politicians *complete* idiots are rare—he knows that the death penalty has a negligible impact on the rate of crime. This has been exhaustively demonstrated. On the other hand, just what is effective in the war against crime remains a matter of hot debate.

But Pataki also knows, as does every other give-'em-the-chair posturer, that dealing out death to the bad guys is an idea that resonates with a frustrated edgy population. So in making this campaign promise his first priority, Governor Pataki, like Marvin, has signaled his willingness to kill—for the sake of perception.

Neither he nor Marvin is very willing to entertain any arguments as to the futility of their positions. The only difference between them, then, is that Marvin is up-front about what he is doing and why, nasty as the whole business is, and that he is willing to pull the trigger himself. (Stringer, 1998, *Grand Central Winter: Stories from the Street*)

In late December of 1968, an intelligent and attractive 11-year-old girl, Mary Bell, was tried in adult court in Newcastle, England, for the inexplicable murders of two toddlers. There was never any serious doubt as to Mary's culpability; she was convicted after a brief, widely publicized trial and eventually served 12 years in prison. During the trial, the media thoroughly vilified Mary, making frequent references to the film *The Bad Seed*, which had been released a decade earlier. However, there were few efforts to better understand the conditions that might lead a child to commit murder.

One notable exception was the work of Gitta Sereny, the renowned European journalist who published *The Case of Mary Bell* in 1972. She has recently produced a book-length analysis of Mary's case, based on extensive follow-up interviews with Mary and others, that has garnered critical acclaim for its sensitive depiction of the brutal abuse to which Mary had been subjected (Sereny, 1998). Sereny's discussions with Mary's social workers and probation officers indicate that Mary has made a crime-free and unexpectedly good adjustment to adult life and is an exemplary mother to her young daughter.

Although Sereny's studies are highly detailed and painstakingly researched, the thoughtful reader is left with a vexing question: How exactly did the effects of these horrific early life experiences and other predisposing factors coalesce in one young girl at one point in time to bring about the murders of two young boys? If Sereny's journalistic accounts, spanning nearly three decades, leave questions about Mary Bell's motivations unanswered, what can the scientific literature tell us about the propensity to commit violence?

Rather than focusing solely on the individual, as do biographers and "true-crime" writers, scientists strive to identify broad factors that are reliably associated with the occurrence of violence in diverse human populations. The effort to identify variables regulating violence across human groups is consistent with the nomothetic approach of contemporary social science. Because their investigative methods are less fine grained and qualitative, scientific studies of violence provide less information about a specific violent episode or person than do biographic accounts; their aim, rather, is to promote greater understanding of the general factors that give rise to violence among individuals, so that effective prevention and treatment interventions can be designed and implemented.

SCOPE AND NATURE OF THE REVIEW

This chapter reviews the scientific literature that addresses the causes of youth violence, with particular attention to issues relevant to social work practitioners. Given that more than 2,000 studies of violence were published before 1990 (Bridges & Weis, 1989), our review is necessarily selective.

In addition to the sheer quantity of the scientific literature relevant to youth violence, the several disciplinary lines of research are largely independent. To date, biological and psychological findings relating to animal and human aggression (Reiss, Miczek, & Roth, 1994; Reiss & Roth, 1994) appear to have had little effect on, and in turn appear to have been only modestly informed by, the results of criminological investigations addressing social causes of violence. Interdisciplinary studies of violence are few. Rather, in most cases, researchers have implicitly adopted a biologically or sociologically deterministic explanatory framework, largely ignoring other potentially important pathogenetic factors.

Confronted by a large, widely scattered, and poorly integrated literature of limited utility for the purposes of prevention or treatment, several researchers have promulgated risk factor models of youth violence. Early risk factor models were largely "laundry lists" of known correlates of youth violence. These models generally failed to consider the temporal relationship of risk factors to violence or to examine the additive and interactive effects of risk factors. Despite these conceptual and methodological limitations, risk factor models gained widespread acceptance during the 1990s as practitioners embraced research-based blueprints for community- and school-based violence prevention.

Recent reviews of risk factors for youth violence (for example, Thornberry, 1998) have improved on earlier efforts by limiting the selection of studies to those in which the risk factor clearly preceded violent offending. Several theorists, further limiting their analyses to studies examining *potentially modifiable* risk factors, have excluded variables such as gender and age, even though they are associated with rates of violent offending (Earls, 1994; J. D. Hawkins et al., 1998). Our approach is to include the malleable variables identified in recent comprehensive risk factor models (J. D. Hawkins et al., 1998; Sampson & Lauritsen, 1994; Thornberry, 1998) and additional factors believed to be important to the etiology of youth violence; this strategy allows for a comparatively encompassing discussion of the causes of youth violence.

Moreover, potentially important causes of youth violence currently regarded as unmodifiable (for example, neurohormonal functioning) may eventually prove treatable. Variables such as gender may also interact with other modifiable risk factors to influence the expression of violence. With respect to the utility of risk factor models, we concur with Thornberry (1998), who noted that

> [identifying] factors that increase risk suggests fruitful areas for exploration in more formal causal analyses . . . can help in isolating variables that mediate or translate increased vulnerability into actually experiencing the outcome . . . helps structure the design of intervention programs by identifying at-risk youth for whom prevention and treatment efforts are most warranted . . . [and] suggests substantive areas or targets for intervention efforts. (p. 50)

We also follow Earls's (1994) recommendation that variables such as ethnicity and gender be discussed as population indicators rather than risk factors because "such variables are most usefully employed to increase precision in identifying and locating vulnerable groups. They may be misused if they are assumed to be part of a mechanism that causes delinquency" (p. 11).

Risk factors for youth violence are presented by level of effect—individual, situational, and neighborhood/community—consistent with the contextual emphasis of the person-in-environment and biopsychosocial models that social workers have preferred. This approach, though useful for didactic purposes, largely ignores the reciprocal and interactive relationships among variables at different levels of effect. Sampson and Lauritsen (1994) have discussed these complex associations insightfully. Table 2-1 presents known risk factors for youth violence identified in this and other reviews (Earls, 1994; J. D. Hawkins et al., 1998; Sampson & Lauritsen, 1994).

INDIVIDUAL-LEVEL FACTORS

Population Indicators

Gender. Violence is an overwhelmingly male phenomenon both in the United States and internationally. Official arrest records and victim surveys indicate that between 85 and 90 percent of all violent offenders are male (Sampson & Lauritsen, 1994). Males are particularly overrepresented in robbery, rape, and manslaughter rates (Hill & Harris, 1981). Although there is some evidence for recent reductions in the male-to-female ratios for some categories of violent crimes, violence continues to be a predominantly male phenomenon (Sampson & Lauritsen, 1994).

Age. Arrests for violent crime peak in late adolescence and early adulthood (Elliott, 1994; Tolan & Gorman-Smith, 1998), an age group that is expected to increase 20 percent in the near future (Farrington & Loeber, 1998). Victim reports and official records indicate that a substantial majority of all violent offenses are committed by people under 30 (Sampson & Lauritsen, 1994).

The average age of offenders varies by offense category. Steffensmeier, Allan, Harer, and Streifel (1989) noted that the mean age of those arrested

Table 2-1. **Risk Factors for Youth Violence**

Individual Factors

Population Indicators
   Male gender
   Age 15–25
   African American or Hispanic American race or ethnicity
   Low SES

Biological Factors
   High testosterone levels
   High levels of lead
   Low resting heart rate
   Low CNS serotonin levels

Psychological Characteristics
   Impulsivity/hyperactivity/restlessness
   Concentration problems
   Risk-taking/sensation-seeking orientation
   Early involvement in problem behaviors (e.g., sexual intercourse)
   Early aggressiveness
   Neuropsychological dysfunction
   Low verbal skills

Family Factors
   Parental criminality and proviolence attitudes
   Child neglect/abuse
   Marital and family conflict
   Low levels of parent–child interaction and family bonding
   Excessively punitive or permissive family management practices
   Frequent changes of residence
   Leaving home before age 16

School Factors
   High rates of truancy
   Suspension
   Dropping out
   Low academic expectations
   Low bonding to school
   Poor school performance
   Enrollment in a school attended by a large number of delinquents

Peer Factors
   Delinquent/violent peers
   Delinquent/violent siblings
   Gang membership

Situational Factors

   Victim–victimizer relationship
   Role of bystanders or witnesses
   Behavior of victim
   Substance abuse
   Presence/availability of a weapon

Macrocontextual Factors

   Neighborhood poverty and population density
   High residential mobility among neighborhood residents
   Community disorganization
   Media influences

for assault (21 years) was higher than that of those arrested for homicide (19 years) or robbery (17 years). Earls (1994) observed that *Uniform Crime Reports* rates (per 1,000) of aggravated assault (7.35) and rape (0.81) peaked at ages 20 to 24, whereas rates of robbery (4.42) peaked at ages 15 to 19. Rates of murder or nonnegligent manslaughter were similar for the 15 to 19 age range (0.45) and the 20 to 24 age range (0.47). Robbery rates appeared to have declined more precipitously over time than did rates of other violent crimes.

In general, violent crime rates among youths age 14 or younger are quite low. Data from the 1990 *Uniform Crime Reports* (Earls, 1994) for males indicated that only three of every 100,000 youths age 14 or younger were arrested for murder or nonnegligent manslaughter and that eight of every 100,000 were arrested for rape. Robbery and aggravated assault rates were also very low. Thus, most crime appears to be committed during a relatively brief developmental window spanning mid- to late adolescence and early adulthood. Earls (1994) observed that perpetrators of most violent acts are between ages 17 and 25.

Race. Studies using official records, victim surveys, and surveys of self-reported violence consistently identify racial differences in rates of violent offending (Hawkins, Laub, & Lauritsen, 1998). *Uniform Crime Reports* data indicated that African American youths comprised 57.7 percent of all juveniles arrested in 1995 for murder or nonnegligent manslaughter, 44.6 percent for forcible rape, 60.2 percent for robbery, and 41.7 percent for aggravated assault. American Indians comprised less than 1 percent of arrestees for these crimes, and Asian/Pacific Islanders comprised less than 2 percent. Because African American youths comprise 15 percent of the U.S. juvenile population, they were substantially overrepresented in the official arrest records.

D. F. Hawkins and colleagues (1998) noted that, although racial differences in rates of violent offending have persisted, they vary in magnitude. Between 1983 and 1992, for example, the ratio of African Americans to Caucasians for violent juvenile crime declined from 7:1 to 5:1; and the racial differential in robbery rates also declined (from 13:1 to 8:1). Findings for youth homicide arrestees showed a much different trend: Arrest ratios of African Americans to Caucasians increased from 5:1 in 1983 to 7:1 in 1992.

Studies asking youths to self-report violent behavior identify relatively high rates of violent offending among African American youths (Elliott & Ageton, 1980), but the differential between African Americans and Caucasians is usually smaller than that identified in studies using official records (Elliott, 1994). Victim surveys also identify significant differences in African American and Caucasian rates of violent offending (for example, Laub, 1987). National Crime Victimization Survey data indicated that 41 percent of juveniles identified by victims were African American and that 51 percent were Caucasian youths (D. F. Hawkins et al., 1998).

Despite current contention about the role of race in violence, "quite surprisingly, criminologists have conducted only a few studies that explore the extent to which socioeconomic disparity accounts for the well-documented differences in rates of violence shown for blacks and whites" (D. F. Hawkins et al., 1998, p. 40). Furthermore, D. F. Hawkins and colleagues argued, the purely individual-level theories that have largely characterized the field to date have poorly accounted for ecological factors that might explain racial differences in rates of violence. In addition to poverty and other macrocontextual factors, situational factors such as drug trafficking, which flow from macro-level conditions, may explain some portion of the African American–Caucasian differential (D. F. Hawkins et al., 1998).

Socioeconomic status. A recent meta-analysis of 34 longitudinal studies of serious or violent delinquency found family socioeconomic status to be one of the strongest predictors of offending between ages 6 and 11, although family socioeconomic status was a much weaker predictor of offending between ages 12 to 14 (Lipsey & Derzon, 1998).

An earlier meta-analysis concluded that the strength of the inverse relationship between socioeconomic status and violent offending depended on the type of data collected (Bridges & Weis, 1989). The findings of Elliott and Ageton (1980), Elliott and Huizinga (1983), and Ageton (1983) largely supported a negative association between socioeconomic status and the incidence of violence. Thornberry and Farnworth (1982) found only a modest inverse association between socioeconomic status and youth violence, but recent findings suggest a more substantial and robust association than previously assumed.

Biological Factors

Heredity. For more than 50 years comparative studies have demonstrated significant differences in aggressive behavior among various strains of rodents. Furthermore, "there is [now] abundant evidence that genetic polymorphisms influence individual differences in aggression and agonistic behavior in rodents" (Carey, 1994, p. 22). However, the role of genetic factors in human aggression is much less clear.

Early efforts to identify a possible Mendelian mode of inheritance of aggression did not yield fruit; nor did studies attempting to relate violence among some males to the presence of an extra Y chromosome (Miczek, Mirsky, Carey, DeBold, & Raine, 1994). Twin and adoption studies do support a genetic contribution to important personality correlates of aggression, although the findings are more compelling for adults than for adolescents. Early twin and adoption studies provided "strong evidence for a family environment effect on juvenile antisocial behavior [but later] studies suggest that genetics cannot be ignored during this period" (Carey, 1994, p. 31).

In summarizing the results of his incisive review of the genetics of violence, Carey (1994) concluded that

> [together] the data do not support a strong role for heredity in violence. On the one hand, the positive correlations between violence in biological parents and alcohol abuse in adopted sons and the trends of the twin correlations suggest a genetic effect. On the other hand, the failure in adoption studies to detect a significant relationship between violent offending and other indices of crime in separated relatives is evidence that any putative genetic factor is weak. (p. 41)

Moreover, the mechanisms by which genetic effects on violence are transmitted are highly complex and nonspecific—that is, genetic influences do not appear to predispose violence directly but rather predispose antisocial behavior generally.

Hormones. The notion that hormones, particularly androgens such as testosterone, are associated with violence is widespread, although controversial. Archer, Birring, and Wu (1998) conducted a meta-analysis examining the findings of 18 studies (most including men ages 18 to 24) and concluded that there was a significant and substantial positive association between testosterone levels and direct measures of aggression.

Brain (1994) evaluated endocrinological findings relating to animal and human aggression and concluded that "it seems unlikely that androgens have a simple causal effect on human aggression and violence, but the patterns of production of sex steroids do appear to alter several factors . . . that predispose individuals toward carrying out actions that can receive this label" (p. 221). Like the role of genetic factors in aggression, the effects of hormonal influences are likely to be far more complex and difficult to ascertain than previously suspected. Miczek, Mirsky, and colleagues (1994) contended that levels of androgens affect, and in turn are affected by, aggression in humans. "However, they are only one of many influences and not the determining factor" (p. 7).

Nutrition. The effects of nutrition generally and of food additives, lead toxicity, high sugar intake, and hypoglycemia specifically have been the subject of a large number of media accounts of youth violence. Reviews of the sugar–hypoglycemia–youth violence literature have identified serious conceptual and methodological deficiencies in this data base, finding little evidence for the putative association between sugar consumption and violence (Kanarek, 1994). Similarly, although the belief that sugar is a cause of hyperactivity is prevalent, available findings do not provide consistent support for an association (for example, Kaplan, Wamboldt, & Barnhart, 1986; Mahan et al., 1988).

Research assessing the effects of some of the more than 2,000 additives now found in commercial food products has largely failed to identify an association between consumption of additives and hyperactivity or violence. Earlier claims (for example, Conners, 1984) about the beneficial effects of a diet free from additives now appear to have been seriously exaggerated (Kanarek, 1994).

High lead intake (which often is due to children's consumption of lead paint chips) appears to have long-term detrimental neurological effects and may be associated with attention problems (Needleman, 1990). Thus, on a theoretical level, one might expect youths who have been exposed to lead to evidence the cognitive, school, and behavioral problems known to increase the risk for violent offending. Although current findings do not support a strong relationship between diet and violence for most youths, additional research on the role of nutrition and diet in youth violence is needed.

Neurochemistry. The literature addressing the role of neurotransmitters—especially GABA, dopamine, norepinephrine, and serotonin—in aggression has grown substantially in recent years. A number of studies (for example, Linnoila, DeJong, & Virkkunen, 1989; Virkkunen, DeJong, Barko, Goodwin, & Linnoila, 1989) indicate that low levels of serotonin in the blood or cerebrospinal fluid are related to aggression, suicide, and impulsivity. Recognition of the role of norepinephrine in the "flight or fight" reaction has also stimulated research addressing its effects on violence. In general, investigation of the neuroanatomical and neurophysiological correlates of youth violence is in its infancy, but may yield clinically useful findings in coming decades.

Psychological and Psychiatric Factors

Impulsivity. Childhood hyperactivity is related to violence in adulthood (for example, Hechtman & Weiss, 1986; Loney, Kramer, & Milich, 1983; Maguin et al., 1995; Mannuzza, Klein, Konig, & Giampino, 1989). Restlessness, poor concentration, impulsivity, and risk taking in childhood also predict later violence (Farrington, 1989a, 1989b; Klinteberg, Andersson, Magnusson, & Stattin, 1993; Maguin et al., 1995). In their meta-analysis, J. D. Hawkins and colleagues (1998) reported weighted mean correlations of .13, .17, .20, and .25 between measures of violence and childhood/adolescent hyperactivity, concentration problems, restlessness, and impulsivity.

Early aggressiveness. Youths who exhibit aggressive behavior in adolescence are at substantial risk for continuing this behavior into adulthood (Farrington, 1989a, 1989b; Loney et al., 1983; McCord & Ensminger, 1995; Olweus, 1977; Stattin & Magnusson, 1989), particularly those youths with an early onset of aggressive and delinquent behavior and alcoholism (Cloninger, 1987; White, 1992).

Problem behaviors and deviant attitudes. The childhood histories of violent adults are often characterized by early engagement in sexual intercourse, drug sales, and other acts involving overt disobedience and deviance

(Farrington, 1989a, 1989b; Maguin et al., 1995; Mitchell & Rosa, 1979; Robins, 1966). Antisocial conduct often occurs in conjunction with dishonest and manipulative behavior (Farrington, 1989a, 1989b; Mitchell & Rosa, 1979), hostility toward authorities, and other antisocial attitudes (Ageton, 1983; Elliott, 1994; Williams, 1994).

Negative emotionality. There appears to be a weak inverse relationship among anxiety, depression and associated childhood conditions such as worrying, and risk for later violent offending (Farrington, 1989a, 1989b; Mitchell & Rosa, 1979). Howard, Kivlahan, and Walker (1996) concluded that internalizing disorders in youths were not related to the age of onset of substance use but were associated with intensity of substance use; thus, internalizing disorders might have indirect effects on violence through intensity of substance use.

Neuropsychological and psychophysiological factors. Some violent offenders may experience neuropsychological dysfunction that accounts for the school failure they frequently experience (Miczek, Mirsky, et al., 1994). The effects of left-hemisphere deficits on language development and later school functioning have recently been investigated (Miczek, Mirsky, et al., 1994). Other studies have identified relatively low resting heart rates in delinquents (Wadsworth, 1976) and high rates of a variety of neuropsychological disorders among both sexually and nonsexually violent offenders (Mirsky & Siegel, 1994). Although the results of these investigations generally support an increased prevalence of neurological abnormalities among violent offenders, no one brain region is implicated in violent offending, and relatively few studies have been conducted specifically with youths (Mirsky & Siegel, 1994).

Family Factors

Parental attitudes and behavior supportive of violence. Baker and Mednick (1984) found a significant positive association between paternal criminality and the likelihood of later violent offending among young Danish men. Farrington (1989a, 1989b) noted that parents' arrests before their son's tenth birthday were associated with the son's self-reported and officially recorded rates of violent crime in early adulthood. Moffitt (1987) and McCord (1979) failed to find an association between parental criminality and rates of violent offending by offspring, though a recent study of risk factors for gang membership in Seattle did identify a significant positive relationship between parental proviolence attitudes and the likelihood that youths later joined a gang (Maguin et al., 1995).

Child abuse and neglect. Several investigations suggest a positive, although weak, association of child abuse with later violent offending (Smith & Thornberry, 1995; Widom, 1989; Zingraff, Leiter, Myers, & Johnson,

1993). Child sexual abuse was found to be inversely associated with the likelihood of later violent offending (Widom, 1989; Zingraff et al., 1993). Child neglect appears to be more strongly correlated with later violence than child physical or sexual abuse (J. D. Hawkins et al., 1998).

Family conflict. Domestic conflict among family members is consistently related to youth violence. Marital and family discord were positively associated with youth violence in studies conducted by Farrington (1989a, 1989b), McCord, McCord, and Zola (1959), and Maguin and colleagues (1995).

Parent–child interaction and bonding to family. Several investigations underscore the protective role of high levels of parent–child interaction. Farrington (1989a, 1989b) found that the more involved a father is in his son's education at age 18, the lower the likelihood of violence by the son at midlife. Williams (1994) reported that higher levels of family involvement and interaction when youths are age 14 were associated with lower levels of self-reported violence at age 16, although this finding was stronger for males than females.

Other than Ageton's (1983) study of the effects of negative family labeling on boys' commission of sexual assaults between ages 13 and 19, few studies have examined associations between family bonding and youth violence. Thornberry (1998) discussed several investigations indicating that low family involvement (Friedman, Mann, & Friedman, 1975; LeBlanc & Lanctot, in press) and impoverished parent–child emotional relationships (Campbell, 1990; Moore, 1991) increased youths' risk of joining a gang.

Family management and disciplinary practices. Excessively punitive or permissive parental disciplinary practices are associated with later youth violence. Authoritarian (Farrington, 1989a, 1989b), punitive (McCord et al., 1959, Wells & Rankin, 1988), and aggressive (McCord, 1979) parenting styles have been implicated in the development of youth violence; yet lax (McCord et al., 1959), passive (Farrington, 1989a, 1989b), and inconsistent (Maguin et al., 1995) family management practices also increase the risk of later youth violence. Poor family management practices increase the risk for gang membership (Moore, 1991; Virgil, 1988; Winfree, Backstrom, & Mays, 1994), which itself is an important risk factor for later violent offending.

Other family factors. Leaving home before age 16 increased youths' risk for later violence, one study found (McCord & Ensminger, 1995). Similarly, childhood separation from one or more parents early in life predicts later youth violence (Farrington, 1989a, 1989b; Henry, Avshalom, Moffitt, & Silva, 1996; Wadsworth, 1976). Frequent changes of residence by age 16 were associated with higher rates of self-reported violence by age 18 among youths participating in the Seattle Social Development Project (Maguin et al., 1995).

School Factors

Truancy and dropping out. Huizinga and Jakob-Chien (1998), who identified high rates of school problems among juvenile offenders participating in the Denver Youth Survey, concluded that

> [there] is clear indication of overlap between school problems and serious delinquency. The greatest overlap of serious offending and school problems was found for truancy and school suspension, and substantially less overlap for school grades and for dropping out of school. There was sufficient overlap for most problems . . . that school problems can be viewed as contemporaneous risk factors for delinquency, and may provide important targets for intervention programs. (p. 59)

Among the many school factors that have been examined are truancy, dropping out, school failure, low attachment and commitment to school, number of schools attended, and enrollment in a school attended by a comparatively large number of delinquents (Denno, 1990; Farrington, 1989a, 1989b; Maguin et al., 1995). Studies of risk factors for gang affiliation identify low academic expectations and school performance–related self-esteem, having gang members as student peers, and educational frustration and stress as important correlates of gang membership (Curry & Spergel, 1992).

Peer Factors

Deviant peers. Delinquent peers and siblings are risk factors for later violent offending (Ageton, 1983; Farrington, 1989a, 1989b; Williams, 1994). Gang membership in particular has potent effects on the risk of later violent offending. Thornberry (1998) observed that rates of youth violence were high during periods of gang membership and declined notably after gang affiliation ended. The facilitation effect of gang membership on youth violence was not due simply to the effects of associating with highly delinquent peers but was largely attributable to the effects of gang membership per se.

SITUATIONAL FACTORS

Situational factors are those "that influence the initiation or outcome of a violent event" (Sampson & Lauritsen, 1994, p. 2). Below we discuss situational and macrocontextual factors identified in the literature as important to the occurrence of youth and adult violence.

Victim–victimizer relationship. Sampson and Lauritsen (1994) observed that "victimization and offending are tightly connected and need to be examined in a more unified perspective that takes account of the structural properties of social environments" (p. 42). It has long been recognized, for example, that the victims and perpetrators of violence tend to evidence common demographic features and may even be significantly overlapping populations (Wolfgang, 1958). There are several reasons why violent offending might increase the risk of victimization and why in turn victimization might increase the risk of violent offending. Victims of violent crime may retaliate against perpetrators if cultural norms support such a response, particularly if they view offenders as unlikely to call or to be aided by the police. Association with other offenders and involvement in deviant lifestyles also increase the likelihood of victimization.

A serious limitation of modern investigations of violence is that "most criminological studies examine either offending or victimization—few data sets are designed to examine victim–offender interrelationships" (Sampson & Lauritsen, 1994, p. 32). The few studies that have been conducted (for example, Gottfredson, 1984; Hough & Mayhew, 1983; Singer, 1981; Sparks, Glenn, & Dodd, 1977) suggest a positive association between violent victimization and violence against others that is not accounted for by sociodemographic correlates of crime (Lauritsen, Sampson, & Laub, 1991).

Behavior of victims. Victim behavior, including type and intensity of resistance, is thought to be related to the likelihood that an encounter that is only potentially violent will escalate, but relatively little is known about the manifold reactions of young victims to aggressive confrontations and their consequences. As with other situational factors, additional research is needed to better assess the social ecology of violent offending among youths. Sampson and Lauritsen (1994) noted that "multilevel models including both demographic and lifestyle measures along with ecological and/or situational measures . . . can provide further insights into the risk factors for violent victimization" (p. 41).

Role of bystanders or witnesses. Another poorly understood but potentially important factor in violence is the role played by witnesses. On a conceptual level, witnesses could either facilitate or discourage expressions of violence, depending on their behaviors before and during the violence. Sampson and Lauritsen (1994) discussed the methodological issues that make situational factors difficult to study. J. D. Hawkins and colleagues (1998) called for "longitudinal researchers to inquire about situational triggers to violent acts in their studies" (p. 143).

Alcohol and drug use. Substance abuse is commonly associated with violent events, but whether drugs cause violence is still a matter of heated debate. The neurological effects of drugs may directly dispose users to the commission of violent acts; conversely, violent crimes may be committed simply to obtain funds with which to buy drugs. Because drug use occurs most frequently in subcultural contexts where violence is comparatively common (Miczek, DeBold, et al., 1994), some association between these behaviors would be expected even if they were causally independent.

Whatever the association, different drugs appear to exert widely vary-ing effects on the propensity to violence. Miczek, DeBold, and colleagues (1994) concluded that marijuana and hallucinogens (including LSD) do not appear to instigate violent acts. There is widespread agreement, however, that alcohol abuse is strongly associated with violence (National Institute on Alcohol Abuse and Alcoholism, 1997). Tinklenber and Ochberg (1981) reported, for example, that 61 percent of the adolescent homicide offenders they studied were alcohol abusers.

At present, traditional accounts of drug use effects suggest that stimu-lants, such as cocaine and amphetamines, increase the likelihood of violence, whereas depressants, such as heroin and benzodiazepines, tend to decrease violence (Miczek, DeBold, et al., 1994). Studies examining dose–response relationships and acute compared with chronic drug administration effects in different populations are rare in the violence area.

Taylor and Hulsizer (1998) discussed a number of recent studies that call into question traditional conceptions of drug class effects on violence. They found that although evidence is emerging that acute cocaine use is related to violence, moderate doses of amphetamines do not appear to increase the likelihood of violence. Furthermore, they concluded, experi-mental findings suggest that central nervous system depressants, such as opi-oids and tranquilizers, are more facilitative of violence than has previously been assumed. Additional research on the endocrinological, neurobiological, pharmacological, and environmental determinants of drug use and the effects of different doses and dosage schedules on the propensity of different populations for violence are needed to inform current public policy and clini-cal practice.

Availability of a weapon. The presence of a weapon, whether held by the perpetrator or the potential victim, may significantly influence the outcome of an altercation. Lowry, Powell, Kann, Collins, and Kolbe (1998) examined the prevalence of and relationship between weapons carrying and physical fighting among more than 10,000 participants ages 12 to 21 in the Youth Risk Behavior Survey. Nearly 15 percent reported carrying a weapon in the previous 30 days (23.7 percent of males), and approximately 39 percent had been in a fight during the previous 12 months. Thus, physical fights and weapons carrying were quite common. Youths ages 12 to 14 had the highest annual rate of physical fighting (49 percent); youths ages 15 to 17 were most likely to report carrying a weapon recently (17 percent).

Adolescents who carried a weapon were more likely to have been involved in a physical fight during the previous year than those who did not. Furthermore, those who carried a handgun were significantly more apt, con-trolling for demographic variables and frequency of fighting, to have received medical care for fight-related injuries. Thus, although many youths feel that carrying a weapon is helpful in avoiding a fight, these data and others (for example, Cook, 1983; Saltzman, Mercy, O'Carroll, Rosenberg, & Rhoades, 1992) suggest that carrying a weapon is associated with a greater likelihood of physical fighting and consequent injury. The actual processes by which the presence of a weapon increases the likelihood of violence or injury have not been adequately investigated.

Other studies suggest that the prevalence of injuries among robbery victims confronted by a firearm-bearing perpetrator is lower than the prevalence of injuries in non-firearm-associated interactions (see Sampson & Lauritsen, 1994). Presumably, victims are more inclined to fight back, and hence suffer injuries, when the robber is not carrying a gun. When injuries do occur during firearm-associated robberies, however, they tend to be serious. Current debate centers on the role of the presence of a gun or weapon per se compared with the offender's intentions or state of mind.

MACROCONTEXTUAL FACTORS

Neighborhood and Community Characteristics

Poverty. Studies of neighborhood poverty and violent crime generally have reported positive associations (for example, Mladenka & Hill, 1976). Seminal research by Shaw and McKay (1942) identified ethnic heterogeneity, poverty, and residential mobility as important factors explaining variations in neighborhood delinquency rates in Chicago. They found that neighborhood rates of delinquency remained stable even after significant changes over time in the ethnic populations comprising an area. "More than any other, this finding led them to reject individualistic explanations of delinquency and focus instead on the processes by which delinquency and criminal patterns of behavior were transmitted across generations in areas of social disorganization and weak social controls" (Sampson & Lauritsen, 1994, pp. 44–45).

Later studies further supported an association between low socioeconomic status and rates of violent crime (for example, Bensing & Schroeder, 1960; Bullock, 1955 Schmid, 1960). In Chicago, Block (1979) found that the percentage of area families living in poverty or headed by a woman was significantly associated with neighborhood homicide and assault rates; similar findings have been reported for other major metropolitan areas (Beasley & Antunes, 1974; Messner & Tardiff, 1986).

Although community characteristics in general, and poverty specifically, have been found to be related to rates of violent crime among youths and adults, they still do "not explain how they are related to poverty and, in turn, how they increase violence. And they do not explain why racial differences in violent crimes tend to disappear when poverty is included as an explanation" (Reiss & Roth, 1993, p. 132).

Neighborhood density and ethnic heterogeneity. Substantial evidence supports the notion that population density is positively associated with rates of violent crime. Areas with a high percentage of multiunit dwellings, a relatively large number of people living within a defined area, or a large proportion of rented, as opposed to owned, housing units tend to evidence comparatively high rates of violence. Controlling for gender, age, and ethnic composition, Sampson (1983) found that youths living in high-density neighborhoods were approximately three times more likely to be robbed than youths living in low-density neighborhoods.

Many widely accepted studies have found that rates of violence are positively related to the proportion of African Americans living in an area (for example, Block, 1979; Smith & Jarjoura, 1988), but there is considerable controversy over the interpretation of these findings. The National Academy of Sciences Panel on the Understanding and Control of Violent Behavior (Reiss & Roth, 1993) identified four studies assessing homicide victimization rates and measures of the racial and ethnic composition of census tracts. All four identified a significant interaction effect: Racial differences evident at lower socioeconomic status levels disappeared at higher income levels. It is apparent that racial and ethnicity effects are seriously confounded with those of socioeconomic status.

Residential mobility. Cross-sectional studies relating neighborhood residential mobility to violent crime (for example, Block, 1979; Sampson, 1985a, 1985b; Smith & Jarjoura, 1988) and longitudinal studies of the effects of neighborhood changes on violent crime (for example, Taylor & Covington, 1988) generally report consistent findings: High rates of mobility are positively associated with violence victimization rates, whereas neighborhood stability is inversely related to the prevalence and incidence of violent events.

Community disorganization. Several studies suggest that community disorganization is related to levels of youth violence. Maguin and colleagues (1995) reported that low attachment to the neighborhood, measures of community disorganization, and neighborhood availability of marijuana at ages 10 and 12 and of marijuana and cocaine at age 16 were positively associated with self-reported violence at age 18. Frequency of exposure to neighborhood violence (Paschall, 1996) and exposure to racial discrimination (McCord & Ensminger, 1995) have also been related to violence among people in late adolescence and early adulthood.

Media influences. Numerous professional and governmental commissions have examined the impact of media portrayals of violence (American Medical Association, 1996; American Psychological Association, 1993; Centers for Disease Control and Prevention, 1991). In general, "these investigations have documented consistently that exposure to media violence . . . contributes to aggressive behavior in viewers and may influence their perceptions about violence in the real world" (Smith & Donnerstein, 1998, p. 175).

The most comprehensive examination of media violence so far conducted, the National Television Violence Study (Kunkel et al., 1995; Kunkel et al., 1996), conclusively established that modern television in the United States is saturated with violence. A majority (57 percent) of the more than 5,000 programs evaluated over the two viewing seasons contained violence, which was stringently defined for study purposes. The violence presented was largely sanitized; 86 percent of all violent episodes depicted no blood or bodily damage, and 74 percent included no punishment or criticism of violence.

Television violence is an important social concern because youths (and adults) watch so much television; 98 percent of American homes have a television and two-thirds of these homes also subscribe to cable TV or have a VCR. American 12- to 17-year-olds watch an average of 20 hours of TV a week, making it one of their principal life activities. African American children watch substantially more television than Caucasian children, and children from lower socioeconomic status homes tend to watch considerably more television than children from higher socioeconomic status homes (Huston et al., 1992; Tangey & Feshbach, 1988).

Current findings suggest that far more public policy attention should be paid to violence on TV. Smith and Donnerstein (1998) recommended that the media

> produce more programs that avoid violence . . . be creative in showing more violent acts being punished—more negative consequences . . . less justification for violent actions . . . consider greater emphasis on strong antiviolence themes, ensure that ratings for violence also take into account the context of the portrayals, [and] ensure that cartoons featuring high-risk portrayals for young children are rated in a way that clearly warns parents. (p. 195)

They also proffered advice to policymakers and parents regarding televised violence.

CONCLUSION

Although numerous risk factors for violence have been identified in prospective, longitudinal studies of youths, including those operating at the individual and micro- and macrocontextual levels, the study of violence is still in its infancy. A recent article in the *New York Times* ("By the Numbers," 1999) discussed what science currently can offer to help prevent events like the school massacre at Littleton, Colorado (the largest in the nation's history), that occurred as this book was being written. Jim Mercy, associate director of the Division of Violence Prevention at the Centers for Disease Control and Prevention, commented, "It would be very hard to predict or identify ahead of time the kinds of kids and the constellation of factors that are likely to lead to that kind of event . . . our understanding of what motivates people to be violent is so imprecise, that this would be a difficult task" ("By the Numbers," 1999, p. 2).

In fact, a number of commentators observed that Littleton—a prosperous and highly educated community—was one of the few counties in the United States with a juvenile assessment center. Eric Harris, one of the gunmen, was under the care of a psychiatrist at the time of the shooting. If a tragic event of this magnitude was not averted in these propitious circumstances, one may well ask what, if any, real utility science and clinical practice have to offer policymakers and the public in the way of violence prevention and treatment strategies.

Our understanding of violence must move from the mere identification of static factors associated with violence to a more dynamic assessment of their interactions over time and in different circumstances and populations. In attempting to identify commonalties in the six multiple-death school shootings that had occurred in the previous 18 months in the United States, Jeffrey Fagan, director of a violence prevention center at Columbia University, noted that unrecognized mental illness, guns, and deeply held grievances were common threads and that "any one of these three risk factors does not produce a violent event. . . . It's their convergence that produces an event" ("By the Numbers," 1999).

More research and more sophisticated statistical and methodological techniques are needed to model a phenomenon as complex, multiply determined, dynamic, and protean as youth violence. However, as our review indicates, we do possess enough information currently to argue that media portrayals of violence should be curtailed and that the child-rearing practices of many parents should be improved. Likewise, early intervention with youths at high risk for violent offending and victimization can be justified and guided by current research findings. With additional research and the political will, the prevalence of violence in this nation can be reduced significantly. Ethical considerations demand that we make violence reduction one of our highest priorities.

REFERENCES

Ageton, S. (1983). The dynamics of female delinquency, 1976–1980. *Criminology, 21,* 555–584.

American Medical Association. (1996). *Physician guide to media violence.* Chicago: Author.

American Psychological Association. (1993). *Violence and youth: Psychology's response.* Washington, DC: Author.

Archer, J., Birring, S. S., & Wu, F.C.W. (1998). The association between testosterone and aggression among young men: Empirical findings and a meta-analysis. *Aggressive Behavior, 24,* 411–420.

Baker, R.L.A., & Mednick, B. R. (1984). *Influences on human development: A longitudinal perspective.* Boston: Kluwer-Nijhoff.

Beasley, R. W., & Antunes, G. (1974). The etiology of urban crime: An ecological analysis. *Criminology, 11,* 439–461.

Bensing, R. C., & Schroeder, O. (1960). *Homicide in an urban community.* Springfield, IL: Charles C Thomas.

Block, R. (1979). Community, environment, and violent crime. *Criminology, 17,* 46–57.

Brain, P. F. (1994). Hormonal aspects of aggression and violence. In A. J. Reiss, K. A. Miczek, & J. A. Roth (Eds.), *Understanding and preventing violence. Volume 2: Biobehavioral influences* (pp. 173–244). Washington, DC: National Academy Press.

Bridges, G., & Weis, J. (1989). Measuring violent behavior: Effects of study design on reported correlates of violence. In N. Weiner & M. Wolfgang (Eds.), *Violent crime, violent individuals.* Newbury Park, CA: Sage Publications.

Bullock, H. A. (1955). Urban homicide in theory and fact. *Journal of Criminal Law, Criminology, and Police Science, 45,* 565–575.

By the numbers: Science looks at Littleton, and shrugs. (1999, May 9). *New York Times,* pp. 1–4.

Campbell, A. (1990). Female participation in gangs. In C. R. Huff (Ed.), *Gangs in America* (pp. 163–182). Newbury Park, CA: Sage Publications.

Carey, G. (1994). Genetics and violence. In A. J. Reiss, K. A. Miczek, & J. A. Roth (Eds.), *Understanding and preventing violence. Volume 2: Biobehavioral influences* (pp. 21–53). Washington, DC: National Academy Press.

Centers for Disease Control and Prevention. (1991). *Position papers from the Third National Injury Conference: Setting the national agenda for injury control in the 1990s.* Washington, DC: Department of Health and Human Services.

Cloninger, C. R. (1987). Neurogenetic adaptive mechanisms in alcoholism. *Science, 236,* 410–416.

Conners, C. K. (1984). Nutritional therapy in children. In G. Galler (Ed.), *Nutrition and behavior* (pp. 159–192). New York: Plenum Press.

Cook, P. J. (1983). The influence of gun availability on violent crime patterns. *Crime and Justice: Annual Review of Research, 4,* 49–89.

Curry, G. D., & Spergel, I. A. (1992). Gang involvement and delinquency among Hispanic and African-American adolescent males. *Journal of Research in Crime and Delinquency, 29,* 273–291.

Denno, D. W. (1990). *Biology and violence: From birth to adulthood.* Cambridge, England: Cambridge University Press.

Earls, F. J. (1994). Violence and today's youth. *Critical Health Issues for Children and Youth, 4,* 4–23.

Elliott, D. (1994). Serious violent offenders: Onset, developmental course, and termination—the American Society of Criminology 1993 presidential address. *Criminology, 32,* 1–21.

Elliott, D., & Ageton, S. (1980). Reconciling race and class differences in self-reported and official estimates of delinquency. *American Sociological Review, 45,* 95–110.

Elliott, D., & Huizinga, D. (1983). Social class and delinquent behavior in a national youth panel: 1976–1980. *Criminology, 21*, 149–177.

Farrington, D. P. (1989a). Early predictors of adolescent aggression and adult violence. *Violence and Victims, 4*, 79–100.

Farrington, D. P. (1989b). Self-reported and official offending from adolescence to adulthood. In M. Klein (Ed.), *Cross-national research in self-reported crime and delinquency* (pp. 399–423). Dordrecht, Netherlands: Kluwer.

Farrington, D. P., & Loeber, R. (1998). Major aims of this book. In R. Loeber & D. P. Farrington (Eds.), *Serious & violent juvenile offenders: Risk factors and successful interventions* (pp. 1–10). Thousand Oaks, CA: Sage Publications.

Friedman, C. J., Mann, F., & Friedman, A. S. (1975). A profile of juvenile street gang members. *Adolescence, 10*, 563–607.

Gottfredson, M. (1984). *Victims of crime: The dimensions of risk* (Home Office Research Study No. 81). London: Her Majesty's Stationery Office.

Hawkins, D. F., Laub, J. H., & Lauritsen, J. L. (1998). Race, ethnicity, and serious juvenile offending. In R. Loeber & D. P. Farrington (Eds.), *Serious & violent juvenile offenders: Risk factors and successful interventions* (pp. 30–46). Thousand Oaks, CA: Sage Publications.

Hawkins, J. D., Herrenkohl, T., Farrington, D. P., Brewer, D., Catalano, R. F., & Harachi, T. W. (1998). A review of predictors of youth violence. In R. Loeber & D. P. Farrington (Eds.), *Serious & violent juvenile offenders: Risk factors and successful interventions* (pp. 106–146). Thousand Oaks, CA: Sage Publications.

Hechtman, L., & Weiss, G. (1986). Controlled prospective fifteen-year follow-up of hyperactives as adults: Non-medical drug and alcohol use and anti-social behavior. *Canadian Journal of Psychiatry, 31*, 557–567.

Henry, B., Avshalom, C., Moffitt, T. E., & Silva, P. A. (1996). Temperamental and familial predictors of violent and nonviolent criminal convictions: Age 3 to age 18. *Developmental Psychology, 32*, 614–623.

Hill, G., & Harris, A. (1981). Changes in the gender patterning of crime, 1953–1977: Opportunity vs. identity. *Social Science Quarterly, 62*, 658–671.

Hough, M., & Mayhew, P. (1983). *The British crime survey: First report* (Home Office Research Study No. 76). London: Her Majesty's Stationery Office.

Howard, M. O., Kivlahan, D., & Walker, R. D. (1996). Cloninger's tridimensional theory of personality and psychopathology: Applications to substance use disorders. *Journal of Studies on Alcohol, 58*, 48–66.

Huizinga, D., & Jakob-Chien, C. (1998). The contemporaneous co-occurrence of serious and violent juvenile offending and other problem behaviors. In R. Loeber & D. P. Farrington (Eds.), *Serious & violent juvenile offenders: Risk factors and successful interventions* (pp. 47–67). Thousand Oaks, CA: Sage Publications.

Huston, A. C., Donnerstein, E., Fairchild, H., Feshbach, N. D., Katz, P. A., Murray, J. P., Rubinstein, E. A., Wilcox, B. L., & Zuckerman, D. (1992). *Big world, small screen: The role of television in American society.* Lincoln: University of Nebraska Press.

Kanarek, R. B. (1994). Nutrition and violent behavior. In A. J. Reiss, K. A. Miczek, & J. A. Roth (Eds.), *Understanding and preventing violence. Volume 2: Biobehavioral influences* (pp. 515–539). Washington, DC: National Academy Press.

Kaplan, H. K., Wamboldt, F. S., & Barnhart, M. (1986). Behavioral effects of dietary sucrose in disturbed children. *American Journal of Psychiatry, 143*, 944–945.

Klinteberg, B. A., Andersson, T., Magnusson, D., & Stattin, H. (1993). Hyperactive behavior in childhood as related to subsequent alcohol problems and violent offending: A longitudinal study of male subjects. *Personality and Individual Differences, 15,* 381–388.

Kunkel, D., Wilson, B. J., Donnerstein, E., Linz, D., Smith, S. L., Blumenthal, E., Gray, T., & Potter, W. J. (1995). Measuring television violence: The importance of context. *Journal of Broadcasting and Electronic Media, 39,* 284–291.

Kunkel, D., Wilson, B. J., Linz, D., Potter, W. J., Donnerstein, E., Smith, S. L., Blumenthal, E., & Gray, T. (1996). Violence in television programming overall. In *University of California, Santa Barbara, Scientific Papers: National Television Violence Study* (pp. 1–172). Studio City, CA: Mediascope.

Laub, J. (1987). Data for a positive criminology. In M. Gottfredson & T. Hirishi (Eds.), *Positive criminology* (pp. 56–70). Newbury Park, CA: Sage Publications.

Lauritsen, J., Sampson, R., & Laub, J. (1991). The link between offending and victimization among adolescents. *Criminology, 29,* 265–291.

LeBlanc, M., & Lanctot, N. (in press). Psychological characteristics of gang members according to the gang structure and its subcultural and ethnic makeup. *Journal of Gang Research.*

Linnoila, M., DeJong, G., & Virkkunen, M. (1989). Family history of alcoholism in violent offenders and impulsive fire setters. *Archives of General Psychiatry, 46,* 613–616.

Lipsey, M. W., & Derzon, J. H. (1998). Predictors of violent or serious delinquency in adolescence and early adulthood. A synthesis of longitudinal research. In R. Loeber & D. P. Farrington (Eds.), *Serious & violent juvenile offenders: Risk factors and successful interventions* (pp. 86–102). Thousand Oaks, CA: Sage Publications.

Loney, J., Kramer, J., & Milich, R. (1983). The hyperkinetic child grows up: Predictors of symptoms, delinquency, and achievement at follow-up: Birth and childhood cohorts. In S. A. Mednick, M. Harway, & K. M. Finello (Eds.), *Handbook of longitudinal research* (Vol. 1, pp. 426–447). New York: Praeger.

Lowry, R., Powell, K. E., Kann, L., Collins, J. L., & Kolbe, L. J. (1998). Weapon-carrying, physical fighting, and fight-related injury among U.S. adolescents. *American Journal of Preventive Medicine, 14,* 122–129.

Maguin, E., Hawkins, J. D., Catalano, R. F., Hill, K., Abbott, R., & Herrenkohl, T. (1995, November). *Risk factors measured at three ages for violence at age 17–18.* Paper presented at the American Society of Criminology, Boston.

Mahan, L. K., Chase, M., Furukawa, S., Sulzbacher, G. G., Shapiro, W. E., Pierson, P., & Bierman, C. W. (1988). Sugar "allergy" and children's behavior. *Annals of Allergy, 61,* 453–458.

Mannuzza, S., Klein, R. G., Konig, P. H., & Giampino, T. L. (1989). Hyperactive boys almost grown up IV: Criminality and its relationship to psychiatric status. *Archives of General Psychiatry, 46,* 1073–1079.

McCord, J. (1979). Some child-rearing antecedents of criminal behavior in adult men. *Journal of Personality and Social Psychology, 37,* 1477–1486.

McCord, J., & Ensminger, M. (1995, November). *Pathways from aggressive childhood to criminality.* Paper presented at the American Society of Criminology, Boston.

McCord, W., McCord, J., & Zola, I. K. (1959). *Origins of crime: A new evaluation of the Cambridge–Somerville youth study.* New York: Cambridge University Press.

Messner, S., & Tardiff, K. (1986). Economic inequality and levels of homicide: An analysis of urban neighborhoods. *Criminology, 24,* 297–318.

Miczek, K. A., DeBold, J. F., Haney, M., Tidey, J., Vivian, J., & Weerts, E. M. (1994). Alcohol, drugs of abuse, aggression, and violence. In A. J. Reiss, K. A. Miczek, & J. A. Roth (Eds.), *Understanding and preventing violence. Volume 2: Biobehavioral influences* (pp. 377–570). Washington, DC: National Academy Press.

Miczek, K. A., Mirsky, A. F., Carey, G., DeBold, J., & Raine, A. (1994). An overview of biological influences on violent behavior. In A. J. Reiss, K. A. Miczek, & J. A. Roth (Eds.), *Understanding and preventing violence. Volume 2: Biobehavioral influences* (pp. 1–20). Washington, DC: National Academy Press.

Mirsky, A. F., & Siegel, A. (1994). The neurobiology of violence and aggression. In A. J. Reiss, K. A. Miczek, & J. A. Roth (Eds.), *Understanding and preventing violence. Volume 2: Biobehavioral influences* (pp. 59–172). Washington, DC: National Academy Press.

Mitchell, S., & Rosa, P. (1979). Boyhood behavior problems and precursors of criminality: A fifteen-year follow-up study. *Journal of Child Psychology & Psychiatry, 22,* 19–33.

Mladenka, K., & Hill, K. (1976). A reexamination of the etiology of urban crime. *Criminology, 13,* 491–506.

Moffitt, T. E. (1987). Parental mental disorder and offspring criminal behavior: An adoption study. *Psychiatry, 50,* 346–360.

Moore, J. W. (1991). *Going down to the barrio: Homeboys and homegirls in change.* Philadelphia: Temple University Press.

National Institute on Alcohol Abuse and Alcoholism. (1997). *Alcohol and health* (Ninth Special Report to the U. S. Congress from the Secretary of Health and Human Services). Washington, DC: Department of Health and Human Services.

Needleman, H. L. (1990). The long-term effects of exposure to lead in childhood. *New England Journal of Medicine, 322,* 83–88.

Olweus, D. (1977). Aggression and peer acceptance in adolescent boys: Two short-term longitudinal studies of ratings. *Child Development, 48,* 1301–1313.

Paschall, M. J. (1996, December). *Exposure to violence and the onset of violent behavior and substance use among black male youth: An assessment of independent effects and psychosocial mediators.* Paper presented at the Society for Prevention Research, San Juan, Puerto Rico.

Reiss, A. J., Miczek, K. A., & Roth, J. A. (Eds.). (1994). *Understanding and preventing violence. Volume 2: Biobehavioral influences.* Washington, DC: National Academy Press.

Reiss, A. J., & Roth, J. A. (Eds.). (1993). *Understanding and preventing violence. Volume 1.* Washington, DC: National Academy Press.

Reiss, A. J., & Roth, J. A. (Eds.). (1994). *Understanding and preventing violence. Volume 3: Social influences.* Washington, DC: National Academy Press.

Robins, L. N. (1966). *Deviant children grown up: A sociological and psychiatric study of sociopathic personality.* Baltimore: Williams & Wilkins.

Saltzman, L. E., Mercy, J. A., O'Carroll, P. W., Rosenberg, M. L., & Rhoades, P. H. (1992). Weapon involvement and injury outcome in family and intimate assaults. *JAMA, 267,* 3043–3047.

Sampson, R. J. (1983). Structural density and criminal victimization. *Criminology, 21,* 276–293.

Sampson, R. J. (1985a). Neighborhood and crime: The structural determinants of personal victimization. *Journal of Research in Crime and Delinquency, 22,* 7–40.

Sampson, R. J. (1985b). Race and criminal violence: A demographically disaggregated analysis of urban homicide. *Crime and Delinquency, 31*, 47–82.

Sampson, R. J., & Lauritsen, J. L. (1994). Violent victimization and offending: Individual-, situational-, and community-level risk factors. In A. J. Reiss & J. A. Roth (Eds.), *Understanding and preventing violence. Volume 3: Social influences* (pp. 1–114). Washington, DC: National Academy Press.

Schmid, C. (1960). Urban crime areas: Part I. *American Sociological Review, 25*, 527–542.

Sereny, G. (1972). *The case of Mary Bell.* London: Eyre Methuen Ltd.

Sereny, G. (1998). *Cries unheard. Why children kill: The case of Mary Bell.* New York: Henry Holt & Co.

Shaw, C., & McKay, H. (1942). *Juvenile delinquency and urban areas.* Chicago: University of Chicago Press.

Singer, S. I. (1981). Homogeneous victim–offender populations: A review and some research implications. *Journal of Criminal Law and Criminology, 72*, 779–778.

Smith, C., & Thornberry, T. P. (1995). The relationship between childhood maltreatment and adolescent involvement in delinquency. *Criminology, 33*, 451–481.

Smith, D. R., & Jarjoura, G. R. (1988). Social structure and criminal victimization. *Journal of Research in Crime and Delinquency, 25*, 27–52.

Smith, S. L., & Donnerstein, E. (1998). Media violence. In R. E. Geen & E. Donnerstein (Eds.), *Human aggression: Theories, research, and implications for social policy* (pp. 139–165). San Diego: Academic Press.

Sparks, R., Glenn, H., & Dodd, D. (1977). *Surveying victims.* London: Wiley.

Stattin, H., & Magnusson, D. (1989). The role of early aggressive behavior in the frequency, seriousness, and types of later crime. *Journal of Consulting and Clinical Psychology, 57*, 710–718.

Steffensmeier, D., Allan, E. A., Harer, M., & Streifel, C. (1989). Age and the distribution of crime. *American Journal of Sociology, 94*, 803–831.

Stringer, L. (1998). *Grand Central winter: Stories from the street.* New York: Seven Stories.

Tangey, J. P., & Feshbach, S. (1988). Children's television viewing frequency: Individual differences and demographic correlates. *Personality and Social Psychology Bulletin, 14*, 145–158.

Taylor, R., & Covington, J. (1988). Neighborhood changes in ecology and violence. *Criminology, 26*, 553–590.

Taylor, S. P., & Hulsizer, M. R. (1998). Psychoactive drugs and human aggression. In R. E. Geen & E. Donnerstein (Eds.), *Human aggression: Theories, research, and implications for social policy* (pp. 139–165). San Diego: Academic Press.

Thornberry, T. P. (1998). Membership in youth gangs and involvement in serious and violent offending. In R. Loeber & D. P. Farrington (Eds.), *Serious & violent juvenile offenders: Risk factors and successful interventions* (pp. 147–166). Thousand Oaks, CA: Sage Publications.

Thornberry, T. P., & Farnworth, M. (1982). Social correlates of criminal involvement: Further evidence on the relationship between social status and criminal behavior. *American Sociological Review, 47*, 505–517.

Tinklenber, J. R., & Ochberg, F. M. (1981). Patterns of adolescent violence: A California sample. In D. A. Hamburg & M. B. Trudeau (Eds.), *Biobehavioral aspects of aggression* (pp. 121–140). New York: Alan R. Liss.

Tolan, P. H., & Gorman-Smith, D. (1998). Development of serious and violent offending careers. In R. Loeber & D. P. Farrington (Eds.), *Serious & violent juvenile offenders: Risk factors and successful interventions* (pp. 68–85). Thousand Oaks, CA: Sage Publications.

Virgil, J. D. (1988). *Barrio gangs: Street life and identity in Southern California.* Austin: University of Texas Press.

Virkkunen, M., DeJong, J., Barko, J., Goodwin, F. K., & Linnoila, M. (1989). Relationship of psychobiological variables to recidivism in violent offenders and impulsive fire setters. *Archives of General Psychiatry, 46,* 600–603.

Wadsworth, M.E.J. (1976). Delinquency, pulse rates and early emotional deprivation. *British Journal of Criminology, 16,* 245–256.

Wells, L. E., & Rankin, J. H. (1988). Direct parental controls and delinquency. *Criminology, 26,* 263–285.

White, H. R. (1992). Drug-use delinquency connection in adolescence. In R. Weisheit (Ed.), *Drugs, crime, and criminal justice* (pp. 215–256). Cincinnati: Anderson.

Widom, C. S. (1989). The cycle of violence. *Science, 244,* 160–166.

Williams, J. H. (1994). *Understanding substance use, delinquency involvement, and juvenile justice system involvement among African-American and European-American adolescents.* Unpublished doctoral dissertation, University of Washington, Seattle.

Winfree, L. T., Backstrom, T., & Mays, G. L. (1994). Social learning theory, self-reported delinquency, and youth gangs: A new twist on a general theory of crime and delinquency. *Youth and Society, 26,* 147–177.

Wolfgang, M. (1958). *Patterns in criminal homicide.* New York: John Wiley & Sons.

Zingraff, M. T., Leiter, J., Myers, K. A., & Johnson, M. (1993). Child maltreatment and youthful problem behavior. *Criminology, 31,* 173–202.

Chapter 3

Assessment of Childhood Aggression and Youth Violence

Mark J. Macgowan

Among the compendia of measures for social workers (Fischer & Corcoran, 1994a, 1994b; Hudson, 1982), there are few instruments related
to violence that are relevant for children or adolescents. Some sources discuss
measures (Chaiken, Chaiken, & Rhodes, 1994; Hersen & Bellack, 1988;
LeBlanc, 1998), and a few include sample instruments (Furlong & Smith,
1994a; McGee, 1996; Wiebush, Baird, Krisberg, & Onek, 1995). Only one
source includes violence-related measures for youths (Dahlberg, Toal, &
Behrens, 1998), with little comment about their application.

This chapter reviews violence-related instruments for children and adolescents and discusses the assessment of youth violence. The chapter first discusses definitional issues, then a conceptual framework for the assessment of
violence, technical criteria for selecting an instrument, and ethical issues
related to using instruments for practice and research. These discussions provide the foundation for an overview of instruments for the assessment of violence in children and youths.

DEFINITIONS AND BOUNDARIES

This chapter is limited to a review of quantitative measures with demonstrated reliability, validity, or both. It includes measures for children (6 to 11
years old) and adolescents (12 to17 years old). The focus is on instruments

measuring interpersonal physical violence, defined as the "perpetration of acts resulting in physical injury or threat of physical injury to another person (including sexual violence)" (J. D. Hawkins et al., 1998, p. 107). This violence excludes self-inflicted harm; collective violence in the form of riots, terrorism, and wars; and instruments where family or community are the level of measurement. Although most of the instruments assess perpetration of violence, the chapter also includes a few measures of victimization.

Measures of aggression are also included for two reasons. First, there is considerable overlap between aggression and violence in the literature: "Studies have rarely differentiated aggressive behavior from violent behavior, although some have indicated differences in the seriousness of the aggressive acts measured (for example, pushing and shoving vs. using a knife)" (Tolan & Guerra, 1994, p. 2). Second, there is strong evidence that early aggression is linked to later violence (Fraser, 1996; Loeber & Farrington, 1998) and is one of the pathways to problem behavior described by Loeber and Hay (1994).

Aggression has been further distinguished as overt and relational (Crick, 1995; Crick & Grotpeter, 1995). Overt aggression is physical; it includes hitting, slapping, or the use of force. Overt aggression has two subtypes: proactive and reactive aggression (Dodge & Coie, 1987). *Proactive aggression* involves the deliberate use of real or threatened physical force and is similar to predatory aggression (Furlong & Smith, 1994b). *Reactive aggression* occurs impulsively and is not goal oriented. It is similar to affective aggression (Furlong & Smith, 1994b).

Relational aggression is a relatively recent conceptualization that refers to "attempts to harm, or threats to harm, another's peer relationships (for example, telling a friend that you will not like her any more unless she does what you tell her to do)" (Crick & Grotpeter, 1995, p. 712; see also Crick, 1995). Relational aggression has emerged as a distinct form of aggression for girls. Those who exhibit the behavior—or who are victims of it—experience adjustment problems such as peer rejection, loneliness, and isolation (Crick & Bigbee, 1998; Crick & Grotpeter, 1995; Grotpeter & Crick, 1996). Although there is no evidence yet to suggest that relational aggression is linked to subsequent violent behavior among girls, as an emerging form of gender-related aggressive behavior, it is important to measure.

This review also addresses anger expression, another concept related to violence. Although conceptually distinct from aggression or violence (Kassinove & Sukhodolsky, 1995), the expression of anger may include physical violence. More specifically, the type of anger of interest here is defined as "socially inappropriate methods for expressing anger and frustration" (Furlong & Smith, 1994b, p. 5); it includes both physical aggression, such as violence, and verbal aggression.

A few measures that assess hyperactivity and attention deficits are included. Both have been strongly linked to aggression and violence. Children identified by parents or teachers as having hyperactivity or attention deficit problems at ages 10, 14, and 16 "had twice the risk of violent behavior by age 18" (J. D. Hawkins et al., 1998, p. 143).

AN ECOLOGICAL–DEVELOPMENTAL ASSESSMENT PERSPECTIVE

Although any measure may be used in assessment, a conceptual framework helps to guide the choice and use of measures. The ecological systems perspective common in social work provides an orientation to assessment. Six principles characterize an ecological systems approach to assessment (Allen-Meares & Lane, 1993):

1. Data should be collected from multiple ecosystems, such as school and the home.

2. Assessment should come from three data sources: the person, significant others, and direct observations.

3. Data should be collected about the person (physical, behavioral, and cognitive–affective domains) and situation (physical environment, behavioral–psychosocial environment, and historic normative environments).

4. A thorough, person-in-environment assessment should include as many of the preceding components as possible. For example, data on aggressive or violent behavior would be collected across different environments, from different sources, and using different methods.

5. The data must be integrated into a comprehensive perspective on the client's situation.

6. The assessment must be linked to intervention approaches that could change person, environment, or both.

There is empirical support for some elements of the ecological perspective on violence assessment. It is widely recognized that violence is caused by multiple and interactive forces at the individual, contextual (family, school, peers, neighborhood), and societal levels (J. D. Hawkins et al., 1998; D. F. Hawkins, Laub, & Lauritsen, 1998; Loeber & Farrington, 1998; Tolan & Guerra, 1994). Tolan and Guerra (1994) note that "this biopsychosocial model suggests that the same type of violence can have several causal pathways and that some violence is dependent on the confluence of multiple factors" (p. 11). Moreover, as we discuss below, different sources of data have inherent measurement biases. For example, in one study, direct observation was able to detect behavior change when behavior ratings failed (Grossman et al., 1997). Multiple informants and multiple methods are advocated for assessing children with externalizing problems (Epps, 1997; Kruesi et al.,

1994; Molina, Pelham, Blumenthal, & Galiszewski, 1998), particularly in the area of clinical violence prediction (Milner & Campbell, 1995). Thus, an ecological approach not only makes sense from a conceptual perspective, but it also has considerable empirical support.

To take the model further, social work assessment of violence might use an ecological–developmental perspective (Fraser, 1996), adding the developmental perspective as a way of understanding aggression and violence in children and adolescents. For example, in assessing children with aggressive behavior, a social worker would evaluate the family environment, including parent and child communication patterns from which children may learn inappropriate ways to respond to conflict, and would assess early social encounters with peers in which a child may use coercive or intimidating behaviors. These types of early social encounters often lead to rejection by peers, and as the child reaches the age when prosocial skills are supported, he or she becomes further isolated from learning opportunities and develops problems in school (Fraser, 1996). Other individual and environmental factors that appear to predispose children to aggression and violence, such as biological conditions, poverty, and exposure to community violence, would also be taken into account (Fraser, 1996; D. F. Hawkins et al., 1998; J. D. Hawkins et al., 1998). Thus, to understand the nature of aggression and violence in children, assessment strategies need to consider academic performance, family functioning and parenting, aggressive behavior among peers, and community and neighborhood influence. Except for family functioning and parenting and biological conditions, many of the measures in this review assess these different areas. Sources for measures of family functioning include Fischer and Corcoran (1994a) and Touliatos, Perlmutter, and Straus (1990). Organic or biomedical conditions are best assessed through referral and consultation.

For aggression that develops in later childhood and adolescence, the influence of contextual and systemic factors outside the family prevails (Fraser, 1996). In particular, school factors such as the quality of teaching and classroom management methods affect the child's bonding to school and influence the risk for aggressive behavior (Fraser, 1996). Peer and neighborhood factors such as the presence of gangs and violence and the opportunity to associate with violent peers also contribute to aggressive behavior. At this stage of development, measures of environmental violence and peer relations become important. Some of the measures reviewed here evaluate these areas.

Although not the focus of this chapter, an important addition to the ecological–developmental perspective is the assessment of protective factors that help to inhibit the development of aggression and violence in children. Protective factors are defined as "both the internal and external forces that help children resist or meliorate risk" (Kirby & Fraser, 1997, p. 16). Although promising research has outlined protective factors related to many childhood problems (Kirby & Fraser, 1997), including delinquency (Williams, Ayers, & Arthur, 1997), there has been little research related specifically to protection from aggression and violence. This chapter focuses on the assessment of violence and aggression, although a few measures (for example, School Social Behavior Scales) include protective factors, such as social competence and academic achievement.

Thus, an ecological–developmental perspective is a broad-based approach incorporating assessment at various levels, including an evaluation of risk and protective factors related to violence. None of the instruments reviewed here is complete in itself, but each may be useful in a biopsychosocial assessment.

TECHNICAL CRITERIA FOR SELECTING A MEASURE

In selecting a measure for practice or research, social workers should consider a number of criteria, including the sample used in the measure's development, the adequacy and appropriateness of norms, culture and race, reliability, validity, and utility. First, the measure should have been developed using representative sampling with respect to gender, race, and ethnicity. The sample should at least be similar to the population of interest to the social worker. The measure should include detailed information about norms (Milner & Campbell, 1995), which should also be based on a sample similar to the target population. These norms should relate to gender, race, and ethnicity and include item means and standard deviations (Table 3-1).

The concern about race and culture in the development and application of measures cannot be overstated. Discriminatory bias may occur when measures are administered to people from ethnic or racial groups for which the measure was not developed (Groth-Marnat, 1997). In view of this problem, at least one compendium of measures for African Americans has been published (Jones, 1996a). In addition to using relevant measures, social workers should be careful to collect assessment data in a manner that is culturally competent (Guerra & Jagers, 1998; Jones, 1996b; Padilla & Medina, 1996; Solomon, 1993). Worker biases or knowledge deficiencies about race or culture may affect the reliability and validity of data collected (Ridley, 1995).

In addition to sampling and norms, social workers should also examine the measure's reliability. The several types of reliability include internal consistency, test–retest, and interrater. Internal consistency, usually indicated by Cronbach's alpha, should be high (Table 3-1). To determine stability, test–retest reliability is often assessed. The same person's scores on the same items at two different points in time are compared; high correspondence is desirable. High stability would indicate that scores are relatively unaffected by changes in situations or times. However, an instrument's stability is also

Table 3-1. **Statistical Criteria for Selecting Instruments to Assess Aggression and Violence**

Criterion Rating	Exemplary	Extensive	Moderate	Minimal	None
Available norms	Means and SDs for several sub-samples and total sample; extensive information for each item	Means and SDs for total and some groups; some item information	Means for some sub-groups; information for some items	Means for total group only; information for 1–2 items	None; no item information
Coefficient α	.80 or better	.70–.79	.60–.69	< .60	Not reported
Test–retest	Scale scores correlate more than .50 for at least a 1-year period	Scale scores correlate more than .40 across a 3–12-month period	Scale scores correlate more than .30 across a 1–3-month period	Scale scores correlate more than .20 across less than a 1-month period	No data reported
Known groups validity	Discriminate between known groups highly significantly; groups also diverse	Discriminate between known groups highly significantly	Discriminate between known groups significantly	Discriminate between known groups	No known groups data
Convergent validity	Highly significant correlations with more than two related measures	Significant correlations with more than two related measures	Significant correlations with two related measures	Significant correlation with one related measure	No significant correlations reported
Divergent validity	Significantly different from four or more unrelated measures	Significantly different from two or three unrelated measures	Significantly different from one unrelated measure	Different from four or more unrelated measures	No difference or no data

SOURCE: Adapted with permission from Robinson, J. P., Shaver, P. R., & Wrightsman, L. S. (1991). Criteria for scale selection and evaluation. In J. P. Robinson, P. R. Shaver, & L. S. Wrightsman (Eds.), *Measures of personality and social psychological attitudes: Volume 1 of measures of social psychological attitudes* (pp. 12–13). San Diego: Academic Press.

affected by the length of time between tests, whether the attitude or behavior being measured is considered a trait or state, and the age of the respondent. Generally, the longer the interval, the lower the temporal stability (Nunnally & Bernstein, 1994). Aggression is a relatively stable construct, particularly at the extremes (highly aggressive or nonaggressive youths) (Moffit, 1993; Tolan & Gorman-Smith, 1998), and relatively high coefficients would be expected, particularly over the short term. For tests of extroversion, considered a relatively stable trait, coefficients in the high .70s to low .80s within a year are typical (Streiner & Norman, 1995). The age of respondents is also relevant. In general, scores of children and adolescents would be more variable than scores of adults, considering their ongoing development. The retest interval for young children should be short (days or a few weeks) and the intervals for any age should rarely exceed six months (Anastasi, 1988).

Interrater reliability is also known as interobserver reliability. If multiple ratings are used, as in direct observation measures, the interrater reliability coefficient should be high, indicating good agreement between raters. Sometimes interobserver reliability is reported as the percentage of agreement between observers. However, this is subject to inflation by chance agreement and by higher frequency behaviors. The kappa statistic, which corrects for chance agreement, is sometimes reported (Vogt, 1999). The standards for interobserver reliability are different depending on whether percentage agreement or kappa is used. For percentage agreement Blythe and Tripodi (1989) suggest that at least 75 percent is adequate. Kappas in the range of .75 and higher are good, between .60 and .74 fair, and below .60 poor (Bloom et al., 1999).

Instruments used for making clinical judgments about individuals should be more reliable than those used for research (Streiner & Norman, 1995). In research studies that aggregate data across many individuals, the sample size helps reduce errors in measurement, and conclusions are based on the total sample, or several samples, not on single scores. Nunnally and Bernstein (1994) note that although a reliability coefficient of .80 may be a good standard for research, if important decisions are being made based on test scores, a reliability of .90 is a bare minimum, and .95 is the desired standard.

In addition to the reliability of a measure, which "sets the upper limits for test validity" (Milner & Campbell, 1995, p. 27), social workers should also consider its validity. The several forms of validity include face, content, criterion-related, and construct. The simplest, face validity, is determined by looking at the items and making a judgment about whether they appear to measure what they are supposed to measure. Sometimes expert judges are involved in a systematic approach to assessing the items. The systematic examination of the content of items is called content validity. An example of a systematic procedure for using expert raters is the Inventory of Knowledge and Attitudes about Violence in Relationships (Rybarik, Dosch, Gilmore, & Krajewski, 1995), reviewed in this chapter. National experts helped to develop and refine the items using a rating scale to judge how well the items measured knowledge and attitudes about violence in relationships (Rybarik et al., 1995).

Criterion-related validity includes concurrent, predictive, and known-groups. Concurrent validity involves determining how well the measure agrees (correlates) with another measure (criterion) the researcher believes is

valid (Vogt, 1999). Predictive validity refers to how well the measure correlates with a measure to be administered in the future. The difference between
concurrent and predictive validity is the time the criterion is applied.
Predictive validity is more difficult to assess because intervening variables
may affect the likelihood of the predicted event (Milner & Campbell, 1995).
Related to the predictive ability of a measure is its predictive accuracy, which
is distinguished from validity:

> [A] prediction equation is valid if there is some statistically significant cor-
> relation between the predictors and the actual outcomes of interest, but it
> is accurate if a sizable proportion of persons predicted to commit violent
> acts turn out in fact to commit such acts, whereas a sizable proportion of
> others turn out not to commit violence. (Chaiken et al., 1994, p. 224)

Despite some advances in prediction, the accuracy of violence prediction is
still generally low (Chaiken et al., 1994; Guerra, 1998).

   Known-groups validity has to do with how well the measure is able to
discriminate between two criterion groups. For example, on any measure of
violence, youths arrested for violent offenses would be expected to score significantly higher than youths with no arrests.

   In assessing criterion validity, the appropriateness of the criterion and
the validity coefficient must be considered. Are there theoretical or empirical grounds for using the criterion? If so, the coefficient may then be examined. In measures intended for clinical applications, both concurrent and
predictive validity coefficients should be statistically significant, and the correlations should be moderate to high (Fischer & Corcoran, 1994a).
Typically, however, predictive validity coefficients are much lower (Milner &
Campbell, 1995). One standard for known-groups validity is shown in Table
3-1, but there is no simple standard for interpreting validity coefficients:
"How high should a validity coefficient be? No general answer to this question is possible, since the interpretation of a validity coefficient must take
into account a number of concomitant circumstances" (Anastasi & Urbina,
1997, p. 143).

   Construct validity validates both the instrument and the theory underlying it: "To establish construct validity, the meaning of the construct must
be understood, and the propositions the theory makes about the relationships between this and other constructs must be identified" (Grinnell, 1993,
p. 186). For construct validity to be supported, the measure should have
both convergent and divergent validity (Fischer & Corcoran, 1994a). In
convergent validity, the construct being tested should be significantly related to a conceptually similar variable. With divergent validity, the measure
should not be associated with dissimilar variables. For example, a measure of
interpersonal violence should be positively related to peer aggression and

negatively related to positive peer relations. General standards are listed in Table 3-1.

Sometimes construct validity is determined using factor analysis, which is often used to determine the dimensionality or structure of a measure. If a measure includes subscales, its heterogeneity should be established through statistical procedures such as factor analysis.

Another issue related to construct validation is a measure's sensitivity to change, particularly if the measure is to be used in outcome evaluation. The point is that the intervention *should* produce change. Improvement in scores would thus be evidence that the measure is sensitive to changes. Some measures that show sensitivity are the Eyberg Child Behavior Inventory (ECBI) and the Sutter–Eyberg Student Behavior Inventory (SESBI). Others, such as the Child Behavior Checklist (CBCL), "may not appear to be sensitive to short-term change" (Achenbach, 1996, p. 99; Webster-Stratton, 1984, 1998).

Utility of the measure is another important concern, particularly for clinical practice. The measure should be relatively brief and easy to score and interpret (Fischer & Corcoran, 1994a). To improve administration accuracy, there should be a training manual or detailed instructions. Manuals should also include reliability and validity findings and information about how to interpret findings (American Psychological Association, 1985). Most commercially published measures and some instruments published in journals include such information. Unfortunately, many others are incomplete, and authors need to be contacted for additional information.

ETHICAL ISSUES IN MEASURING VIOLENCE AMONG CHILDREN AND ADOLESCENTS

In using instruments to assess aggression and violence, practitioners and researchers face several ethical issues. The first has to do with competence in using measures. The National Association of Social Workers (NASW) *Code of Ethics* (National Association of Social Workers, 1996) has general provisions about working within the bounds of competence. With respect to school social work, the NASW Education Commission Task Force (1993) has established standards requiring social workers in schools to be skilled and competent in using evaluative measures. More detailed competency standards have been developed by the interdisciplinary Joint Committee on Testing Practices, which identified 86 competencies for the proper administration of measures, 12 of which are considered basic proficiencies (Hood & Johnson, 1997). Furthermore, some measures require specific competence. For example, distributors and publishers of measures often require purchasers to have had graduate-level coursework in measurement in addition to supervision (see, for example, Sigma Assessment Systems, Inc., 1999).

The need for competence might seem obvious, but when queried about the appropriate circumstances in which to use a screening scale about child abuse potential, a number of professionals described situations that were inconsistent with the purpose of the measure (Milner, as cited in Milner & Campbell, 1995). A standard of competence is especially important in the clinical prediction of violence (Webster, 1997). Social workers must ensure that they have met the standards for using measures and must work within the bounds of their competence.

Another ethical issue is the potential for unintentional racism and classism in predicting and classifying violent or dangerous clients: "Race, ethnicity, and class have a way of unmindfully influencing clinical judgment. Is it possible for the clinician to remain 'objective' when making an assessment of dangerousness? Will the clinician be influenced by his or her identification with victim or the offender?" (Limandri & Sheridan, 1995, p. 15). Moreover, in creating risk equations there is the possibility of ecological fallacy in making decisions about individuals based on group data. Guerra has noted that

> although [these general] outcomes can be reasonably estimated at the aggregate level, a given individual's future behavior is extremely difficult to predict. Because risk factors often include static contextual variables (for example, neighborhood violence, income level), minority youth from poor urban neighborhoods are likely to score higher on risk, which should also result in higher false positive rates for those groups of juveniles. (1998, p. 397)

Although age, gender, and race are generally predictive of violence (Chaiken et al., 1994), such characteristics are beyond one's ability to change and should be interpreted carefully when predicting or classifying violent clients (LeBlanc, 1998; Wiebush et al., 1995).

One other ethical issue in using assessment to predict or to make classification decisions is balancing individual rights and the need to protect the public (Limandri & Sheridan, 1995). On the one hand, there is the need to keep assessment minimal, not to overpredict dangerousness (that is, to keep false positives to a minimum), and to avoid stigmatization through negative labeling. On the other hand, underpredicting dangerousness (false negatives) puts the community at risk. There are several ways this ethical issue may be addressed. The first is to improve the accuracy of risk assessments to help reduce the likelihood of false positives. Another option is to move from an individualistic risk assessment approach in which individual children are screened to a community-focused model such as the one described by Hawkins and Catalano (1992).

In working with dangerous youths, clinicians and researchers may face the need to warn potential victims, as established by the *Tarasoff* ruling (*Tarasoff v. Board of Regents of the University of California*, 17 C.3d 425 [1976]).

Because clinical prediction of violence has many limitations, social workers are likely to err on the side of caution and warn rather than maintain confidentiality (Milner & Campbell, 1995). Here is where professional competence and adequate administrative support in assessment become critical.

In summary, an ecological–developmental perspective provides a general framework for assessment, and the technical standards may further help in selecting measures for practice. Ethical considerations suggest additional guidelines for the proper use of assessments for aggression and violence among children and youths.

MEASURING INSTRUMENTS

The instruments reviewed in this chapter are organized by method of assessment: structured interviews, self-reports, behavior-rating scales, sociometric methods, direct observation, and archival record reviews.

Structured Interviews

In most cases, social workers will undertake a face-to-face interview with potentially aggressive and violent children or adolescents. Interviews may be structured, semistructured, unstructured, or behavioral (Merrell, 1994). The degree of difference between structured, semistructured, and unstructured interviewing is the amount of worker directiveness, use of ordered and systematic questions or ratings, and degree of latitude in departing from structured activities. Behavioral interviewing is often structured; its main purpose is to identify the problem behavior and the conditions maintaining it (Merrell, 1994).

Structured interviews have several strengths, particularly in comparison with unstructured interviews. They reduce criterion variance—the error caused by vague guidelines for symptom patterns—and information variance—"the variability in amount and type of information derived" (Groth-Marnat, 1997, p. 89) caused by differences in question phrasing or content. Structured interviews also reduce the amount of clinical judgment, allowing for more accurate comparisons among cases (Groth-Marnat, 1997). In addition, structured assessment instruments limit the likelihood of missing relevant symptoms (Groth-Marnat, 1997); often there are concomitant problems associated with violence among children and adolescents (Bailey, 1997).

Structured interviews also have limitations. Highly structured methods are inflexible, limiting clinician exploration of other salient areas. Using a highly structured approach might lead to an emphasis on the content of the interview at the expense of the interpersonal context. It is particularly important to consider the implications or effects of this approach in attending to issues of race and culture; several resources address issues of culture in the interviewing context (Guerra & Jagers, 1998; Kadushin & Kadushin, 1990; Padilla & Medina, 1996; Ridley, 1995; Solomon, 1993). Workers may need to adapt a highly structured interview accordingly. Also, since most structured interviews are used for diagnostic purposes, the earlier cautions about labeling apply.

Two popular structured diagnostic interviews for children and adolescents with conduct problems are the Diagnostic Interview for Children and Adolescents (DICA) and the Diagnostic Interview Schedule for Children (DISC–C) and Parents (DISC–P) (Table 3-2). The DICA and DISC–C are often used for the assessment of DSM-IV Axis I disorders, particularly opposition defiant disorder (Lehmann & Dangel, 1998). Both instruments have been used in epidemiological studies and can be administered by a layperson. The DICA was revised in 1991 to include child, adolescent, and parent versions (Reich, Shayka, & Taibleson, 1991a, 1991b, 1991c). The revised version has been used with young offenders (Ulzen & Hamilton, 1998). A recent study of a Spanish adaptation found good test–retest reliability (Ezpetela, de la Osa, Domenech, Navarro, & Losilla, 1997).

Self-Reports

One strength of self-report measures is that they tap clients' feelings, perceptions, and attitudes (Hudson, 1997). They are thus recommended for assessing internalizing problems (Merrell, 1994). On the other hand, self-reports are limited by response bias problems such as social desirability (participants' responding in socially acceptable ways rather than the way they really feel) and acquiescent responding (participants' agreeing or disagreeing with certain responses out of politeness, not based on what they really believe) (Paulhus, 1991). There is evidence that children and adolescents may not report their aggressive and violent behavior accurately (Hilton, Harris, Rice, Krans, & Lavigne, 1998; Huesmann, Eron, Guerra, & Crawshaw, 1994; Merrell, 1994). Thus, self-reports need to be carefully checked against other measures of aggression or violence. The self-report instruments reviewed here include measures of personality, attitudes or beliefs, attributional bias, behavioral measures, and exposure to environmental violence.

Personality measures. The self-report measures of personality are mostly used with older children or adolescents (Table 3-3). All these measures include aggression subscales. The Jesness Inventory of Adolescent Personality (JIAP) is an inventory of attitudes and behavior related to delinquency. It has been used in studies involving juvenile offenders (Oliver, Hall, & Neuhaus, 1993) and adolescents with conduct disorders (Roberts & Schmitz, 1990). The measure has been criticized for its obsolete norms—it is more than 30

Table 3-2. **Structured Interviews to Assess Aggression and Violence**

Name of Measure (Source)	Description	Targeted/Tested Group	Reliability	Validity
Diagnostic Interview for Children & Adolescents (DICA) and Parents (DICA–P) (Herjanic & Reich, 1982)	Assesses psychopathology. Takes 60–90 minutes to complete. Part 1 includes 19 questions for a joint interview with parent and child; Part 2: child and parent interviewed separately and administered 247 items; Part 3 includes observational data collected from the interview. May be administered by a trained layperson.	Ages 6–17	Test–retest good: .76–.90. Interrater findings between interviewers: .85–.89; between child and parent: .19–.54 (Groth-Marnat, 1997).	DICA can distinguish between children referred to psychiatric clinic and those referred to pediatric clinic, although there is overlap among children ages 6–8 (Groth-Marnat, 1997).
Diagnostic Interview Schedule for Children (DISC–C) and Parents (DISC–P) (Fisher, Wicks, Shaffer, Piacentini, & Lapkin, 1992)	Assesses psychopathology. DISC–C contains 264 items; DISC–P has 302 items. Child version takes about 60 minutes to administer, parent version about 70 minutes. May be administered by a trained layperson.	Ages 9–17	Strong interrater reliability and test–retest (Groth-Marnat, 1997).	Concurrent: correlation with CBCL weak but with DICA–R strong. Known groups: psychiatric referrals had more symptom scores than those referred to pediatric clinic, but mostly for children with severe diagnoses and symptoms (Groth-Marnat, 1997).

years old—but is recommended for assessing socialized aggressive conduct disorder (Merrell, 1994).

The Minnesota Multiphasic Personality Inventory (MMPI) is the most widely used measure of personality (Groth-Marnat, 1997). The MMPI has often been used in criminal justice settings for classification purposes; its use has helped reduce violence in those settings (Chaiken et al., 1994). The adolescent version of the MMPI (MMPI–A) (Butcher et al., 1992) is relatively new, although the original MMPI has been used with adolescents for many years. The basic scale is the same as that of the adult version, but the content includes new items related to adolescents. Although a number of the basic clinical subscales (for example, Psychopathic Deviate) have items related to aggressive behavior, the Anger and Conduct Problems content subscales are

Table 3-3. **Self-Reports to Assess Aggression and Violence**

Name of Measure (Source)	Description	Targeted/Tested Group	Reliability	Validity
		Comprehensive Personality Measures		
Jesness Inventory of Adolescent Personality (JIAP) (Jesness, 1988)	Assesses externalizing disorders; provides scores on 11 personality characteristics including social maladjustment, manifest aggression, and asocial behavior; 155 items	Norms on 970 delinquents and 1,075 nondelinquent males ages 8–18; 450 delinquent and 811 nondelinquent females ages 12–19; California sample	Split-half reliability: .62–.88; Test–retest: .40–.79, with Social Maladjustment and Manifest Aggression among the most stable subscales (Merrell, 1994)	Concurrent validity supported among JIAP subscales, MMPI, and California Personality Inventory; sensitive to treatment changes with youth offenders (Merrell, 1994)
MMPI–Adolescent (Butcher et al., 1992)	Assessment of psychopathology; includes seven validity scales, 10 basic clinical scales, and 15 content scales; 478 true–false items	Ages 14–18; norming sample: 805 males, 815 females, generally representative (Groth-Marnat, 1997)	Basic and Content scales have adequate internal consistency and test–retest reliability (Hood & Johnson, 1997).	Concurrent validity of the content scales appears good and validity of the basic scales seems strong (Hood & Johnson, 1997).
Youth Self-Report (Achenbach, 1991c)	Measures problem behavior and social competence. Problem items scored along two broad-band scales (Internalizing/ Externalizing) and eight narrow-band syndromes including Aggression; 126 items	Ages 11–18; N = 1,315; nationally representative norming sample with respect to race, SES, and urbanism (Merrell, 1994)	One-week test–retest: Broad-band: .83–.87; narrow-band: .39–.83 (Merrell, 1994)	Correlates well with CBCL and Teacher Report Form (.40 range); significant relationship with DSM-III Conduct Disorder and Delinquency subscale; some poor validity findings when used as a screening tool for psychopathology and in assessing girls hospitalized for behavior problems (Merrell, 1994)
		Attitudes, Beliefs, or Fantasies		
Acceptance of Couple Violence (Foshee, Fothergill, & Stuart, as cited in Dahlberg et al., 1998)	Measures acceptability of couple violence; three subscales: Male-on-Female Violence, Female-on-Male Violence, and Acceptance of General Dating Violence; 11 items	Grades 8–9	Alphas: For Male-on-Female violence: .74; for Female-on-Male violence: .71; for Acceptance of General Dating Violence: .73	Not reported

(Continued on next page)

Table 3-3. *(continued)*

Name of Measure (Source)	Description	Targeted/Tested Group	Reliability	Validity
		Attitudes, Beliefs, or Fantasies		
Aggression Approval Scale (Guerra, Huesmann, & Hanish, 1995; Huesmann, Guerra, Miller, & Zelli, 1992; Huesmann, Guerra, Zelli, & Miller, 1992)	Assesses children's beliefs about the appropriateness of aggression; 35 items	$N = 293$, grades 2–4 in four inner-city Chicago schools, 85% African American; 155 males, 138 females	Full scale alpha: .90; three-month test–retest: .48	Children's scores correlated significantly with self-reports of aggressive behavior for girls and boys and with peer nominations of aggressive behavior for boys.
Aggressive Fantasies Scale (Nadel et al., 1996; reprinted in Dahlberg et al., 1998)	Measures level of aggressive fantasies and daydreams; seven items	$N = 664$, grades 7 and 8; 33% Latina, 28% Latino, 21% African American females, 17% African American males	Alpha: .69	Correlated (.30) significantly (p < .001) with Violent Behaviors Committed Checklist
Attitude toward Violence (Bosworth & Espelage, cited in Dahlberg et al., 1998)	Measures acceptability of violence; six items	Grades 6–8	Alpha: .67	Not reported
Beliefs Supporting Aggression (Slaby & Guerra, 1988; Legitimacy of Aggression subscale reprinted in Dahlberg et al., 1998)	Measures beliefs in five subscales: Legitimacy, Aggression Increases Self-Esteem, Aggression Helps to Avoid a Negative Image, Victims Deserve Aggression, and Victims Don't Suffer; 18 items	$N = 66$ incarcerated adolescents	Alphas on five subscales: .67, .53, .68, .72, and .37; 10-week test–retest (Kendall's tau): .86	First four belief subscales strongly associated with violent behavior
Inventory of Knowledge and Attitudes about Violence in Relationships (Rybarik, Dosch, Gilmore, & Krajewski, 1995)	30 items in main inventory: 18 true–false items about knowledge, 12 items about attitudes; eight open-ended help-seeking items	$N = 99$, grade 7 students, M age 12.3 years; 57 males, 42 females; 78% Caucasian, 9% Asian American, 5% American Indian, 3% Hispanic, 4% other; Midwestern city	Alpha: Knowledge: .32, Attitude: .72. Two-week test–retest: Knowledge: overall: .57, girls: .58, boys: .52; Attitude: overall: .67, girls: .52, boys: .70	Content validity determined by national panel of expert jurors who rated the acceptability of items using a Likert scale. Item discrimination analyses found 11 knowledge items and one attitude item discriminated and best elicited knowledge or attitudes. In other validity tests, gender differences were found on attitude measure.

(Continued on next page)

Table 3-3. *(continued)*

Name of Measure (Source)	Description	Targeted/Tested Group	Reliability	Validity
		Attitudes, Beliefs, or Fantasies		
Normative Beliefs about Aggression Scale (Huesmann & Guerra, 1997); Revision of the Aggression Approval Scale (Huesmann, Guerra, Miller, & Zelli, 1992)	Measures children's belief about the acceptability of aggression; 20 items	N = 1,550, grades 1 and 4; 38.3% African American, 36.6% Hispanic, 18.1% Caucasian; 52% girls	Alphas high (minimum .84) for total measure across grades and race/ethnic groups. One-year test–retest with a subsample (N = 846) on overall scale: .31 (relatively stable across sex and race/ethnicity). Test–retest with first graders: .13	Validity subsample was 1,070. Scale correlated with peer-nominated aggression and teacher ratings of aggression, more for boys than girls (Huesmann & Guerra, 1997). Nadel et al. (1996) found scale significantly ($p < .001$) but modestly correlated (.24) with Violent Behaviors Committed Checklist.
		Attributional Bias		
Home Interview (Dodge, 1980; Aber, Brown, Jones, & Samples, as cited in Dahlberg et al., 1998)	Measures children's attributions of hostile or benign intent; six scenarios with four questions per scenario	Grades 1–6, urban sample	Alpha: .70	Not reported
Peer Relations Assessment (Graham, Hudley, & Williams, 1992; Hudley & Graham, 1993; measure reprinted in Dahlberg et al., 1998)	Measures children's attributions for hypothetical peer provocations in three subscales: Bias, Anger, and Preferred Behavior; eight scenarios, eight questions per scenario	Two study samples (N = 110) grades 3–6, 7, and 8; mostly African American boys, but included Latinos	Six-week test–retest: Bias subscale: .68, Anger: .74, Preferred Behavior: .71 (Dahlberg et al., 1998)	Not reported
		Behavioral Measures		
Aggression Scale (Orpinas, cited in Dahlberg et al., 1998)	Frequency of self-reported aggressive behaviors; 11 items	Grades 6–8	Alpha: .87.; good stability; intraclass correlation coefficient .85	Positive correlations with predictor variables of violence
Dating Violence Victimization and Perpetration (Foshee et al., 1996; reprinted in Dahlberg et al., 1998)	Two measures of physical and sexual violence in teen dating relationships, 18 items each: Victimization and Perpetration	N = 1,965, ages 12–17; 50.4% females; 75.9% Caucasian, 20.2% African American, 3.9% other	Alphas: Victimization: .90; Perpetration: .93	Not reported

(Continued on next page)

Table 3-3. *(continued)*

Name of Measure (Source)	Description	Targeted/Tested Group	Reliability	Validity
		Behavioral Measures		
Social Experience Questionnaire–Self Report (Crick & Bigbee, 1998)	Measures overt (five items) and relational (five items) aggression victimization and prosocial recipient acts (five items).	$N = 857$ (two studies), grades 3–6; 52% boys; mostly Caucasian, but about 25% African American; Midwest sample	Alphas (study 1, study 2): Overt: .78, .89; Relational: .80, .91; Prosocial: .77, .90	Three subscales generally validated by factor analysis except one or two overt victimization items cross-loaded
State–Trait Anger Expression Inventory (STAXI) (Spielberger, 1988; Spielberger, Reheiser, & Sydeman, 1995)	Measures experience, expression, and control of anger in five main scales: State Anger (10 items), Trait Anger (10 items), Anger-In (eight items), Anger-Out (eight items), and Anger Control (eight items). Trait Anger is subdivided into two four-item subscales: Angry Temperament and Angry Reaction.	$N = 2,469$, norming sample ages 12–18, males and females; Florida sample, no data on race/ethnicity (Furlong & Smith, 1994a)	Alphas of .82–.90 for State Anger, Trait Anger, Angry Temperament, and Anger-In; .65–.75 for Angry Reaction and Anger-Out (Furlong & Smith, 1994a)	STAXI scores correlated with the Buss–Durkee Hostility Inventory (Furlong & Smith, 1994a). Anger-In correlated (.47) with systolic and diastolic blood pressure of 1,114 high school students (Spielberger et al., 1995).
Victimization (Orpinas & Kelder, as cited in Dahlberg et al., 1998)	Measures frequency of being teased, pushed, or threatened in the previous week; 10 items	Grades 6–8	Alpha: .85	Correlated well (.51) with the Aggression Scale (reviewed above)
		Environmental Violence Exposure		
Children's Exposure to Community Violence (Richters & Martinez, as cited in Dahlberg et al., 1998)	Frequency of exposure to violence at home, neighborhood, or school; 12 items	African American males ages 12–16	Alpha: .84	Not reported
Exposure to Violence Checklist (Nadel et al., 1996; checklist reprinted in Dahlberg et al., 1998)	Measures direct or indirect (violence witnessed or rumored) violence victimization; 135 items	N = 664, grades 7 and 8; 33% Latina, 28% Latino, 21% African American females, 17% African American males	Not reported	Six factors "tapped direct and vicarious victimization in: (1) school, (2) the community, and (3) the family" (Nadel et al., 1996, p. 113)

(Continued on next page)

Table 3-3. *(continued)*

Name of Measure (Source)	Description	Targeted/Tested Group	Reliability	Validity
		Environmental Violence Exposure		
Screen for Adolescent Violence Exposure (SAVE) (Hastings & Kelley, 1997)	Assesses adolescent exposure to school, home, and community violence; three subscales for each setting: Traumatic Violence, Indirect Violence, Physical/ Verbal Abuse; 32 items	N = 1,250 inner-city adolescents, mostly African American; approximately 55% girls; Southern sample	Alphas for each scale: range of .90–.94; subscale alphas: range of .58–.91. Two-week test–retest: range of .53–.92	Exploratory and confirmatory factor analyses supported subscales. Known-groups validity: All scales successfully classified participants according to low- and high-violence status. Convergent and divergent validity supported by highly significant correlations with several measures of violence and low correlations with a few unrelated measures.

the most relevant in assessing violence and aggression. The Anger subscale includes a number of items related to overt aggression, such as throwing things, smashing objects, or fighting. The MMPI–A takes one hour to complete (45 minutes with computer administration). To reduce administration time, some testers use only the basic validity and standard clinical scales, which include the first 350 items of the MMPI–A (Groth-Marnat, 1997).

There have been concerns about the social validity of the MMPI and the MMPI–A. On the original MMPI, some differences in scores were noted between African American and Caucasian respondents, but there were no systematic differences among American Indian, Hispanic, and Asian American respondents (Groth-Marnat, 1997). In view of this and other research, a cautious approach in using the MMPI with African American and Hispanic subjects has been advocated (Sturmer & Gerstein, 1997; Whitworth & Unterbrink, 1994). The MMPI–A has not been as widely tested, but a recent examination with Hispanics found elevated T-score means on a number of subscales (though not on the Anger or Conduct Problems subscales) and below-average scores for girls on some subscales, including Anger (Gumbiner, 1998). Additional testing to examine the social validity of the MMPI–A is needed.

The Youth Self-Report (YSR) is the self-report version of the multiaxial CBCL. It was intended to be used in conjunction with the CBCL and the Teacher Report Form (TRF), although it is often used on its own. Its strengths lie in its usability. However, it lacks validity scales to assess deviant responding (Merrell, 1994) and is not the best choice for assessing children or adolescents with problems specifically related to aggression and violence (Merrell, 1994).

Of the three personality measures designed for children and adolescents with conduct problems, the JIAP is perhaps the most appropriate. It is considered a more specific measure of delinquency than the MMPI (Roberts & Schmitz, 1990).

Attitudes or beliefs. Self-reports are the best method for assessing attitudes or beliefs. Table 3-3 includes five instruments assessing violence-related beliefs and two assessing attitudes about dating violence. These measures are mostly used in research or in prevention programs. Several are available in Dahlberg and colleagues (1998). The two dating violence attitude measures are important because there are very few such tested measures. Both assess attitudes about the acceptability of violence in dating relationships; one includes items related to knowledge about violence.

Attributional bias. Social cognitive researchers have explored how children's perceptions of peers in social situations differ and how they relate to subsequent aggressive behavior. Researchers have found differences between aggressive and nonaggressive children in their attributions of intent. Specifically, aggressive children are more likely than nonaggressive children to attribute hostile intentions to others (Crick, 1995; Crick & Dodge, 1994; Dodge & Crick, 1990; Dodge, Price, Bachorowski, & Newman, 1990). To assess hostile attribution bias, researchers have typically used vignettes like those in the Home Interview or the Peer Relations Assessment (Table 3-3). The Home Interview was originally developed by Dodge (1980), but has since been adapted by others. The version reviewed in Table 3-3 is the adapted version.

Behavioral measures. Behavioral measures include instruments measuring a range of constructs, including aggression (several forms), anger, and dating violence. The Social Experience Questionnaire (SEQ) assesses overt and relational aggression victimization. As noted earlier, relational aggression, which includes relationship-damaging behaviors, is more characteristic of girls than boys (Crick, 1995; Crick & Bigbee, 1998; Crick & Grotpeter, 1995; Grotpeter & Crick, 1996). The SEQ also includes a few items related to prosocial acts.

A measure not cited in Table 3-3 because of its lack of formal reliability or validity is the Violent Victimization Survey (McGee, 1996). Recently developed for students attending predominantly African American high schools, the instrument consists of 40 statements related to weapons carrying and personal exposure to community and school violence. The measure has face validity.

One measure of anger expression is the State–Trait Anger Expression Inventory (STAXI). The inventory has five main scales that measure the experience of anger as an emotional state (State Anger) and as a personality trait (Trait Anger) and that measure the frequency of anger expression (Anger-In, Anger-Out, and Anger Control). The Anger-Out scale includes verbal expressions, such as insults or threats, and physical expressions of anger, such as slamming doors and assaulting people. The STAXI is relatively brief, easy to administer (Feindler, 1995), and available in several languages.

One measure cited in Table 3-3 assesses dating violence perpetration and victimization for middle and high school students. Because there are few reliable and valid measures of dating aggression among youths, many use adaptations of the Straus Conflict Tactics Scale (Straus, 1979) developed for adults. The Dating Violence Victimization and Perpetration measure includes items related to physical and sexual violence, but not items related to psychological abuse.

Exposure to environmental violence. Environmental factors play a significant role in violence. Exposure to violence, availability of drugs, and involvement of neighborhood adults in drug use or crime predict subsequent violence (Gorman-Smith & Tolan, 1998; J. D. Hawkins et al., 1998). Three measures of exposure to community violence are included in Table 3-3. The Violent Victimization Survey (McGee, 1996) noted previously also includes items related to exposure to community and school violence.

Behavior-Rating Instruments

Behavior-rating scales "provide a standardized format for the development of summative judgments about a child or adolescent's behavior characteristics, supplied by an informant who knows the subject well" (Merrell, 1994, p. 66). The measures cited in Table 3-4 are completed by teachers, parents, or others who know the child or adolescent well.

As with the other measures, there are advantages and disadvantages to rating scales (Merrell, 1994). Costing less in both time and money than direct observations, rating scales can capture behavior over time and in different settings. They also gather information from people who know the subject best. However, rating scales are subject to response bias and error variance (Merrell, 1994). Forms of response bias include rating a subject favorably out of positive regard rather than on what is being measured (halo bias), rating all subjects either too critically or too positively (leniency or severity), and rating using only midpoints, avoiding extremes on the scale (central tendency effects) (Merrell, 1994). Error variance may be introduced in three forms: source variance, in which different raters respond differently to the rating format; setting variance, in which informants tend to rate differently in different environments because of varying properties in those settings;

Table 3-4. **Behavior Rating Instruments to Assess Aggression and Violence**

Name of Measure (Source)	Description	Targeted/Tested Group	Reliability	Validity
Aggressive Behavior (Dodge & Coie, 1987)	Assesses reactive and proactive aggression; six items; teacher scored	Two study samples (N = 598), grades 1–6; mostly male and African American; samples from North Carolina and Indiana	Alphas for studies 1 and 2: proactive aggression: .91, .87; reactive aggression: .90, .88; scores stable over short time span	Factor structure generally supported. Teacher ratings significantly related to independent observer ratings of proactive and reactive aggression. Other discriminant validity data supportive.
Behavior Problem Checklist–Revised (Quay & Peterson, 1987)	Measures problem behavior in six subscales: Conduct Disorder, Socialized Aggression, Attention Problems, Anxiety–Withdrawal, Psychosis, and Motor Excess; 89 items	Ages 5–15; different and diverse norming samples used, although none national or representative	Alphas of subscales: range of .70–.95. Interrater between teachers: .52–.85; between mothers and fathers: .55–.93 across subscales. Two-month test–retest: .49–.93.	Subscales determined through factor analysis. Measure distinguished children with problems from normal samples. Convergent validity supported in several studies (Merrell, 1994). Good correlations (.60) between Conduct Disorder subscale and playground observations of aggressive behavior (Merrell, 1994).
Child Behavior Checklist (CBCL) and Teacher Report Form (TRF) (Achenbach, 1991a, 1991b)	Assesses problem behavior on eight subscales, one on Aggression. Two versions, parent (CBCL) and teacher (TRF), each with 120 items	Ages 4–18 (CBCL), 5–18 (TRF); large norming samples for both versions	Test–retest: CBCL one week: . 80–mid-.90s; 18 months: .47–.76; TRF one week: .90; 15 days: .84; two months: .74; four months: .68. Interrater for CBCL between parents: .66; for TRF between teachers and aides: .42–.72 (Merrell, 1994)	Discriminant validity: Both versions discriminated between clinical and nonclinical samples with high accuracy. Concurrent validity: CBCL and TRF had strong correlations with Conners Parent Rating Scale (.91), Conners Teacher Rating Scale (.85 on overall), and Revised Behavior Problem Checklist (.92 overall) (Merrell, 1994).
Eyberg Child Behavior Inventory (Robinson, Eyberg, & Ross, 1980)	Assesses conduct problems; 36 items, each rated on two scales: Problem scale (yes–no) and Intensity scale (seven-point scale); parent-completed	N = 1,003, ages 2–16; 52% male; 78% Caucasian, 8% African American, 7% Asian American; Northwest (Burns & Patterson, 1990)	Alphas: Problem scale: .91; Intensity scale: .93 (Burns & Patterson, 1990). Test–retest: .86 (Eyberg & Ross, 1978)	Good concurrent validity using the CBCL, particularly the externalizing dimension (Boggs, Eyberg & Reynolds, 1990). Good known-groups validity (Burns & Patterson, 1990; Eyberg & Robinson, 1983; Eyberg & Ross, 1978). Appears sensitive to intervention effects (Eyberg & Robinson, 1983).

(Continued on next page)

Table 3-4. *(continued)*

Name of Measure (Source)	Description	Targeted/Tested Group	Reliability	Validity
Conners Rating Scale (Conners, 1990; Goyette, Conners, & Ulrich, 1978)	Applies to a wide range of problems, often used to assess ADHD; two parent and two teacher-scored scales; most widely used: 48-item parent version (CPRS–48) and 39-item teacher version (CTRS–39)	Norming samples: CPRS–48: N = 529, ages 3–17; almost half male; mostly Caucasian. CTRS–39: N = 9,583, ages 3–14; Canadian sample	CPRS–48: M interrater between parents: .51 (Goyette et al., 1978). CTRS–39: interrater on subscales: .39–.94. Test–retest: one month: .72–.91, one year: .33–.55 (Merrell, 1994)	Scales discriminated between ADHD and non-ADHD children (Zaparniuk & Taylor, 1997), learning disabled and regular education students, boys referred from juvenile court and a control group, behavioral-disordered and non–special education students (Merrell, 1994). Convergent validity with several measures, including CBCL (Merrell, 1994). Predictive validity of CTRS–39 good using hyperactivity at age 10 as criterion, based on ratings at age 7 (Merrell, 1994).
Iowa–Conners Teacher's Rating Scale (Atkins & Milich, 1988; Loney & Milich, 1982)	Assesses attention deficit disorder and aggression; two subscales of five items each: Inattention/Overactivity (I/O), and Aggression (AG)	Ages 6–12	Alphas: For norming sample: I/O: .87; AG: .85; for clinic sample: I/O: .80; AG: .87. One-week test–retest: I/O: .89; AG: .86 (Atkins & Milich, 1988)	Significant r's found between I/O and hyper-activity factor of Conners Teacher Rating Scale (CTRS) and between AG subscale and Conduct Problems subscale of CTRS. AG correlated with peer ratings of aggres-sion; other evidence for concurrent and construct validity cited by authors (Atkins & Milich, 1988)
School Social Behavior Scales (Merrell, 1993a, 1993b)	Two scales assessing Social Competence (32 items) and Anti-social Behavior (33 items); school personnel rated.	N = 1,858 standard-ization sample, grades K–12; 1,025 boys, 833 girls; 87% Caucasian, 8% African American, 2.7% Hispanic, .9% Asian American, .6% American Indian; geographically rep-resentative	Alphas (internal consistency and split half): .91–.98. Three-week test–retest: Social Competence: .76–.83, Antisocial: .60–.73. Interrater between teachers and aides: Social Competence: .72–.83, Antisocial: .53–.71.	Scales structure supported through factor analysis. Concurrent validity: moderate to high correlations with Waksman Social Skills Rating Scale, Conners Teacher Rating Scale, Walker–McConnell Scale of Social Competence and School Adjustment. Correlations with CBCL–Direct Observation Form from low to moderate. Good known-groups validity.

(Continued on next page)

Table 3-4. *(continued)*

Name of Measure (Source)	Description	Targeted/Tested Group	Reliability	Validity
Sutter–Eyberg Student Behavior Inventory (SESBI) (Burns & Owen, 1990; Funderburk & Eyberg, 1989; Sutter & Eyberg, 1984)	Assesses conduct problems; yields a Problem score (yes/no) and an Intensity score (seven-point scale); 36 items; teacher scored	Ages 2–17; samples not large, mostly Caucasian; less data available on 8- to 17-year-olds	Alphas: Problem scale: .93–.96; Intensity scale: .95–.98. Test-retest: Problem scale: .89–.98; Intensity scale: .90–.94. Interrater: Problem scale: .84–.87; Intensity scale: .85–.95.	Concurrent validity: Intensity scale correlated (.94) with Conners Rating Scales; both scales correlated with Preschool Behavior Questionnaire–Externalizing. Other validity: CBCL External-izing scale correlated with Problem scale (.71), with Intensity scale (.87). Good known-groups validity.
Systematic Screening for Behavior Disorders (SSBD) (Walker & Severson, 1990; Walker et al., 1990; Walker, Severson, Nicholson, Kehle, Jenson, & Clark, 1994)	Three stages to assess internalizing and externalizing behavior problems. Stage 1: all stu-dents screened; stage 2: targeted students assessed using two mea-sures; stage 3: targeted students observed in class and playground.	Grades 1–5; boys and girls, mostly white non-Hispanics; samples from Northwest: Washington, Oregon, and Utah	Mean alphas for stage 2 scales: .92. Interobserver reliability for stage 3 observations: 95% for classroom, 88% for playground (Walker et al., 1994).	Concurrent validity: Correlated with school record profiles (Walker et al., 1990). Discriminant validity: students correct-ly classified into exter-nalizing, internalizing, and nonranked groups based on scores at stages 2 and 3 (Walker et al., 1990, 1994).

and temporal variance, in which ratings may change over time (Merrell, 1994). To reduce these limitations, Merrell (1994) recommends aggrega-tion—getting ratings from a variety of sources, in different settings, and using different methods.

Most of the behavior-rating instruments listed in Table 3-4 are compre-hensive, including subscales of aggression or violence. One measure exclu-sively related to aggression is Dodge and Coie's (1987) measure of aggressive behavior, which assesses both reactive and proactive aggression. Dodge and Coie do not reproduce a complete version of the measure, but Dahlberg and colleagues (1998) include one in their compendium of instruments.

The Behavior Problem Checklist–Revised (BPC–R) is a measure of anti-social behavior widely used in both research and clinical settings. Its Conduct Disorder and Socialized Aggression subscales include items related to vio-lence. The measure can be completed by anyone familiar with the child, such as a parent or teacher. There is a Spanish language version (Curtis & Schmidt, 1993). The biggest limitation of the BPC–R is the lack of representative national norms.

The CBCL and the TRF are also widely used in clinical practice and research. Violence research (for example, Grossman et al., 1997) often uses the Aggression subscale, which covers a range of aggressive behavior from arguing to physically attacking others. Both measures have strong psychometric properties and have minimal or no effects related to gender or race (Merrell, 1994). However, subjects with low SES on the CBCL have had higher problem behavior scores (Merrell, 1994). Nevertheless, the measure has been called "perhaps the best rating scale currently available for assessing severe symptoms of childhood psychopathology" (Merrell, 1994, p. 75) and has been recommended for clinical social work (Lowe, 1998). It is not a good short-term outcome measure, because it does not appear to be sensitive to short-term treatment change (Achenbach, 1996; Webster-Stratton, 1984, 1998).

The Conners Rating Scale (CRS) assesses a range of problems, including aggression. The CRS is often used to assess attention deficit hyperactivity disorder (ADHD), which has been strongly linked to later violence (J. D. Hawkins et al., 1998). Because it is relatively brief, the CRS has been recommended as a screening tool (Merrell, 1994). The most common parent version is the CPRS–48; the most common teacher version is the CTRS–39.

Another measure often used to assess ADHD is the Iowa–Conners Teacher's Rating Scale (ICTRS), which is easily administered and appears to be reliable and valid for children with externalizing problems. Though items were derived from the CRS, the ICTRS is better able to discriminate inattention–overactivity from aggression (Atkins & Milich, 1988; Deblinger & Atkins, 1988).

Other comprehensive measures are the Eyberg Child Behavior Inventory (ECBI) for parents and the Sutter–Eyberg Student Behavior Inventory (SESBI) for teachers. The ECBI is widely used to measure a range of problems, including aggression. Recommended for use with children and adolescents with conduct problems, it is relatively easy to administer and score and is reportedly sensitive to treatment effects (Eyberg & Robinson, 1983; Webster-Stratton, 1984). This instrument is not yet commercially published but has been reproduced in Fischer and Corcoran (1994a).

The SESBI is relatively brief. Like the ECBI, it has been observed to be sensitive to treatment change in children (McNeil, Eyberg, Eisenstadt, Newcomb, & Funderburk, 1991). The SESBI has been revised into a 38-item measure (Rayfield, Eyberg, & Foote, 1998).

The School Social Behavior Scales (SSBS) measure social competence and antisocial behavior; they have been used in both research and clinical settings (Grossman et al., 1997). The antisocial subscales include Hostile–Irritable, Antisocial–Aggressive, and Disruptive–Demanding. Reviews have been generally positive (Furlong & Smith, 1994a; Welsh, 1998), with calls for more representative samples (Welsh, 1998).

Multiple-gating or multiple-stage strategies have been developed to screen large numbers of children for conduct problems in juvenile justice (Loeber, Dishion, & Patterson, 1984) and educational settings (Lochman et al., 1995). Multiple-gating refers to progressively more intense levels of assessment using multiple domains (for example, academics, behavior), multiple informants (teacher, children, parents), multiple methods (teacher ratings, observations), and multiple settings (school, home). Loeber and colleagues (1984) found that a three-stage process increased predictive accuracy and saved money over single-stage methods using full assessments.

One norm-based three-stage multiple-gating method developed for schools is Systematic Screening for Behavior Disorders (SSBD), which is used to screen for internalizing and externalizing behavior problems. At stage 1 teachers screen all students. Those meeting the internalizing/externalizing criteria are screened at the next level. At stage 2 teachers use two instruments, a 23-item Likert rating scale of adaptive and maladaptive behaviors and a 33-item binomial-scaled Critical Events Index. At stage 3 students who exceed the stage 2 cutoffs are observed by trained observers in class (Academic Engaged Time) and on the playground (using the Peer Social Behavior observation code). Those exceeding the normative cutoffs at stage 3 are referred for further evaluation. The norming samples, which were from the northwestern United States, consisted of 4,500 students for stage 2 and 1,275 students for stage 3. Reviews of the system have been generally favorable (Kelley, 1998; Merrell, 1994; Zlomke & Spies, 1998). However, there is a need for norming samples that are more geographically, racially, and ethnically diverse.

Sociometric Methods

Sociometric methods of measuring aggression and violence have been used mostly in research contexts. Often used to assess peer relations, sociometric methods are generally reviewed favorably for their technical qualities (Merrell, 1994). The most common sociometric method used to identify aggressive children is peer nomination, which is also used to assess relational aggression (Crick & Grotpeter, 1995).

Three peer nomination measures are reviewed in Table 3-5, two completed by children and one completed by teachers. The Peer Nominated Index of Aggression has appeared in several iterations. The original measure by Eron and colleagues (Eron, Walder, & Lefkowitz, 1971; Huesmann et al., 1994) included 22 items but was later modified to 24. This chapter cites the 24-item version. All versions include the 10 items related to aggression often used by researchers (Eron et al., 1971; Huesmann et al., 1994; Huesmann, et al., 1992).

The Peer Nomination Instrument (PNI) includes items related to overt and relational aggression (Crick & Bigbee, 1998; Crick & Grotpeter, 1995).

The PNI has been used in different versions; the Relational, Overt, and Prosocial subscales have been used in one study (Grotpeter & Crick, 1996), and the Overt and Relational subscales in another (Crick & Bigbee, 1998), with slight modifications to the number of items in the subscales. With all versions, the psychometric properties have been favorable.

Table 3-5. **Sociometric Measures to Assess Aggression and Violence**

Name of Measure (Source)	Description	Targeted/Tested Group	Reliability	Validity
Peer-Nominated Index of Aggression (Eron, Walder, & Lefkowitz, 1971; reprinted in Dahlberg et al., 1998)	Measures peer assessments of aggressive behavior. Each child in class nominates any child who fits any of the questions related to six domains: Aggression, Prosocial, Popularity, Rejection, Victimization, and Hyperactivity; 24 items	Grades 1–6; urban samples; measure used in many countries (Huesmann, Guerra, Miller, & Zelli, 1992; Huesmann, Guerra, Zelli, & Miller, 1992)	Alphas: about .95. One-month test–retest: approximately .91 (Huesmann, Guerra, Zelli, & Miller, 1992)	Construct validity supported in many studies; predictive validity supported by correlations with aggression, violence, delinquency, and criminal behavior over three, 11, and 22 years (Huesmann, Eron, Guerra, & Crawshaw, 1994).
Peer Nomination Instrument (PNI) (Crick & Bigbee, 1998; Crick & Grotpeter, 1995)	Assesses peer perceptions of social adjustment. Includes a peer sociometric (two studies) and four subscales: Relational Aggression (four items), Overt Aggression (three items), Prosocial Behavior (five items), and Isolation (three items)	N = 857 (two studies), grades 3–6; 52% boys; mostly Caucasian, but about 25% African American; Midwest sample	Alphas: Overt: .94; Relational: .83; Prosocial: .91; Isolation: .92 (Crick & Grotpeter, 1995). One-month test–retest: Relational: .82; Overt: .90 (Crick, 1996)	Four subscales supported by factor analysis.
Teacher Predictions of Peer Nominations–Aggression (Huesmann, Eron, Guerra, & Crawshaw, 1994)	Teachers' perceptions of how children will rate another child on aggression, prosocial behavior, popularity, rejection, victimization, and hyperactivity. Two versions, one by question (number of children who would nominate each child on each question), the other by child (percent of peers who would nominate child); 22 items, 10 related to aggression	N = 179, grades 3–5; 82 boys, 97 girls; all African American; low SES; inner-city school in large Midwestern city	Alphas for two versions: .97 and .95	Teacher predictions highly correlated with Peer Nomination Inventory (PNI). Correlations with PNI also high by gender.

A different strategy in the sociometric measurement of aggression has been to use teachers to predict peer nominations of aggression. The Teacher Predictions of Peer Nominations instrument (Huesmann et al., 1994) measures teachers' perceptions of how children will rate a child on each item. Although the measure has undergone only limited testing, the psychometric properties are good.

Direct Observations

Self-reports and rating scales are considered indirect assessment methods because they assess perceptions about behaviors (Doke, 1988; Stein & Karno, 1994). A highly regarded direct method of gathering data about aggression and violence is direct observation (McMahon & Forehand, 1988; Merrell, 1994). The importance of this method was recently shown when direct observations in naturalistic settings detected behavior change that other behavior-rating methods missed (Grossman et al., 1997). Furthermore, the biggest change in aggressive behavior was observed on the playground and in the cafeteria, highlighting the need for observations outside the classroom where aggressive behavior is less likely.

There are, however, limitations to direct observation. Errors can come from "observer bias, observer drift (that is, changes in observer sensitivity or vigilance), errors in data computation, and ambiguity in defining target behaviors" (Doke, 1988, p. 297). Subject-related errors include reactivity, in which behaviors change as a result of being observed. A related problem is behavior that is context related.

There are several ways to minimize these measurement problems. To reduce observer errors, detailed manuals are needed that clearly define the behavioral domains to be observed and the methods of computing data. To reduce bias and drift, observers must have extensive initial training and then retraining (Merrell, 1994) that includes interobserver agreement testing that meets the standards cited earlier. Often, the training uses videotaped scenarios in which high interobserver reliabilities are achieved before real observations begin.

To reduce reactivity, observers are instructed to be as unobtrusive as possible and to include a habituation time for children and adolescents to get used to the observer's presence. Another method is to discard early observations. To reduce the problem of context-related behavior, observations should be compared with behaviors in real-life settings. Observations should be made in several settings to address behaviors that are situation specific (Merrell, 1994). Also, the child's or adolescent's behavior should be compared with the behavior of other children or adolescents in the same setting. This has been described as collecting social comparison data (Merrell, 1994).

Three recording systems are used in the observational systems reviewed in Table 3-6: event, interval, and time sampling. Event recording counts how many times a target behavior occurs within a specified period. For example, the event-recording method used with the CBCL Direct Observation Form requires respondents to record behavior during a 10-minute period. In interval recording, an observation period is divided into equal intervals, and the observer records whether the target behavior occurs in the interval. For example, in the Dyadic Parent–Child Interaction Coding System, any externalizing behaviors that occur during five-minute periods in each of the three contexts (child-directed interaction, parent-guided interaction, and cleanup) are recorded, for a total of 15 minutes. In the third method, time sampling, the presence of the target behavior is observed at predetermined intervals. For example, with the Behavior Observation Checklist, observations are made every 10 seconds for each child and repeated for the duration of the meeting.

The measures cited in Table 3-6 have all been used to assess aggressive behavior in multiple settings, including schools, camps, and clinic offices. Observation systems have been used primarily in research projects but are practical, with some adaptations, for clinical settings (Foster, Bell-Dolan, & Burge, 1988).

Assessment of School Records

Often social work practitioners and researchers review files as part of an assessment. Historical information "is important in helping to build up a picture of the development of aggressive and violent behavior" (Epps, 1997, p. 53). The School Archival Record Search (SARS) was developed to systematize the collection of school-based behavioral information. Although the reliability and validity of the SARS are weak (Table 3-7), the instrument helps to reduce biases in data collection and allows comparisons across cases. There is no equivalent for assessing agency-based records, but Blythe, Tripodi, and Briar (1994) have described six criteria for doing so.

APPLICATIONS TO PRACTICE

How does one choose which measure to use? In an ecological–developmental assessment, one would want to use multiple methods, informants, settings, and domains. One would want to examine all development and norming samples to make sure they were similar to the target clients. The reliability and validity of the instrument should be acceptable. Certainly no measure should be used without an adequate understanding of its strengths and weaknesses and the proper method of administration.

Table 3-6. **Direct Observation Methods to Assess Aggression and Violence**

Name of System (Source)	Description, Domains, Number of Items	Setting	Sample	Recording System	Reliability/ Validity
Behavior Coding System (Harris & Reid, 1981)	Measures coercive and aggressive behavior; eight categories	Classroom, playground	N = 53, 10 in grades 1–2, 43 in grades 5–6; boys	Interval	Interobserver reliability: classrooms: 93%; playground: 86%
Behavior Observation Checklist (Feldman, Caplinger, & Wodarski, 1983)	Records prosocial (eight items), nonsocial (11 items), and antisocial (five items) behaviors	Children in summer camp, community center	N = 701; M age: 11.2 years; all boys; 65% Caucasian, 34% African American	Time sampling	189 reliability checks over three years; average interobserver agreement: 92.2%
Child Behavior Checklist–Direct Observation Form (Achenbach, 1986)	Assesses internalizing and externalizing child problems and on-task behavior; three parts: 96-item rating scale, event and time-sampling methods	Classroom, other group settings	Ages 5–14; normed on 287 nonreferred children	Time sampling, event, and interval	Good interrater reliability and discriminant validity (McConaughy, Achenbach, & Gent, 1988)
Dyadic Parent–Child Interaction Coding System (Robinson & Eyberg, 1981)	Assesses externalizing behaviors of children in parent–child interactions in three contexts: child-directed interaction, parent-directed interaction, and cleanup; 24 parent and child behaviors coded	Agency/clinic office	N = 42, ages 2–7 (Robinson & Eyberg, 1981)	Interval	Alphas: .92 for child and .91 for parent behaviors. Interrater: .65–1.00 (Aragona & Eyberg, 1981; Eyberg & Matarazzo, 1980). Correctly classified 94% of families; predicted 61% of variance in parent reports of behavior problems
Social Interaction Observation System (Asher, Neckerman, & Pavlidis, 1994)	Assesses social interactions among children and between children and teachers in three domains: Prosocial/Neutral, Verbal Negative, Physical Negative.	Classroom, playground, cafeteria	N = 790, grades 2–3; 53% male; 79% Caucasian. Sample from Washington.	Interval	M kappa values: Prosocial/Neutral: .92; Physical Negative: .50; Verbal Negative: .45 (Grossman et al., 1997)

Table 3-7. **Records Screening Instrument to Assess Aggression and Violence**

Name of Measure (Source)	Description	Targeted/Tested Group	Reliability	Validity
School Archival Record Search (Walker, Block, Todis, Barckley, & Severson, 1988; Walker, Block, Todis, & Severson, 1991)	Search and coding system for school records: demographics, attendance, achievement test information, failure, disciplinary contacts, within-school referrals, certification for special education, placement out of regular classroom, receiving chapter I services, out-of-school referrals, negative narrative comments; 11 items	Grades 1–12; 307 cases in Oregon, 216 in Washington (Walker et al., 1990); no race/ethnic data reported	Interobserver reliability: 96% (Walker et al., 1990); no record of stability of items over time (Crawford, 1998)	Factor analysis: three student profiles: disruption, needs assistance, and low achievement (Walker et al., 1990); concern about multicollinearity of items (Crawford, 1998) and insufficient validity testing (Crawford, 1998; Fitzpatrick, 1998)

Two case examples illustrate the use of several measures. The first is a youth admitted to a juvenile assessment facility, and the second is a child referred to a mental health agency.

T., AGE 14

T. is a 14-year-old Hispanic youth arrested for assaulting a boy in school and breaking the boy's nose. He has fought with other youths during the past year, both on and off school grounds. T. was referred to the Juvenile Assessment Center (JAC), a combination day treatment and assessment facility where youths are assessed over a three-week period.

Initial assessment process

While at the JAC, T. met with professional staff members (social worker, psychologist, nurse, teacher) who undertook assessments for their respective areas. Lucinda Smith, MSW, is the clinical social worker. Her responsibility was to complete an evaluation that considered individual, family, school, and environmental factors. Lucinda used multiple sources in her assessment, including the client, family members, JAC personnel, school staff members, case records, and her own observations.

Because Lucinda was not Hispanic, she was careful to undertake a culturally informed assessment (Delva, 1995). She examined her own knowledge and values in working with T. and his mother to determine where she might miss or misunderstand the information collected. For example, in the interviews with T., she asked him about his own ethnic identity—how it benefitted him, but also how it has been a challenge for him. Lucinda continued to be mindful of culture and language in her selection and administration of measures.

Choice of measures

Lucinda chose measures that were psychometrically sound and clinically useful and that drew from different sources. She also chose measures that she was competent to administer, score, and interpret. To assess for broad-based problems from multiple perspectives, Lucinda chose the Child Behavior Checklist (CBCL) and related instruments. Using an interpreter, Lucinda first engaged T.'s mother and then administered the Spanish version of the CBCL. She administered to T. the CBCL's companion Youth Self Report (YSR). Also, JAC youth supervisors filled out the Direct Observation Form (DOF) while T. was in the classroom, in the recreation area, and on breaks in the common area. To specifically assess anger and violence, T. completed the State–Trait Anger Expression Inventory (STAXI). With the information collected from multiple measures, sources, and environments, Lucinda gained an overview of T.'s strengths and areas of need, as well as a specific understanding about his anger and violence. The data gathered from these measures, along with family and other information about the context and circumstances of the violence, shaped Lucinda's assessment report. Her findings, although comprehensive on their own, would contribute to a larger picture of T.'s situation using findings from the rest of the multidisciplinary team. These data would culminate in a treatment plan.

R., AGE 8

R. is an eight-year-old Caucasian boy referred by his mother for defiant and aggressive behavior at home and in school during the past year. At home, R.'s mother reported that R. generally refused to do what he was told and often had temper tantrums. She said her son had been disruptive at school and had bullied others. The family was referred to the children's mental health agency where they were assigned to Don Smith, MSW, the clinical social worker.

Initial assessment process

Don wanted to use measures that would provide information about R.'s situation but that would also serve as a baseline to measure progress. He interviewed R. and R.'s mother first together and then separately. During these meetings over two weeks, Don administered several measures. He wanted to collect data from multiple sources including R., R.'s mother, and the school. The family signed releases allowing Don to speak with school personnel and allowing them to share information.

Choice of measures

Don used a structured interview and rating scales to collect information from R.'s mother and the school. He used the DICA to systematically assess for a range of problems, including oppositional defiant disorder. To focus more on externalizing behaviors such as conduct problems, Don administered the relatively brief ECBI. He asked R.'s teacher to complete the SESBI. Don believed that these measures would gather reliable and valid clinical data and that the ECBI and SESBI would provide baseline data to assess progress over time.

These two cases illustrate how a few of the measures could be used. No measure should be viewed as complete on its own. Don was careful to assess R.'s mother's situation, including collecting information about parenting issues and broader issues such as financial resources. Both Lucinda and Don made sure to collect data on strengths and resources.

CONCLUSION

Further research in the measurement of violence in children and youths is needed. First, most of the measures reviewed need further psychometric testing. Many have had insufficient validity testing. There is also a need to further develop gender- and culture-sensitive instruments that are normed on different racial and cultural groups (Guerra, 1998; Guerra & Jagers, 1998). Diversity within groups should be recognized. Measures that are relevant for subgroups—particularly Hispanic subgroups—should be developed.

There is a repeated call to intervene early to prevent violence (for example, Loeber & Farrington, 1998; Slaby, 1998; Walker et al., 1994; Wilson, 1998). A promising approach for early screening is the multiple-gating method. This strategy needs to be further refined to identify the optimal number of gates, the age at which to screen, where to screen, and the best predictors to include (LeBlanc, 1998). Another approach to the early identification of violent youths is to screen when youths become involved in the juvenile justice system for relatively minor offenses. Effective screening tools need to be developed that could be routinely administered when children and youths enter the system for the first time (Loeber & Farrington, 1998).

Developing effective screening or multiple-gating methods requires first identifying accurate and appropriate predictors. A few instruments were reviewed in this chapter because they measure predictors of subsequent violence (for example, aggression, hyperactivity, and attention deficits). Yet there is little conclusive data about what predicts later violence. Most of what is known about predictors has been based on studies using arrest or delinquency as the predictor criterion (J. D. Hawkins et al., 1998; Lipsey & Derzon, 1998). There is a need to improve the predictive accuracy of violence risk assessments (Guerra, 1998; LeBlanc, 1998; Wiebush et al., 1995) to reduce the number of false positives and false negatives. Significant social costs and benefits ride on this issue (LeBlanc, 1998).

This chapter has mostly identified problem-based assessment instruments, but a comprehensive research agenda that also emphasizes the identification of protective factors will allow future reviewers to identify "assets or supports that can be mobilized to promote healthy development" (Guerra, 1998, p. 397).

REFERENCES

Achenbach, T. M. (1986). *Child Behavior Checklist–Direct Observation Form* (rev. ed.). Burlington, VT: University Associates in Psychiatry.

Achenbach, T. M. (1991a). *Manual for the Child Behavior Checklist 4–18 and 1991 profile*. Burlington, VT: University of Vermont Department of Psychiatry.

Achenbach, T. M. (1991b). *Manual for the Teacher's Report Form and 1991 profile*. Burlington, VT: University of Vermont Department of Psychiatry.

Achenbach, T. M. (1991c). *Manual for the Youth Self-Report and 1991 profile*. Burlington, VT: University of Vermont Department of Psychiatry.

Achenbach, T. M. (1996). The Child Behavior Checklist (CBCL) and related instruments. In L. I. Sederer & B. Dickey (Eds.), *Outcomes assessment in clinical practice* (pp. 97–99). Baltimore: Williams & Wilkins.

Allen-Meares, P., & Lane, B. A. (1993). Grounding social work practice in theory: Ecosystems. In J. Rauch (Ed.), *Assessment: A sourcebook for social work practice* (pp. 3–13). Milwaukee: Families International, Inc.

American Psychological Association. (1985). *Standards for educational and psychological tests*. Washington, DC: Author.

Anastasi, A. (1988). *Psychological testing* (6th ed.). New York: Macmillan.

Anastasi, A., & Urbina, S. (1997). *Psychological testing* (7th ed.). Englewood Cliffs, NJ: Prentice-Hall.

Aragona, J. A., & Eyberg, S. M. (1981). Neglected children: Mother's report of child behavior problems and observed verbal behavior. *Child Development, 52,* 596–602.

Asher, K., Neckerman, H. J., & Pavlidis, K. (1994). *Social Interaction Observation System (SIOS): Observer training manual* (4th ed.). Seattle: Harborview Injury Prevention and Research Center, University of Washington.

Atkins, M. S., & Milich, R. (1988). Iowa–Conners Teacher Rating Scale. In M. Hersen & A. S. Bellack (Eds.), *Dictionary of behavioral assessment techniques* (pp. 273–274). New York: Pergamon Press.

Bailey, S. (1997). Psychiatric assessment of the violent child and adolescent: Towards understanding and safe intervention. In V. Varma (Ed.), *Violence in children and adolescents* (pp. 37–47). London: Jessica Kingsley.

Bloom, M., Fischer, J., & Orme, J. G. (1999). *Evaluating practice: Guidelines for the accountable professional* (3rd ed.). Boston: Allyn & Bacon.

Blythe, B. J., & Tripodi, T. (1989). *Measurement in direct social work practice*. Newbury Park, CA: Sage Publications.

Blythe, B., Tripodi, T., & Briar, S. (1994). *Direct practice research in human service agencies.* New York: Columbia University Press.

Boggs, S. R., Eyberg, S., & Reynolds, L. A. (1990). Concurrent validity of the Eyberg Child Behavior Inventory. *Journal of Clinical Child Psychology, 19,* 75–78

Burns, G. L., & Owen, S. M. (1990). Disruptive behaviors in the classroom: Initial standardization of a new teacher rating scale. *Journal of Abnormal Child Psychology, 18,* 515–525.

Burns, G. L., & Patterson, D. R. (1990). Conduct problem behaviors in a stratified random sample of children and adolescents: New standardization data on the Eyberg Child Behavior Inventory. *Psychological Assessment, 2,* 391–397.

Butcher, J. N., Williams, C. L., Graham, J. R., Archer, R. P., Tellegen, A., Ben-Porath, Y. S., & Kraemmer, B. (1992). *MMPI–A (Minnesota Multiphasic Personality Inventory–Adolescent): Manual for administration, scoring, and interpretation.* Minneapolis: University of Minnesota Press.

Chaiken, J., Chaiken, M., & Rhodes, W. (1994). Predicting violent behavior and classifying violent offenders. In A. J. Reiss & J. A. Roth (Eds.), *Understanding and preventing violence: Vol. 4. Consequences and control* (pp. 217–295). Washington, DC: National Academy Press.

Conners, C. K. (1990). *Conners rating scales manual.* North Tonawanda, NY: Multihealth Systems.

Crawford, J. (1998). School Archival Records Search. In J. C. Impara & B. S. Plake (Eds.), *Thirteenth mental measurements yearbook* [SilverPlatter Online Edition]. Lincoln, NE: Buros Institute of Mental Measurements.

Crick, N. R. (1995). Relational aggression: The role of intent attributions, feelings of distress, and provocation type. *Development and Psychopathology, 7,* 313–322.

Crick, N. R. (1996). The role of relational aggression, overt aggression, and prosocial behavior in the prediction of children's future adjustment. *Child Development, 67,* 2317–2327.

Crick, N. R., & Bigbee, M. A. (1998). Relational and overt forms of peer victimization: A multiinformant approach. *Journal of Consulting and Clinical Psychology, 2,* 337–347.

Crick, N. R., & Dodge, K. A. (1994). A review and reformulation of social-information processing mechanisms in children's social adjustment. *Psychological Bulletin, 115,* 74–101.

Crick, N. R., & Grotpeter, J. K. (1995). Relational aggression, gender, and social–psychological adjustment. *Child Development, 66,* 710–722.

Curtis, P. A., & Schmidt, L. L. (1993). A Spanish translation of the Revised Behavior Problem Checklist. *Child Welfare, 72,* 453–460.

Dahlberg, L. L., Toal, S. B., & Behrens, C. B. (Eds.). (1998). *Measuring violence-related attitudes, beliefs, and behaviors among youths: A compendium of assessment tools.* Atlanta: Centers for Disease Control and Prevention, National Center for Injury Prevention and Control, Division of Violence Prevention.

Deblinger, E., & Atkins, M. S. (1988). Conners Teacher Rating Scales. In M. Hersen & A. S. Bellack (Eds.), *Dictionary of behavioral assessment techniques* (pp. 152–153). New York: Pergamon Press.

Delva, J. (1995). Assessment and prevention of aggressive behavior among youths of color: Integrating cultural and social factors. *Social Work in Education, 17,* 83–91.

Dodge, K. A. (1980). Social cognition and children's aggressive behavior. *Child Development, 51,* 162–170.

Dodge, K. A., & Coie, J. D. (1987). Social-information-processing factors in reactive and proactive aggression in children's peer groups. *Journal of Personality and Social Psychology, 53,* 1146–1158.

Dodge, K. A., & Crick, N. (1990). Social-information processing bases of aggressive behavior in children. *Personality and Social Psychology Bulletin, 16,* 8–22.

Dodge, K. A., Price, J. M., Bachorowski, J.-A., & Newman, J. P. (1990). Hostile attribution biases in severely aggressive adolescents. *Journal of Abnormal Psychology, 99,* 385–392.

Doke, L. A. (1988). Measurement of chronic aggression: Direct quantitative methods. In M. Hersen & A. S. Bellack (Eds.), *Dictionary of behavioral assessment techniques* (pp. 297–298). New York: Pergamon Press.

Education Commission Task Force. (1993). *Standards for the practice of school social work services.* Washington, DC: NASW Press.

Epps, K. J. (1997). Psychological assessment and monitoring of violent children and adolescents. In V. Varma (Ed.), *Violence in children and adolescents* (pp. 48–64). London: Jessica Kingsley.

Eron, L. D., Walder, L. O., & Lefkowitz, M. M. (1971). *Learning of aggression in children.* Boston: Little, Brown, and Co.

Eyberg. S. M., & Matarazzo, R. G. (1980). Training parents as therapists: A comparison between individual parent–child interaction training and parent group didactic training. *Journal of Clinical Psychology, 36,* 492–499.

Eyberg, S. M., & Robinson, E. A. (1983). Conduct problem behavior: Standardization of a behavior rating scale with adolescents. *Journal of Clinical Child Psychology, 12,* 347–354.

Eyberg, S. M., & Ross, A. W. (1978). Assessment of child behavior problems: The validation of a new inventory. *Journal of Clinical Child Psychology, 7,* 113–116.

Ezpetela, L., de la Osa, N., Domenech, J. M., Navarro, J. B., & Losilla, J. M. (1997). Test–retest reliability of the Spanish adaptation of the Diagnostic Interview for Children and Adolescents. *Psicothema, 9,* 529–539.

Feindler, E. L. (1995). Ideal treatment package for children and adolescents with anger disorders. In H. Kassinove (Ed.), *Anger disorders: Definition, diagnosis, and treatment* (pp. 173–195). Washington, DC: Taylor & Francis.

Feldman, R. A., Caplinger, T. E., & Wodarski, J. S. (1983). *The St. Louis conundrum: The effective treatment of antisocial youths.* Englewood Cliffs, NJ: Prentice-Hall.

Fischer, J., & Corcoran, K. (1994a). *Measures for clinical practice: A sourcebook. Volume 1: Couples, families and children.* New York: Free Press.

Fischer, J., & Corcoran, K. (1994b). *Measures for clinical practice: A sourcebook. Volume 2: Adults.* New York: Free Press.

Fisher, P., Wicks, J., Shaffer, D., Piacentini, J., & Lapkin, J. (1992). *National Institute of Mental Health Diagnostic Interview Schedule for Children users' manual.* New York: State Psychiatric Institute, Division of Child and Adolescent Psychiatry.

Fitzpatrick, R. (1998). School Archival Records Search. In J. C. Impara & B. S. Plake (Eds.), *The thirteenth mental measurements yearbook* [SilverPlatter Online Edition]. Lincoln, NE: Buros Institute of Mental Measurements.

Foshee, V. A., Linder, G. F., Bauman, K. E., Langwick, S. A., Arriaga, X. B., Heath, J. L., McMahon, P. M., & Bangdiwala, S. (1996). The Safe Dates project: Theoretical basis, evaluation design, and selected baseline findings. *Youth Violence Prevention, 12,* 39–47.

Foster, S. L., Bell-Dolan, D. J., & Burge, D. A. (1988). Behavioral observation. In A. S. Bellack & M. Hersen (Eds.), *Behavioral assessment: A practical handbook* (pp. 119–160). New York: Pergamon Press.

Fraser, M. (1996). Aggressive behavior in childhood and early adolescence: An ecological–developmental perspective on youth violence. *Social Work, 41,* 347–361.

Funderburk, B. W., & Eyberg, S. M. (1989). Psychometric characteristics of the Sutter–Eyberg Student Behavior Inventory: A school behavior rating scale for use with preschool children. *Behavioral Assessment, 11,* 297–313.

Furlong, M. J., & Smith, D. C. (1994a). Assessment of youth's anger, hostility, and aggression using self-report and rating scales. In M. Furlong & D. Smith (Eds.), *Anger, hostility, and aggression: Assessment, prevention and intervention strategies for youth* (pp. 167–244). Brandon, VT: Clinical Psychology Publishing Co.

Furlong, M. J., & Smith, D. C. (1994b). Prevalence, definitional, and conceptual issues. In M. Furlong & D. Smith (Eds.), *Anger, hostility, and aggression: Assessment, prevention and intervention strategies for youth* (pp. 1–11). Brandon, VT: Clinical Psychology Publishing Co.

Gorman-Smith, D., & Tolan, P. (1998). The role of exposure to community violence and developmental problems among inner-city youth. *Development and Psychopathology, 10,* 101–116.

Goyette, C. H., Conners, C. K., & Ulrich, R. F. (1978). Normative data for revised Conners Parent and Teacher Rating Scales. *Journal of Abnormal Child Psychology, 6,* 221–236.

Graham, S., Hudley, C., & Williams, E. (1992). Attributional and emotional determinants of aggression among African-American and Latino young adolescents. *Developmental Psychology, 28,* 731–740.

Grinnell, R. (1993). *Social work research and evaluation* (4th ed.). Itasca, IL: Peacock.

Grossman, D. C., Neckerman, H. J., Koepsell, T. D., Liu, P.-Y., Asher, K. A., Beland, K., Frey, K., & Rivara, F. P. (1997). Effectiveness of a violence prevention curriculum among children in elementary school. *JAMA, 277,* 1605–1611.

Groth-Marnat, G. (1997). *Handbook of psychological assessment* (3rd ed.). New York: Wiley.

Grotpeter, J. K., & Crick, N. R. (1996). Relational aggression, overt aggression, and friendship. *Child Development, 67,* 2328–2338.

Guerra, N. G. (1998). Serious and violent juvenile offenders: Gaps in knowledge and research priorities. In R. Loeber & D. P. Farrington (Eds.), *Serious & violent juvenile offenders: Risk factors and successful interventions* (pp. 389–404). Thousand Oaks, CA: Sage Publications.

Guerra, N. G., Huesmann, L. R., & Hanish, L. (1995). The role of normative beliefs in children's social behavior. In N. Eisenberg (Ed.), *Review of personality and social psychology, development and social psychology: The interface* (pp. 140–158). Thousand Oaks, CA: Sage Publications.

Guerra, N. G., & Jagers, R. (1998). The importance of culture in the assessment of children and youth. In V. C. McLoyd & L. Steinberg (Eds.), *Studying minority adolescents: Conceptual, methodological and theoretical issues* (pp. 167–181). Hillsdale, NJ: Lawrence Erlbaum.

Gumbiner, J. (1998). MMPI–A profiles for Hispanic adolescents. *Psychological Reports, 82,* 659–672.

Harris, A. M., & Reid, J. B. (1981). The consistency of a class of coercive child behaviors across school settings for individual subjects. *Journal of Abnormal Child Psychology, 9,* 219–227.

Hastings, T. L., & Kelley, M. L. (1997). Development and validation of the Screen for Adolescent Violence Exposure (SAVE). *Journal of Abnormal Child Psychology, 25,* 511–520.

Hawkins, D. F., Laub, J. H., & Lauritsen, J. L. (1998). Race, ethnicity, and serious juvenile offending. In R. Loeber & D. P. Farrington (Eds.), *Serious & violent juvenile offenders: Risk factors and successful interventions* (pp. 30–46). Thousand Oaks, CA: Sage Publications.

Hawkins, J. D., & Catalano, R. F. (1992). *Communities that care.* San Francisco: Jossey-Bass.

Hawkins, J. D., Herrenkohl, T., Farrington, D. P., Brewer, D., Catalano, R. F., & Harachi, T. W. (1998). A review of predictors of youth violence. In R. Loeber & D. P. Farrington (Eds.), *Serious & violent juvenile offenders: Risk factors and successful interventions* (pp. 106–146). Thousand Oaks, CA: Sage Publications.

Herjanic, B., & Reich, W. (1982). Development of a structured psychiatric interview for children: Agreement on diagnosis comparing child and patient interviews. *Journal of Abnormal Psychology, 10,* 325–336.

Hersen, M., & Bellack, A. A. (Eds.). (1988). *Dictionary of behavioral assessment techniques.* New York: Pergamon Press.

Hilton, N. Z., Harris, G. T., Rice, M. E., Krans, T. S., & Lavigne, S. E. (1998). Antiviolence education in high schools: Implementation and evaluation. *Journal of Interpersonal Violence, 13,* 726–742.

Hood, A., & Johnson, R. W. (1997). *Assessment in counseling* (2nd ed.). Alexandria, VA: American Counseling Association.

Hudley, C., & Graham, S. (1993). An attributional intervention to reduce peer directed aggression among African-American boys. *Child Development, 64,* 124–138.

Hudson, W. (1982). *The clinical measurement package: A field manual.* Homewood, IL: Dorsey Press.

Hudson, W. W. (1997). Assessment tools as outcomes measures in social work. In E. J. Mullen & J. L. Magnabosco (Eds.), *Outcomes measurement in the human services: Cross-cutting issues and methods* (pp. 68–80). Washington, DC: NASW Press.

Huesmann, L. R., Eron, L. D., Guerra, N. G., & Crawshaw, V. B. (1994). Measuring children's aggression with teacher's predictions of peer nominations. *Psychological Assessment, 6,* 329–336.

Huesmann, L. R., & Guerra, N. G. (1997). Children's normative beliefs about aggression and aggressive behavior. *Journal of Personality and Social Psychology, 72,* 408–419.

Huesmann, L. R., Guerra, N. G., Miller, L., & Zelli, A. (1992). The role of social norms in the development of aggressive behavior. In A. Frączek & H. Zumkley (Eds.), *Socialization and aggression* (pp. 139–151). New York: Springer.

Huesmann, L. R., Guerra, N. G., Zelli, A., & Miller, L. (1992). Differing normative beliefs about aggression for boys and girls. In K. Bjorkqvist & N. Pirkko (Eds.), *Of mice and women: Aspects of female aggression* (pp. 77–87). San Diego: Academic Press.

Jesness, C. F. (1988). *Jesness Inventory of Adolescent Personality.* North Tonawanda, NY: Multi-Health Systems.

Jones, R. L. (1996a). *Handbook of tests and measurements for black populations.* Hampton, VA: Cobb & Henry.

Jones, R. L. (1996b). Handbook of tests and measurements for black populations: Introduction and overview. In R. L. Jones (Ed.), *Handbook of tests and measurements for black populations* (Vol. 1, pp. 3–15). Hampton, VA: Cobb & Henry.

Kadushin, A., & Kadushin, G. (1990). *The social work interview* (4th ed.). New York: Columbia University Press.

Kassinove, H., & Sukhodolsky, D. G. (1995). Anger disorders: Basic science and practice issues. In H. Kassinove (Ed.), *Anger disorders: Definition, diagnosis, and treatment* (pp. 1–26). Washington, DC: Taylor & Francis.

Kelley, M. L. (1998). Systematic Screening for Behavior Disorders. In J. C. Impara & B. S. Plake (Eds.), *The thirteenth mental measurements yearbook* [SilverPlatter Online Edition]. Lincoln, NE: Buros Institute of Mental Measurements.

Kirby, L. D., & Fraser, M. (1997). Risk and resilience in childhood. In M. W. Fraser (Ed.), *Risk and resilience in childhood: An ecological perspective* (pp. 10–33). Washington, DC: NASW Press.

Kruesi, M. J., Hibbs, E. D., Hamburger, S. D., Rapoport, J. L., Keysor, C. S., & Elia, J. (1994). Measurement of aggression in children with disruptive behavior disorders. *Journal of Offender Rehabilitation, 21,* 159–172.

LeBlanc, M. (1998). Screening of serious and violent juvenile offenders. In R. Loeber & D. P. Farrington (Eds.), *Serious & violent juvenile offenders: Risk factors and successful interventions* (pp. 167–193). Thousand Oaks, CA: Sage Publications.

Lehmann, P., & Dangel, R. F. (1998). Oppositional defiant disorder. In B. A. Thyer & J. S. Wodarski (Eds.), *Handbook of empirical social work practice. Volume 1: Mental disorders* (pp. 91–116). New York: Wiley.

Limandri, B. J., & Sheridan, D. J. (1995). Prediction of intentional interpersonal violence: An introduction. In J. C. Campbell (Ed.), *Assessing dangerousness: Violence by sexual offenders, batterers, and child abusers* (pp. 1–19). Thousand Oaks, CA: Sage Publications.

Lipsey, M. W., & Derzon, J. H. (1998). Predictors of violent or serious delinquency in adolescence and early adulthood: A synthesis of longitudinal research. In R. Loeber & D. P. Farrington (Eds.), *Serious & violent juvenile offenders: Risk factors and successful interventions* (pp. 86–105). Thousand Oaks, CA: Sage Publications.

Lochman, J. E., & the Conduct Problems Research Group. (1995). Screening of child behavior problems for prevention programs at school entry. *Journal of Consulting and Clinical Psychology, 63,* 549–559.

Loeber, R., Dishion, T. J., & Patterson, G. R. (1984). Multiple gating: A multistage assessment procedure for identifying youths at risk for delinquency. *Journal of Research in Crime and Delinquency, 21,* 7–32.

Loeber, R., & Farrington, D. P. (1998). Executive summary. In R. Loeber & D. P. Farrington (Eds.), *Serious & violent juvenile offenders: Risk factors and successful interventions* (pp. xix–xxv). Thousand Oaks, CA: Sage Publications.

Loeber, R., & Hay, D. F. (1994). Developmental approaches to aggression and conduct problems. In M. Rutter & D. F. Hay (Eds.), *Development through life: A handbook for clinicians* (pp. 488–515). Oxford, England: Blackwell Scientific.

Loney, J., & Milich, R. (1982). Hyperactivity, inattention, and aggression in clinical practice. In M. Wolraich & D. Routh (Eds.), *Advances in developmental and behavioral pediatrics* (Vol. 3, pp. 113–147). Greenwich, CT: JAI Press.

Lowe, L. A. (1998). Using the Child Behavior Checklist in assessing conduct disorder: Issues of reliability and validity. *Research on Social Work Practice, 8,* 286–301.

McConaughy, S. H., Achenbach, T. M., & Gent, C. L. (1988). Multiaxial empirically based assessment: Parent, teacher, observational, cognitive, and personality correlates of child behavior profile types for 6 to 11 year old boys. *Journal of Abnormal Child Psychology, 16,* 485–509.

McGee, Z. T. (1996). The violent victimization survey. In R. L. Jones (Ed.), *Handbook of tests and measurements for black populations* (Vol. 2, pp. 613–620). Hampton, VA: Cobb & Henry.

McMahon, R. J., & Forehand, R. (1988). Conduct disorders. In E. J. Marsh & L. G. Terdal (Eds.), *Behavioral assessment of childhood disorders* (2nd ed.) (pp. 105–153). New York: Guilford Press.

McNeil, C. B., Eyberg, S., Eisenstadt, T. H., Newcomb, K., & Funderburk, B. (1991). Parent child interaction therapy with behavior problem children: Generalization of treatment effects to the school setting. *Journal of Clinical Child Psychology, 20,* 140–151.

Merrell, K. W. (1993a). *School Social Behavior Scales.* Austin, TX: Pro-Ed., Inc.

Merrell, K. W. (1993b). Using behavior rating scales to assess social skills and antisocial behavior in school settings: Development of the school social behavior scales. *School Psychology Review, 22,* 115–133.

Merrell, K. W. (1994). *Assessment of behavioral, social, and emotional problems: Direct & objective methods for use with children and adolescents.* New York: Longman.

Milner, J. S., & Campbell, J. C. (1995). Prediction issues for practitioners. In J. C. Campbell (Ed.), *Assessing dangerousness: Violence by sexual offenders, batterers, and child abusers* (pp. 20–40). Thousand Oaks, CA: Sage Publications.

Moffit, T. E. (1993). Adolescence-limited and life-course-persistent antisocial behavior: A developmental taxonomy. *Psychological Review, 100,* 674–701.

Molina, B. S., Pelham, W. E., Blumenthal, J., & Galiszewski, E. (1998). Agreement among teachers' behavior ratings of adolescents with a childhood history of attention deficit hyperactivity disorder. *Journal of Clinical Child Psychology, 27,* 330–339.

Nadel, H., Spellmann, M., Alvarez-Canino, T., Lausell-Bryant, L., & Landsberg, G. (1996). The cycle of violence and victimization: A study of the school-based intervention of a multidisciplinary youth-violence prevention program. *American Journal of Preventive Medicine, 12(5),* 109–119.

National Association of Social Workers. (1996). *Code of ethics.* Washington, DC: Author. (Available: http://www.socialworkers.org/CODE.HTM)

Nunnally, J., & Bernstein, I. H. (1994). *Psychometric theory* (3rd ed.). New York: McGraw-Hill.

Oliver, L. L., Hall, G.C.N., & Neuhaus, S. M. (1993). A comparison of the personality and background characteristics of adolescent sex offenders and other adolescent offenders. *Criminal Justice & Behavior, 20,* 359–370.

Padilla, A. M., & Medina, A. (1996). Cross-cultural sensitivity in assessment: Using tests in culturally appropriate ways. In L. A. Suzuki, P. J. Meller, & J. G. Ponterotto (Eds.), *Handbook of multicultural assessment: Clinical, psychological, and educational applications* (pp. 3–28). San Francisco: Jossey-Bass.

Paulhus, D. L. (1991). Measurement and control of response bias. In J. P. Robinson, P. R. Shaver, & L. S. Wrightsman (Eds.), *Measures of personality and social psychological attitudes: Volume 1 of measures of social psychological attitudes* (pp. 17–59). San Diego: Academic Press.

Quay, H. C., & Peterson, D. R. (1987). *Manual for the Behavior Problem Checklist.* Coral Gables, FL: Author.

Rayfield, A., Eyberg, S. M., & Foote, R. (1998). Revision of the Sutter–Eyberg Student Behavior Inventory. *Educational & Psychological Measurement, 58,* 88–98.

Reich, W., Shayka, J. J., & Taibleson, C. (1991a). *Diagnostic Interview for Children and Adolescents (DICA–RA): Adolescent Version.* St. Louis: Washington University.

Reich, W., Shayka, J. J., & Taibleson, C. (1991b). *Diagnostic Interview for Children and Adolescents (DICA–RC): Child Version.* St. Louis: Washington University.

Reich, W., Shayka, J. J., & Taibleson, C. (1991c). *Diagnostic Interview for Children and Adolescents (DICA–RP): Parent Version.* St. Louis: Washington University.

Ridley, C. R. (1995). *Overcoming unintentional racism in counseling and therapy : A practitioner's guide to intentional intervention.* Thousand Oaks, CA: Sage Publications.

Roberts, G., & Schmitz, K. (1990). The MMPI and Jesness Inventory as measures of effectiveness on an inpatient conduct disorders treatment unit. *Adolescence, 25,* 989–996.

Robinson, E. A., & Eyberg, S. (1981). The dyadic parent–child interaction coding system: Standardization and validation. *Journal of Consulting and Clinical Psychology, 49,* 245–250.

Robinson, E. A., Eyberg, S. M., & Ross, A. W. (1980). The standardization of an inventory of child conduct problem behaviors. *Journal of Clinical Child Psychology, 9,* 22–29.

Robinson, J. P., Shaver, P. R., & Wrightsman, L. S. (1991). Criteria for scale selection and evaluation. In J. P. Robinson, P. R. Shaver, & L. S. Wrightsman (Eds.), *Measures of personality and social psychological attitudes: Volume 1 of measures of social psychological attitudes* (pp. 1–16). San Diego: Academic Press.

Rybarik, M. F., Dosch, M. F., Gilmore, G. D., & Krajewski, S. S. (1995). Violence in relationships: A seventh grade inventory of knowledge and attitudes. *Journal of Family Violence, 10,* 223–251.

Sigma Assessment Systems, Inc. (1999). U.S. qualifications form [Online]. Port Huron, MI: Author. (Available: http://www.sigmaassessmentsystems.com/usqual.htm)

Slaby, R. G. (1998). Preventing youth violence through research-guided intervention. In P. K. Trickett & C. J. Schellenbach (Eds.), *Violence against children in the family and the community* (pp. 371–399). Washington, DC: American Psychological Association.

Slaby, R. G., & Guerra, N. G. (1988). Cognitive mediators of aggression in adolescent offenders: 1. Assessment. *Developmental Psychology, 24,* 580–588.

Solomon, A. (1993). Clinical diagnosis among diverse populations: A multicultural perspective. In J. Rauch (Ed.), *Assessment: A sourcebook for social work practice* (pp. 345–355). Milwaukee: Families International, Inc.

Spielberger, C. D. (1988). *Manual for the State–Trait Anger Expression Inventory (STAXI).* Odessa, FL: Psychological Assessment Resources.

Spielberger, C. D., Reheiser, E. C., & Sydeman, S. J. (1995). Measuring the experience, expression, and control of anger. In H. Kassinove (Ed.), *Anger disorders: Definition, diagnosis, and treatment* (pp. 49–67). Washington, DC: Taylor & Francis.

Stein, S., & Karno, M. (1994). Behavioral observation of anger and aggression. In M. Furlong & D. Smith (Eds.), *Anger, hostility, and aggression: Assessment, prevention and intervention strategies for youth* (pp. 245–283). Brandon, VT: Clinical Psychology Publishing Co.

Straus, M. (1979). Measuring intrafamily conflict and violence: The Conflict Tactics (CT) Scales. *Journal of Marriage and the Family, 41,* 75–88.

Streiner, D. L., & Norman, G. R. (1995). *Health measurement scales: A practical guide to their development and use* (2nd ed.). Oxford: Oxford University Press.

Sturmer, P. J., & Gerstein, L. H. (1997). MMPI profiles of black Americans: Is there a bias? *Journal of Mental Health Counseling, 19,* 114–129.

Sutter, J., & Eyberg, S. M. (1984). *Sutter–Eyberg Student Behavior Inventory.* (Available from Sheila Eyberg, Department of Clinical and Health Psychology, Box J-165, Health Sciences Center, University of Florida, Gainesville, FL 32610)

Tarasoff v. Board of Regents of the University of California, 17 C.3d 425 (1976).

Tolan, P. H., & Gorman-Smith, D. (1998). Development of serious and violent offending careers. In R. Loeber & D. P. Farrington (Eds.), *Serious & violent juvenile offenders: Risk factors and successful interventions* (pp. 68–85). Thousand Oaks, CA: Sage Publications.

Tolan, P. H., & Guerra, N. (1994). *What works in reducing adolescent violence: An empirical review of the field* (Monograph prepared for the Center for the Study and Prevention of Violence). Boulder: University of Colorado.

Touliatos, J., Perlmutter, B. F., & Straus, M. A. (Eds.). (1990). *Handbook of family measurement techniques.* Newbury Park, CA: Sage Publications.

Ulzen, T.P.M., & Hamilton, H. (1998). The nature and characteristics of psychiatric comorbidity in incarcerated adolescents. *Canadian Journal of Psychiatry, 43,* 57–63.

Vogt, W. P. (1999). *Dictionary of statistics and methodology* (2nd ed.). Thousand Oaks, CA: Sage Publications.

Walker, H. M., Block, A., Todis, B., Barckley, M., & Severson, H. (1988). *The School Archival Records Search (SARS).* Eugene, OR: Oregon Research Institute.

Walker, H. M., Block, P. A., Todis, B., & Severson, H. H. (1991). *School Archival Records Search.* Longmont, CO: Sopris West, Inc.

Walker, H. M., & Severson, H. (1990). *Systematic Screening for Behavior Disorders (SSBD).* Longmont, CO: Sopris West, Inc.

Walker, H. M., Severson, H. H., Nicholson, F., Kehle, T., Jenson, W. R., & Clark, E. (1994). Replication of the Systematic Screening for Behavior Disorders (SSBD) procedure for the identification of at-risk children. *Journal of Emotional Disorders, 2,* 66–77.

Walker, H. M., Severson, H. H., Todis, B. J., Block-Pedego, A. E., Williams, G. J., Harring, N. G., & Barckley, M. (1990). Systematic Screening for Behavior Disorders (SSBD): Further validation, replication, and normative data. *Remedial and Special Education, 11,* 32–46.

Webster, C. D. (1997). A guide for conducting risk assessments. In C. D. Webster & M. A. Jackson (Eds.), *Impulsivity: Theory, assessment and treatment* (pp. 343–358). New York: Guilford Press.

Webster-Stratton, C. (1984). Randomized trial of two parent-training programs for families with conduct-disordered children. *Journal of Consulting and Clinical Psychology, 52,* 666–668.

Webster-Stratton, C. (1998). Preventing conduct problems in Head Start children: Strengthening parenting competencies. *Journal of Consulting and Clinical Psychology, 66,* 715–730.

Welsh, L. A. (1998). School Social Behavior Scales. In J. C. Impara & B. S. Plake (Eds.), *The thirteenth mental measurements yearbook* [SilverPlatter Online Edition]. Lincoln, NE: Buros Institute of Mental Measurements.

Whitworth, R. H., & Unterbrink, C. (1994). Comparison of MMPI–2 clinical and content scales administered to Hispanic and Anglo-Americans. *Hispanic Journal of Behavioral Sciences, 16,* 255–264.

Wiebush, R. G., Baird, C., Krisberg, B., & Onek, D. (1995). Risk assessment and classification for serious, violent, and chronic juvenile offenders. In J. C. Howell, B. Krisberg, J. D. Hawkins, & J. J. Wilson (Eds.), *Serious, violent, and chronic juvenile offenders* (pp. 171–212). Thousand Oaks, CA: Sage Publications.

Williams, J. H., Ayers, C. D., & Arthur, M. W. (1997). Risk and protective factors in the development of delinquency and conduct disorder. In M. W. Fraser (Ed.), *Risk and resilience in childhood: An ecological perspective* (pp. 140–170). Washington, DC: NASW Press.

Wilson, J. Q. (1998). Foreword: Never too early. In R. Loeber & D. P. Farrington (Eds.), *Serious & violent juvenile offenders: Risk factors and successful interventions* (pp. ix–xi). Thousand Oaks, CA: Sage Publications.

Zaparniuk, J., & Taylor, S. (1997). Impulsivity in children and adolescents. In C. D. Webster & M. A. Jackson (Eds.), *Impulsivity: Theory, assessment and treatment* (pp. 158–179). New York: Guilford Press.

Zlomke, L. C., & Spies, R. (1998). Systematic Screening for Behavior Disorders. In J. C. Impara & B. S. Plake (Eds.), *The thirteenth mental measurements yearbook* [SilverPlatter Online Edition]. Lincoln, NE: Buros Institute of Mental Measurement.

Prevention, Treatment, and Recent Practice Innovations

Chapter 4

Child Abuse and Youth Violence

Melissa Jonson-Reid

> In the winter of 1998, a 17-year-old boy climbed to the top of a river bluff and threw a 3-year-old girl more than 100 feet to the ground. On finding her still alive he attempted to drown her, then repeatedly stabbed her and left her to die. He had apparently grown tired of babysitting. The young man had a history of maltreatment and was in and out of foster homes for about 11 years prior to his placement with the grandmother of the murdered child. (Bell Jr., 1998)

The association between child maltreatment and youth violence is vividly illustrated in this excerpt. Violent behavior among previously maltreated children—particularly in such extreme forms—is rare; the majority of maltreated children do not become violent adolescents (Jonson-Reid & Barth, 1998; Smith & Williams, 1992; Widom, 1989, 1996). However, a small proportion of abused and neglected children accounts for a significant proportion of all youth violence (Chesney-Lind, 1997; Jonson-Reid & Barth, 1998; Smith & Williams, 1992; Widom, 1989). Therefore, reducing child maltreatment may have a significant effect on the larger problem of violent behavior among adolescents.

The prevention of violent behavior among children and youths who experience abuse and neglect is hampered by serious gaps in knowledge about how and why maltreatment increases the risk of violence (Jonson-Reid, 1998; Widom, 1989). Researchers are only beginning to examine complex interactions among individual, family, and community variables that increase or decrease the likelihood of violent behavior after abuse or neglect. Little is known about the efficacy of interventions to alleviate the personal damage caused by abuse and neglect (Cicchetti & Toth, 1995; Jonson-Reid & Barth, 1998; Pearce & Pezzot-Pearce, 1997).

The goal of this chapter is to identify and review approaches to preventing youth violence that address underlying issues of childhood abuse and neglect. It discusses risk factors and causal theories about the relationship between maltreatment and violence and outlines promising violence prevention and intervention techniques using case examples. We begin with a discussion of child abuse in the United States.

CHILD ABUSE IN THE UNITED STATES

Child welfare agencies define maltreatment to include *physical abuse, sexual abuse, emotional abuse, neglect,* or *other* (for example, abandonment or threats of harm) (U.S. Department of Health and Human Services, 1998). These categories are used to discuss maltreatment here.

For every 1,000 children in the United States, 44 were reported to child welfare agencies for abuse or neglect in 1996 (U.S. Department of Health and Human Services, 1998), though studies assessing unreported cases of child maltreatment suggest that the actual incidence of maltreatment in the United States is much higher (Sedlak & Broadhurst, 1996). Official data indicated that only about one million maltreatment cases were substantiated in 1996, implying that on investigation these cases had sufficient evidence to convince child protection officials that the child had been maltreated (U.S. Department of Health and Human Services, 1998). In comparison, findings from the *Third National Incidence Study of Child Abuse and Neglect* (NIS-III) revealed that approximately 1.5 million children were maltreated according to a harm standard more stringent than state definitions (Sedlak & Broadhurst, 1996). The majority of reported and unreported cases of maltreatment in 1996 involved neglect (Sedlak & Broadhurst, 1996).

Who Maltreats Children?

Child abuse is commonly associated with the primary caregiver of a child. Approximately 80 percent of maltreatment reports identify a parent as the perpetrator (U.S. Department of Health and Human Services, 1998). However, children are also abused by strangers and siblings (Besharov, 1990; Finkelhor & Dzuiba-Leatherman, 1994; Kashani & Allan, 1998). Because studies of childhood victimization use a variety of measures (for example, official statistics and self-reports from victims), actual rates of victimization by perpetrator type are difficult to estimate.

Who Is Maltreated?

More than half the cases substantiated by child welfare agencies are children under six years old. Neglect is the most prevalent type of maltreatment reported for young children (Berrick, Needell, Barth, & Jonson-Reid, 1998). Among older children, reports of physical and sexual abuse are as prevalent as neglect (Jonson-Reid & Barth, 1998).

Boys and girls are about equally likely to experience maltreatment (U.S. Department of Health and Human Services, 1998). In one study of older children, however, Jonson-Reid and Barth (1998) found that girls comprised more than 60 percent of maltreatment reports. Yet the National Family Violence Resurvey reported that school-age boys were physically abused more often than girls (Straus & Gelles, 1992). Several studies indicate that girls are more frequent victims of sexual abuse than boys (Finkelhor & Dzuiba-Leatherman, 1994; Sedlak & Broadhurst, 1996).

Children reared in poverty appear to face a much higher risk of maltreatment than other children (Drake & Zuravin, 1998). The *Third National Incidence Study* (NIS-III), which attempts to estimate the actual incidence of maltreatment rather than counting youths who were reported to child protection authorities, found that children from families with annual incomes below $15,000 were more than 20 times more likely to experience maltreatment than children raised in wealthier families (Sedlak & Broadhurst, 1996). This does not, of course, mean that poor caregivers are abusive by nature. Poor families face substantial stress in the home and community (for example, weak social supports, substance abuse, unemployment) (Coulton, Korbin, Su, & Chow, 1995; Dembo, Williams, Wothke, Schmeidler, & Brown, 1992; Garbarino & Kostelny, 1992). These factors may be more responsible for higher rates of abuse and neglect in poor households than is income per se.

The co-occurrence of poverty and maltreatment confounds current understanding of ethnic variations in rates of maltreatment. For example, youths of color are referred to child protection services at higher rates than are Caucasian youths (U.S. Department of Health and Human Services, 1998). However, youths of color are also more likely than Caucasian children to be poor, making it difficult to assess any independent contribution of ethnicity to child maltreatment. Interestingly, the NIS-III study reported no difference in incidence of maltreatment by ethnicity after controlling for income (Sedlak & Broadhurst, 1996). Debate continues about whether ethnic variations in the rate of reporting reflect actual differences between ethnic groups or the underlying effect of poverty (Coulton & Pandey, 1992; Sedlak & Broadhurst, 1996).

CHILD ABUSE AND VIOLENT BEHAVIOR IN CHILDREN AND YOUTHS

This section reviews what is known about the relationship between childhood victimization and subsequent involvement in aggressive behavior, dating violence, and violent delinquency.

Aggressive Behavior

Exposure to abuse and neglect during childhood is associated with aggressive behavior in youths (Pearce & Pezzot-Pearce, 1997). Debate continues about which aspects of abuse and neglect are most detrimental. For example, Manly, Cicchetti, and Barnett (1994) found a significant increase in fighting behaviors among children who experienced chronic abuse. Wolfe and McGee (1994) reported that boys who experienced abuse and neglect early in childhood were more likely to display aggression than boys who had not been abused or neglected. Vissing, Straus, Gelles, and Harrop (1991) found that combinations of emotional and physical maltreatment, in addition to severity of abuse, were associated with onset of childhood aggression.

Forms of violence that coexist with child maltreatment may also make unique contributions to childhood aggression. In the 1985 National Family Violence Resurvey, children who were both victims of abuse and witnesses to domestic violence were six times more likely than children from nonviolent homes to assault another child outside the home (Hotaling, Straus, & Lincoln, 1989). In studies of the impact of community violence on aggressive behavior, family conflict has been noted to have a strong relationship to community violence as well as to aggressive behavior (Attar, Guerra, & Tolan, 1994).

Dating Violence

There is growing evidence of a relationship between history of abuse and dating violence (Jonson-Reid & Bivens, in press). Gray and Foshee (1997), surveying 185 middle and high school students, found a relationship among witnessing spousal abuse, experiencing physical child abuse, and later participation in physically violent dating relationships. In a study of 1,353 rural high school students, Smith and Williams (1992) reported a relationship between severe abuse by parents and justification by adolescents of violence against dates. Additional empirical studies are needed to better understand the relationship between prior episodes of abuse and date violence.

Violent Delinquency

Many studies have examined the relationship between maltreatment and delinquency; few have investigated the connection between maltreatment and violent behavior (Jonson-Reid, 1998; Schwartz, Rendon, & Hsieh,

1994). The following discussion reviews studies examining violent behavior among adolescents who have been maltreated.

Age and gender. A recent study of incarcerated adolescents found that maltreatment victims older than 14 were more likely to be incarcerated for serious or violent offenses than victims younger than 13 (Jonson-Reid & Barth, no date). The timing of the abuse report, however, was not a significant factor in discriminating between those who were committed for a violent offense and those incarcerated for a drug-related or property crime. In a study of children who experienced official court intervention for abuse or neglect before age 12, Widom (1991) found that children placed in foster care between the ages of seven and 11 were more likely to be arrested for a violent crime than children placed in foster care before age seven. It is not known whether age at placement corresponded to age at the time of the maltreatment incident in this study.

Rivera and Widom (1990) and Maxfield and Widom (1996) found an increased risk of violent behavior among abused females compared with nonabused females but not for abused males compared with nonabused males. Jonson-Reid and Barth (no date) found an increase in risk of serious offending for both maltreated female and male children and youths compared with those without maltreatment reports. The increase in risk, however, varied by gender: It was much higher for females reported for abuse than for females in the population who did not have maltreatment reports.

Other studies suggest that the link between gender and maltreatment may depend on age at the time of victimization. Females have been shown to be at greater risk than males for aggression following maltreatment in preadolescence (Pakiz, Reinherz, & Giaconia, 1997). In contrast, males have been found to suffer greater negative effects of maltreatment when it occurs early in childhood (Wolfe & McGee, 1994).

It is possible that the increased risk of violent behavior among females reported for maltreatment may be due to gender differences in reaction to abuse or neglect. Females tend to display fewer externalized behaviors than males (Kashani & Allan, 1998; Sadker & Sadker, 1993; Wolfe & McGee, 1994). Because internalized behaviors may draw less attention, females may experience longer episodes of abuse or neglect than males. Chronic maltreatment is related to more negative developmental outcomes (Cicchetti, 1996), suggesting that gender differences in violence may be partially explained by chronicity of abuse. The notion of chronicity underlying the age-related findings is supported by a 1990 study by the American Correctional Association, which reported that 30 percent of females in juvenile corrections institutions experienced abuse 11 or more times; most were not yet nine years old when the abuse occurred (see Chesney-Lind, 1997).

Ethnicity. There is mixed evidence about whether violent behavior after maltreatment differs by ethnicity. Rivera and Widom (1990) found that maltreated African American males were more likely to be arrested for violent offenses than nonmaltreated African American males. This was not true of Caucasian males. Because the study relied on officially recorded delinquency, this finding may be confounded by the fact that youths of color are more likely to gain attention from juvenile justice authorities and receive harsher criminal penalties than Caucasians who commit similar crimes (Pope & Feyerherm, 1992; Walker, Spohn, & DeLone, 1996). Jonson-Reid and Barth (1998) found no difference in incarceration rates for violent offenses among African American, Caucasian, and Hispanic youths with histories of investigated maltreatment reports.

Type of maltreatment. Most studies of violent behavior after maltreatment have focused on abuse rather than neglect. Yet neglect may have a greater effect than abuse on the likelihood of future delinquent behavior—though its impact on violent behavior is still being debated (Jonson-Reid & Barth, 1998; Maxfield & Widom, 1996). For example, Zingraff, Leiter, Myers, and Johnsen (1993) found neglect to be the sole significant predictor of violent offending in a study of adjudicated delinquents. After controlling for family structure, however, Jonson-Reid and Barth (1998) found that neglect was not significantly related to violent offending. Neglect was a stronger influence than abuse on the likelihood of incarceration for a violent offense among youths who came from census tracts with high levels of violent crime (Jonson-Reid & Barth, 1998).

The likelihood of violent behavior may increase according to the severity, frequency, and type of abuse experienced during childhood. One study found that the duration of child welfare involvement (used as a proxy for severity and chronicity) was related to increased levels of aggressive behavior (Manly et al., 1994). Smith and Thornberry (1995) found that chronicity and severity were predictive of more arrests and self-reports of serious and violent delinquency. Jonson-Reid and Barth (no date) found that having three or more maltreatment reports was predictive of incarceration for serious and violent delinquent offenses.

Additional Factors Influencing the Relationship between Maltreatment and Violence

Child maltreatment and youth violence are the product of many risk factors. A brief overview of other factors affecting the relationship between maltreatment and violent conduct follows.

Media and societal norms. Children who live in the United States are exposed to violence at the societal level as well as in the home and community. The association between the observation of media violence and an increased tendency toward aggression has been confirmed (Donnerstein, Slaby, & Eron, 1993). Similarly, some theorists suggest that societal norms condoning violence for the pursuit of individuality may encourage or provoke violent behavior (Gil, 1996; Kappeler, 1995). It is not known, however, how much these influences increase the likelihood of violence among maltreated children.

Family and community violence. A child who lives in poverty is more likely to experience violence between significant adults in the home and violence in the community (Cooley-Quille, Turner, & Beidel, 1995; Osofsky, Wewers, Hann, & Fick, 1993). Because children and youths who experience abuse and neglect are often poor, they may also have a higher risk of exposure to other types of interpersonal violence.

The relative impact of child abuse versus family and community violence is a new area of study. Thornberry (1994) suggested that the effects of witnessing or experiencing violence are cumulative. He found that 60 percent of youths reporting either personal abuse or domestic violence engaged in violent behavior. More than 73 percent of those who experienced both maltreatment and domestic violence later became violent. Jonson-Reid and Barth (1998) found that high rates of violent crime in the census tract of residence increased the likelihood of incarceration as a violent offender among youths with investigated maltreatment reports. Cooley-Quille and colleagues (1995) and Durant, Cadenhead, Pendergast, Slavens, and Linder (1994) found that family conflict was highly correlated with community violence. Researchers studying the influence of family versus community violence, however, have found the impact difficult to assess because of the comorbidity of other forms of violence.

Substance abuse and mental health. Maltreatment is associated with mental health distress and substance abuse, problems that are also strongly associated with violence. Child maltreatment is linked to increases in mental health distress (Cicchetti & Toth, 1995; Garland, Landsverk, Hough, & Ellis-MacLeod, 1996; Silverman, Reinherz, & Giaconia, 1996); there appears to be a strong relationship between mental health distress and violent behavior (Foley, Carlton, & Howell, 1996; Lewis, 1992; Ulzen & Hamilton, 1998). Abused and neglected children also have higher levels of risk for substance abuse than children who have not been maltreated (Dembo et al., 1992; Esbensen & Huizinga, 1991; Vega, Zimmerman, Warheit, Apospori, & Gil, 1993). Substance abuse is related to other problems, such as mental health distress and school failure, that have been found to increase the likelihood of delinquency and violence (Brook & Cohen, 1992; Stiffman, Dore, & Cunningham, 1996; Vega et al., 1993).

Neurophysiological factors. It remains uncertain how neurophysiological factors should be placed along a potential causal chain from trauma to violence. Some researchers attempting to understand biogenetic relationships to violence suggest that aggressive children are born with certain traits that may

Table 4-1. **Risk Factors for Violence among Abused and Neglected Children**

Systemic Domain	Risk Factor
Individual	Neurological injury or biochemical malfunction History of chronic maltreatment Mental health disorders, substance abuse
Family	Domestic violence, parental criminality, poverty
Community	Community poverty, community violence
Public service sector	Multiple placements in foster care Early juvenile offending patterns School failure

directly increase the probability of violence (Reiss Jr. & Roth, 1993). Other investigators similarly suggest that some children are born with difficult temperaments that strain parent–child relationships (Gjone & Stevenson, 1997). It may be that children with such temperaments decrease the likelihood of positive relationships with parent figures, which in turn may contribute to child abuse (Karr-Morse & Wiley, 1998; Pearce & Pezzot-Pearce, 1997). Still others are exploring the possibility that maltreatment results in neurochemical reactions that alter the normal course of brain development (Perry, 1997). Risk factors for violence among maltreated children are summarized in Table 4-1.

WHY DOES MALTREATMENT INCREASE THE RISK FOR VIOLENCE?

There are numerous theories to explain the relationship between maltreatment and violence. Several of the more prominent theories are reviewed here.

Social Learning Theory

The relationship between child maltreatment and violent behavior has often been described as a "cycle of violence." Cycle of violence theories are loosely based on social learning theory (Bandura, 1986). A simplified explanation of the cycle of violence is that abused children later turn violent because they repeat the behaviors they witness as victims. This theoretical approach suggests that the appropriate course of action is to "unlearn" the behaviors, using a behavior management or information-processing approach. Practitioners operating within this framework might attempt to link maltreated children to prosocial mentors or role models.

Social Control Theory

Social control theory suggests that a child or youth may behave in a violent manner because of weak social bonds with prosocial adults or peers (Hirschi, 1969). Gottfredson and Hirschi (1990) emphasize the relationship between prosocial bonds at a young age and the ability to develop self-control skills during adolescence. This theoretical perspective suggests that increasing self-control skills in early childhood—perhaps through parent–child intervention programs—is critical to preventing violent behavior.

Social Disorganization and Oppression Theories

Certain sociological, feminist, and critical schools of criminology suggest a similar process to social control theory at a macro level. They believe that community and societal dysfunction prevent certain groups from attaining personal and economic status through appropriate interpersonal relationships (Gil, 1996; Shaw & McKay, 1942). For example, Ogbu (1983, 1988) states that youths develop pathways to success according to a status mobility system that includes parental guidance, education, and economic opportunity. When mobility is blocked by societal inequities, youths develop oppositional social identities. Because maltreated children and youths are often poor and lack positive family resources, they may reside in communities characterized by low-performing schools and limited social and educational opportunities. This approach to understanding violent behavior suggests that practitioners must develop positive opportunities for youths, such as youth employment programs, school-based interventions, and community outreach.

Attachment Theory

Though attachment theory has its origins in psychological rather than sociological thought, its underlying concepts are not dissimilar to social control theory. Attachment theory suggests that a child's failure to develop a healthy attachment to a parent figure in the first year or two of life may lead to serious psychosocial problems (Berrick et al., 1998). It is posited that abuse and neglect disrupt the normal development of attachment, which later translates into interpersonal difficulties such as an inability to empathize with others or to regulate reactions to emotion (Berrick et al., 1998; Fonagy, Target, Steele, & Steele, 1997; Kennedy & McCarthy, 1998; Pearce & Pezzot-Pearce, 1997). These deficits in relationships and perceptions of relationships and emotions may in turn result in violent behavior (Fonagy et al., 1997). Intervention methods based on attachment theory include individual child and youth counseling and techniques to improve parent–child relationships (Kennedy & McCarthy, 1998).

Cognitive and Moral Development Theory

Cognitive and moral development theorists believe that interpersonal dynamics lead to the development of mental scripts for processing social information and internalizing norms. Dysfunctional parent–child relationships, like those present in many maltreating homes, may inhibit the child's ability to appropriately assess interpersonal communication and behaviors. In turn, these processing difficulties can result in aggressive responses to conflict (Astor, 1994; Rutter & Rutter, 1993). An excellent illustration is found in a case reported by Pearce and Pezzot-Pearce (1997):

> A means of processing had become so ingrained in a previously severely abused child that he perceived his peers as attacking during a game of tag. He had become so accustomed to chasing resulting in brutal attacks that he was unable to recognize the fact that the children were not running toward him, but were smiling, laughing and obviously engaged in a game. (p. 44)

Cognitive–behavioral skills training and information-processing interventions are consistent with this theory.

Posttraumatic Stress Disorder

Violent behavior among children and youths who have been victims of abuse or neglect has been associated with traumatic reaction or posttraumatic stress disorder (Carlson, Furby, Armstrong, & Shlaes, 1998; Steiner, Garcia, & Matthews, 1997; Zeanah & Scheeringa, 1997). This psychological reaction to stress may manifest itself in feelings of hopelessness, an inability to form interpersonal relationships, psychic numbing, or other emotional and psychosomatic difficulties (Carlson et al., 1998). Violence may result from various behaviors related to posttraumatic stress disorder (PTSD), such as an uncontrollable reenactment of past abuse or lack of empathy with a victim because of the numbing effect. Though research on the prevalence of PTSD among abused children is just emerging, children and youths who experience repeated abusive events—particularly those that are experienced as random and uncontrollable—seem to have the greatest risk for developing PTSD (Carlson et al., 1998; Pearce & Pezzot-Pearce, 1997). Traumatic and attachment perspectives are often combined in the therapeutic literature on treating abused and neglected children, as illustrated later in this chapter. Individual and group counseling are used to address PTSD.

Biogenetic Explanations

While various studies have documented the association between physiological abnormalities and violent behavior, the relative impact of these factors compared with experience and environmental conditions is a matter of great debate (Knoblich & King, 1992; Reiss Jr. & Roth, 1993). Some investigators suggest that children may be born with temperaments or disabilities that make them more vulnerable to abuse and violent behavior (Gjone & Stevenson, 1997; Karr-Morse & Wiley, 1998). Neurodevelopmental research has focused on the possibility that abuse and neglect, particularly during infancy and early childhood, may negatively affect brain development, because of either physical injury or neurochemical alterations in response to trauma (Otnow Lewis et al., 1988; Perry, 1997). Altered neural structures may prevent children from developing impulse control skills (Perry, 1997). The range of potential biological influences, however, is as broad as the family, community, and societal risk factors already discussed. Nor is there reason to believe, with rare exceptions, that biogenetic traits act independently of environmental influences on the causal path toward aggressive behavior. This perspective is associated with psychopharmacological intervention.

Resiliency-Based Theories

Another way of asking why maltreatment is associated with violent behavior is to ask why some maltreated children do not become violent. The term resilient is often used to describe such individuals (Garmezy, 1991). This area of inquiry is far from theoretically unified; debate continues about the meaning and utility of the concept of resiliency (Kinard, 1998). Some researchers hypothesize that maltreated children may develop limited resilience that protects them from becoming violent. At the same time, such resiliency may not rule out other emotional problems or long-lasting difficulties maintaining jobs or relationships (Herrenkohl, Herrenkohl, & Egolf, 1994). Like risk factors, resiliency traits may also vary with a child's individual characteristics and family and community environment. The accumulation of stressors in relation to the number or strength of resiliency factors may determine future outcomes for maltreated children (Luthar & Zigler, 1991; Radke-Yarrow & Brown, 1993). Practitioners operating from a resiliency perspective should focus on increasing the number and quality of resiliency factors in a youth's life in an attempt to offset the negative impact of maltreatment.

Integrated Theories

Investigators examining violent behavior after childhood maltreatment are increasingly using integrated or augmented theories that include a developmental perspective. The social developmental model (Catalano & Hawkins, 1996), eco-transactional and eco-developmental frameworks (Cicchetti & Lynch, 1993; Jonson-Reid & Barth, 1998), and life-course theories of crime (Sampson & Laub, 1992) suggest that children may experience the impact of child maltreatment differently based on the presence or absence of other individual, family, and social risk factors. Such a theoretical perspective supports multilevel approaches to intervention, such as multisystemic treatment (Henggeler, Schoenwald, Borduin, Rowland, & Cunningham, 1998).

ASSESSING RISK OF VIOLENCE AMONG ABUSED AND NEGLECTED CHILDREN: EXAMPLES

Using maltreatment as a screen for future violent behavior is complicated by findings suggesting that most victims of abuse and neglect do not become violent. Risk factors for violence discussed above and in chapter 2 should be considered in any assessment of violence. Assessment tools summarized by the Centers for Disease Control and Prevention and reported in Dahlberg, Toal, and Behrens (1998) are an excellent source for screening instruments, as are the strategies outlined in chapter 3. These tools should be used in combination with the assessment of risks associated with maltreatment to develop intervention plans.

The following case examples illustrate problems in assessing maltreated youths for propensity of violence.

> Jeremy was six years old and lived with a foster family along with some of his older siblings—at least one of whom was developmentally delayed. He was referred to a school social worker for violent episodes with peers. A review of Jeremy's history revealed he had been exposed to multiple risk factors for later violent behavior. His mother had been a multiple drug user throughout her pregnancy with Jeremy. The family environment was characterized by poverty and neglect. Jeremy had experienced several hospitalizations during his early childhood, once due to physical abuse from an older sibling and another related to an explosion in the house that resulted in his highly visible permanent scars. Despite the chronic neglect and history of severe medical trauma, Jeremy had only recently been permanently removed from his family of origin.

This case illustrates how multiple risk factors interact in the lives of abused children. By age six, Jeremy had experienced possible prenatal damage, prolonged neglect, physical abuse by siblings, repeated injuries, and the deprivation associated with chronic poverty.

The next case highlights adolescent manifestations of prior maltreatment (adapted from Kashani & Allan, 1998).

Tom was admitted to inpatient treatment at age 13. After years of physical abuse by his father, Tom was removed from the home and his father sentenced to prison for the physical abuse of Tom and the sexual abuse of Tom's older sister. The physical abuse consisted of severe beatings for minor misconduct or because his father had been drinking. Tom later began running away from foster placements. He set a barn on fire, hit his head against walls and mutilated himself when upset, stole several lethal weapons, and assaulted adults and peers.

On the surface, the severe physical abuse suggests a cycle-of-violence explanation of Tom's behavior. The presence of psychological and perhaps physiological harm, however, indicates a more complicated causal chain that may include PTSD, cognitive processing difficulties, neuropsychological damage, or some combination thereof.

These cases suggest that it is important during assessment to consider physiological problems associated with maltreatment. A thorough assessment of a child or adolescent's health should be conducted by appropriate professionals immediately after an abuse or neglect report is made. This may reveal physiological conditions that require medical intervention. Families of abused and neglected children may not seek or understand how to access health care. Without treatment, health risks may result in developmental damage not amenable to psychosocial intervention.

PROMISING PREVENTION AND TREATMENT APPROACHES

The many direct and indirect links between child maltreatment and violent behavior suggest that abused and neglected children should be a prime focus of violence prevention efforts. Unfortunately, we know that some abused and neglected children remain unidentified (Sedlak & Broadhurst, 1996), making it difficult to develop programs that can serve the entire population. In considering this dilemma, this section first highlights prevention strategies that have potential for addressing the needs of those children whose maltreatment is undetected. This is followed by an examination of interventions for children and youths with recognized histories of abuse and neglect. Psychopharmacological intervention is not discussed. While some childhood mental health disorders or neurological abnormalities may call for psychopharmacological intervention, an adequate exploration of these options is beyond the scope of this chapter. Prevention and treatment approaches are summarized in Figure 4-1.

Figure 4-1.   **Prevention and Treatment Programs Organized by Child Population**

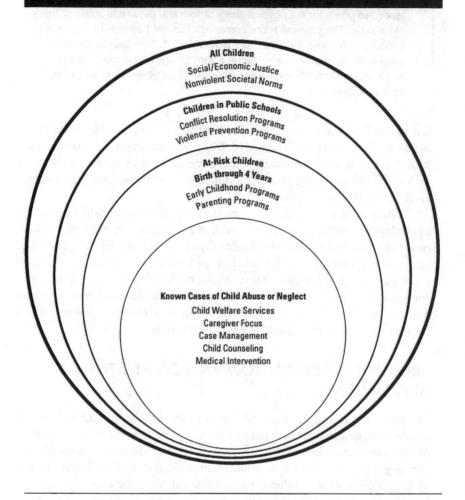

All Children
Social/Economic Justice
Nonviolent Societal Norms

Children in Public Schools
Conflict Resolution Programs
Violence Prevention Programs

At-Risk Children
Birth through 4 Years
Early Childhood Programs
Parenting Programs

Known Cases of Child Abuse or Neglect
Child Welfare Services
Caregiver Focus
Case Management
Child Counseling
Medical Intervention

Universal Prevention Approaches

Changing social norms, early childhood programs, and school-based strategies are interventions that can affect children who have suffered both detected and undetected maltreatment.

Changing social norms. Numerous strategies for social action and policy change have been suggested to reduce youth violence. These include reducing violent images portrayed in the media, limiting the availability of weapons, and alleviating inequity in social and economic opportunities (see Gil, 1998;

Howell, 1995; Murray, 1997). Social change interventions may well contribute to positive individual and family-level violence prevention efforts.

Early childhood programs. Delinquency, child development, and child maltreatment researchers have long promoted the benefits of early intervention. Supportive parenting—particularly during the preschool years—may buffer the effects of early family adversity and harsh discipline (Pettit, Bates, & Dodge, 1997). Early childhood interventions such as Home Visitation 2000 and the Prenatal and Early Childhood Nurse Home Visitation Project have demonstrated increases in educational and social skills and reductions in antisocial behavior among high-risk children (Howell, 1995; Kazdin, 1994). These programs targeting low-income families teach young parents how to care for and supervise their children. These interventions also emphasize cognitive development in children (Howell, 1995; Karr-Morse & Wiley, 1998).

The Perry Preschool Program combines a cognitively oriented child education curriculum with weekly meetings between teacher, mother, and child to encourage positive and productive parent–child interaction. Follow-up evaluations found significant reductions in later criminal and violent behavior among child participants compared with controls (Howell, 1995). If these programs were universally available to families of very young children, children who experience abuse and neglect unreported to child welfare authorities might experience similar benefits.

School-based programs. Recent school shootings in Littleton, Colorado, and Conyers, Georgia, suggest an urgent need for school-based violence prevention programs. School personnel are among the most frequent reporters of child abuse and neglect because of their daily contact with students (Berrick et al., 1998). The vast majority of children in the United States, and nearly all low-income children, attend public schools, a statistic that suggests the majority of children who are abused and neglected also attend public schools. By default, these children are participants in all schoolwide efforts to reduce violent behavior. It is not known whether such efforts are sufficient to offset risk attributable to maltreatment, although school-based trauma recovery programs have been successful in helping children exposed to community violence (Murphy, Pynoos, & James, 1997).

Interventions for Children and Youths with Known Maltreatment Histories

Before discussing intervention strategies for children and youths with known maltreatment histories, it is important to discuss client safety. In accordance with social work ethics, legal requirements, and sound therapeutic practice, the selection of intervention strategies must be based on the ability to maintain a safe environment (Kashani & Allan, 1998; National Association of Social Workers, 1996; Pearce & Pezzot-Pearce, 1997). When intervening with children and youths who remain in the home after an abuse and neglect report, practitioners should be alert to signs of continuing maltreatment or the accumulation of risks that signal maltreatment is likely to recur. In addition to involving the child welfare system, practitioners may empower a child by developing a safety plan the child can execute should the need arise. Of course, at the point of referral for services some youngsters may already be removed from the source of maltreatment, as in the case of children in foster care. Although removal may reduce concern for the client's physical safety, efforts to create an emotionally safe environment remain crucial to the treatment plan whether or not the child remains with the original caretaker (Brohl, 1996; Pearce & Pezzot-Pearce, 1997). Successful prevention of violent behavior is unlikely when a child is concerned with immediate threats.

Mandated child welfare services. The child welfare system is generally conceptualized as a child protection response to child abuse reports and investigations (Lindsey, 1994). Child welfare systems provide in-home services for families who are at risk or who have documented incidents of maltreatment and out-of-home placement and adoption services. An expansion of services within the child welfare system, perhaps by accessing other agency services more systematically, is a second source of interventions for children who are reported as victims of child maltreatment (Bloom, 1998).

Only three studies have focused on the potential mediating effect of child welfare services on later delinquency (Jonson-Reid & Barth, 1998; Runyan & Gould, 1985; Widom, 1991). Runyan and Gould (1985) and Widom (1991) found that foster placement neither increased nor decreased the likelihood of delinquency unless a child had multiple placements; neither study included a comparison group that did not receive in-home or foster care services. In contrast, by using a contemporary sample with a nonservice comparison group, Jonson-Reid and Barth (1998) found that in-home and foster care services decreased the risk of incarceration among maltreated African American and Hispanic youths. Repeated child welfare contacts, indicators of failed attempts to protect children from ongoing harm (for example, repeat reports or moves in and out of foster care), decreased the benefit. Additional analysis of child characteristics, services provided, and other familial and community factors is necessary to understand whether child welfare services played a causal or preventive role in the development of serious and violent behavior among youths. Future research should identify child-level outcomes for specific child welfare intervention strategies.

Parent support. Maltreating parents often do not have adequate information about child development and have poor coping strategies that lead to inappropriate discipline and supervision (Moore, Armsden, & Gogerty, 1998). A combination of education in child development and training in using appropriate disciplinary procedures and coping strategies may help prevent further abuse, reducing the likelihood of later negative consequences like violence (DePanflis, 1996; Feindler & Becker, 1994; Kashani & Allan, 1998; E. Moore et al., 1998). Parent training, particularly long-term, has been successful in reducing aggressive behaviors among children identified as antisocial or aggressive (Kazdin, 1994; Tremblay et al., 1992). The Childhaven Program is an example that combines parenting and early childhood education. The program provides day care services for high-risk and maltreated children while parents participate in support groups, counseling, and other services. After 12 months, parents who participated in the program were found to be better organized and more supportive of child development than parents in a control group. Children in the program had significantly less antisocial behavior and aggression than a control group (E. Moore et al., 1998).

Caregiver involvement in therapy. Therapists have noted the value of including caregivers in therapeutic interventions with children (Briesmeister & Schaefer, 1998; Henggeler et al., 1998). A family-based treatment approach, multisystemic treatment (MST), has been successful in reducing antisocial behavior in children and youths and in improving parent–child relations among abusive and neglectful families (Henggeler et al., 1998). To date, MST has not been evaluated to examine its effect on antisocial behavior among previously maltreated children.

Some therapists suggest that interventions with caregivers should explore a caregiver's family history as it contributes to current abusive behavior in the home (Kennedy & McCarthy, 1998; Pearce & Pezzot-Pearce, 1997). For example, a caregiver's experience may cause distortions in his or her ability to correctly perceive and react to a child's behavior (Feindler & Becker, 1994). Empathy expressed for past trauma experienced by the perpetrator has been reported as a method of obtaining a commitment to intervention and challenging the client's use of aggression (Kashani & Allan, 1998). Identifying past problems may help a family make lasting and positive changes that will support the recovery of a child.

Empowering caregivers. Personal guilt resulting from an abusive incident and a confusing array of helping professionals often lead to uncertainty among caregivers during treatment. If the family is still involved in the child welfare system, caregivers should be educated about the process of court intervention and about services available (Pearce & Pezzot-Pearce, 1997). This may require helping the original caregiver to collaborate with foster parents to support the positive development of the child (Bloom, 1998). Parents and other caregivers should also be educated about the consequences of abuse and be prepared for the fact that the child's recovery may not be immediate (Kennedy & McCarthy, 1998). Children and youths may continue for some time to test the commitment of caregivers or display behaviors related to the traumatic experience (Kashani & Allan, 1998; Pearce & Pezzot-Pearce,

1997). Practitioners can help parents understand children's reactions and promote positive means of dealing with the situation.

Case management. The primary role of a practitioner is often to identify appropriate services for maltreated children after abuse. For example, children in foster care face numerous obstacles to receiving appropriate educational support, one of which is a high mobility rate (Ayasse, 1995). Movements due to placement or school failure can thwart attempts to address a child's needs, making good assessment skills and knowledge of treatment resources imperative. A continuation of the case vignette profiling Jeremy illustrates the case management role.

> *Jeremy II.* Observations from the home, teacher, foster parent, and school social worker combined with available background information suggested that Jeremy's violent behavior might reflect serious emotional needs that went beyond the ability of a regular school setting to address. Triggering services for emotional disturbance in the school setting can take time and must be preceded by evidence that other attempts to remediate the behaviors were tried and failed. Because aggressive behavior can lead to disciplinary action that removes a child from school, Jeremy was in jeopardy of having to leave the school before the assessment was completed. The case manager focused on maintaining Jeremy in the present environment until educational testing could be completed without compromising his safety or that of his peers. Working closely with the teacher, family, and school officials, the case manager implemented an interim intervention plan that safeguarded the other students while allowing the assessment to proceed. When the results indicated that Jeremy was eligible for services for severe emotional disturbance, he was placed in a therapeutic day treatment program. Follow-up calls revealed that Jeremy was progressing very well.

Mentors. Mentors are often part of delinquency and violence prevention efforts. The use of mentors is based on findings that a relationship with a positive, caring adult can be a protective factor in the lives of high-risk youths (Werner, 1993). Although the concept of mentoring is supported by social control and attachment theories of violent behavior, empirical evaluations have failed to demonstrate significant positive results (Howell, 1995). Short-term mentoring relationships may simply be an inadequate replacement for a long-term caring relationship with an adult.

Counseling. Several investigators have put forth counseling approaches for abused and neglected children; none of the approaches, however, has been rigorously evaluated (Cicchetti & Toth, 1995; Gil, 1991; Pearce & Pezzot-Pearce, 1997). Generally these approaches are characterized by respect for the child or adolescent's experiences, consideration of the child's physical and psychological safety, and the development of positive coping strategies (Gil, 1991; Kashani & Allan, 1998; Kennedy & McCarthy, 1998; Pearce & Pezzot-Pearce, 1997). Counseling strategies are usually limited by their goal of reducing harm associated with maltreatment rather than preventing violent behavior specifically.

Interventions to increase attachment and reduce trauma. Some recent empirical and therapeutic work addressing abused and neglected children has emphasized interventions on the basis of attachment- and trauma-based theories (Carlson, Furby, Armstrong, & Shlaes, 1998; Moore, Moretti, & Holland, 1998; Price & Landsverk, 1998). These interventions typically include steps to help victims process traumatic experiences, identify and express feelings, and develop new coping and cognitive strategies to raise self-esteem (Brohl, 1996; Pearce & Pezzot-Pearce, 1997). Art and play therapy are among the strategies used to develop attachments and reduce trauma (Gil, 1991). Unfortunately, the effects of attachment- and trauma-based approaches have not been evaluated.

Cognitive and information processing. Cognitive techniques, including self-instruction and skills training, have been used alone or as part of a larger program to decrease aggressive responses associated with problems in processing social information (Kazdin, Siegel, & Bass, 1992; Pearce & Pezzot-Pearce, 1997; Price & Landsverk, 1998). Cognitive treatment and skills training programs have been effective in preventing and reducing aggressive and antisocial behavior (Howell, 1995; Kazdin, 1994; Phillips, Schwean, & Saklofske, 1997).

Summary. The intervention methods discussed in this section reflect the variety of approaches practitioners are using to prevent violence. Because empirical evaluation is lacking, none of the approaches can be suggested as a single best practice for violence prevention among abused and neglected youths. Rather, readers should consider this review as a menu from which items should be selected after careful assessment of each case.

CONCLUSION

Most maltreated children do not become violent. Therefore, it is important not to stigmatize or stereotype abused and neglected children as the violent perpetrators of tomorrow. Furthermore, the complex array of risk and protective factors discussed in this chapter does not suggest a single etiological path from maltreatment to violent behavior. This means that careful assessments conducted from an ecological perspective are vital in planning appropriate services.

Additional research is necessary to inform the selection of prevention methods. For example, studies identifying the interaction of multiple risk factors over time may help identify typologies to guide the selection of intervention methods. Researchers and practitioners must work together to systematically evaluate practice strategies given what is known about risk factors and developmental influences.

Despite serious gaps in knowledge, there is reason for optimism. In particular, early childhood programs show promise of diminishing violent behavior related to abuse and neglect. Furthermore, though evaluative research on interventions with maltreated children is scarce, the substantial literature on risk factors, causal theories, and evaluations of interventions with other at-risk groups of children can help practitioners select strategies that closely match the dynamics of a particular case.

Of course, the best means of preventing violence associated with abuse and neglect is to prevent the abuse and neglect. Until that can be achieved, practitioners must support research-based practice that will uncover new ways to prevent children from moving down the path from victim to victimizer.

REFERENCES

Astor, R. A. (1994). Children's moral reasoning about family and peer violence: The role of provocation and retribution. *Child Development, 65,* 1054–1067.

Attar, B., Guerra, N., & Tolan, P. (1994). Neighborhood disadvantage, stressful life events, and adjustment in urban elementary-school children. *Journal of Clinical Child Psychology, 23,* 391–400.

Ayasse, R. (1995). Addressing the needs of foster children: The foster youth services program. *Social Work in Education, 17,* 207–216.

Bandura, A. (1986). *Social foundations of thought and action.* Newark, NJ: Prentice-Hall.

Bell Jr., B. (1998, December 9). Missouri will investigate youth who said he threw girl from bluff; Family services agency placed boy, 17, in home in September; "Out of blue" action is assailed. *St. Louis Post-Dispatch,* p. A17.

Berrick, J., Needell, B., Barth, R., & Jonson-Reid, M. (1998). *The tender years: Toward developmentally-sensitive child welfare services for very young children.* New York: Oxford University Press.

Besharov, D. (1990). *Recognizing child abuse: A guide for the concerned.* New York: Free Press.

Bloom, M. (1998). Primary prevention and foster care. *Child Welfare, 20,* 667–696.

Briesmeister, J., & Schaefer, C. (Eds.). (1998). *Handbook of parent training: Parents as co-therapists for children's behavior problems.* New York: Wiley.

Brohl, K. (1996). *Working with traumatized children.* Washington, DC: Child Welfare League of America Press.

Brook, J., & Cohen, P. (1992). A developmental perspective on drug use and delinquency. In J. McCord (Ed.), *Facts, frameworks, and forecasts. Advances in criminological theory* (Vol. 3, pp. 231–252). New Brunswick, NJ: Transaction Publishers.

Carlson, E., Furby, L., Armstrong, J., & Shlaes, J. (1998). A conceptual framework for the long-term psychological effects of traumatic child abuse. *Child Maltreatment, 2,* 272–295.

Catalano, R. F., & Hawkins, J. D. (1996). The social development model: A theory of antisocial behavior. In J. D. Hawkins (Ed.), *Delinquency and crime: Current theories* (pp. 149–197). New York: Cambridge University Press.

Chesney-Lind, M. (1997). *The female offender: Girls, women and crime.* Thousand Oaks, CA: Sage Publications.

Cicchetti, D., (1996). Child maltreatment: Implications for developmental theory and research. *Human Development, 39,* 18–39.

Cicchetti, D., & Lynch, M. (1993). Toward an ecological/transactional model of community violence and child maltreatment: Consequences for children's development. *Psychiatry, 56,* 96–118.

Cicchetti, D., & Toth, S. (1995). A developmental psychopathology perspective on child abuse and neglect. *Journal of the American Academy of Child and Adolescent Psychiatry, 34,* 541–565.

Cooley-Quille, M., Turner, S., & Beidel, D. (1995). Assessing community violence: The children's report of exposure to violence. *Journal of the American Academy of Child and Adolescent Psychiatry, 34,* 201–208.

Coulton, C., Korbin, J., Su, M., & Chow, J. (1995). Community level factors and child maltreatment rates. *Child Development, 66,* 1262–1276.

Coulton, C., & Pandey, S. (1992). Geographic concentration of poverty and risk to children in urban neighborhoods. *American Behavioral Scientist, 35,* 238–257.

Dahlberg, L., Toal, S., & Behrens, C. (1998). *Measuring violence-related attitudes, beliefs, and behaviors among youths: A compendium of assessment tools.* Atlanta: U.S. Department of Health and Human Services, Centers for Disease Control and Prevention.

Dembo, R., Williams, L., Wothke, W., Schmeidler, J., & Brown, C. (1992). The role of family factors, physical abuse, and sexual victimization experiences in high risk youths' alcohol and other drug use and delinquency: A longitudinal model. *Violence and Victims, 7,* 233–246.

DePanfilis, D. (1996). Social isolation of neglectful families: A review of social support assessment and intervention models. *Child Maltreatment, 1,* 37–52.

Donnerstein, E., Slaby, R., & Eron, L. (1993). *The mass media and youth aggression.* In L. Eron, J. Gentry, & P. Schlegel (Eds.), *Reason to hope: A psychosocial perspective on violence and youth* (pp. 219–250). Washington, DC: American Psychological Association.

Drake, B., & Zuravin, S. (1998). Bias in child maltreatment reporting: Revisiting the myths of classlessness. *American Journal of Orthopsychiatry, 68,* 295–305.

Durant, R., Cadenhead, C., Pendergrast, R., Slavens, G., & Linder, C. (1994). Factors associated with the use of violence among urban black adolescents. *American Journal of Public Health, 84,* 612–617.

Esbensen, F., & Huizinga, D. (1991). Juvenile victimization and delinquency. *Juvenile Victimization, 23,* 202–228.

Feindler, E., & Becker, J. (1994). Interventions in family violence involving children and adolescents. In L. Eron, J. Gentry, & P. Schlegel (Eds.), *Reason to hope: A psychosocial perspective on violence and youth* (pp. 405–432). Washington, DC: American Psychological Association.

Finkelhor, D., & Dziuba-Leatherman, J. (1994). Victimization of children. *American Psychologist, 49,* 173–183.

Foley, H., Carlton, C., & Howell, R. (1996). The relationship of attention deficit hyperactivity disorder and conduct disorder to juvenile delinquency: Legal implications. *Bulletin of the American Academy of Psychiatry and the Law, 24,* 333–345.

Fonagy, P., Target, M., Steele, M., & Steele, H. (1997). The development of violence and crime as it relates to the security of attachment. In J. Osofsky (Ed.), *Children in a violent society* (pp. 150–182). New York: Guilford Press.

Garbarino, J., & Kostelny, K. (1992). Child maltreatment as a community problem. *Child Abuse and Neglect, 16,* 455–464.

Garland, A., Landsverk, J., Hough, R., & Ellis-MacLeod, E. (1996). Type of maltreatment as a predictor of mental health services use for children in foster care. *Child Abuse and Neglect, 20,* 675–688.

Garmezy, N. (1991). Children in poverty: Resilience despite risk. *Psychiatry, 56,* 127–136.

Gil, E. (1991). *The healing power of play: Working with abused children.* New York: Guilford Press.

Gil, D. (1996). Preventing violence in a structurally violent society: Mission impossible. *American Journal of Orthopsychiatry, 66,* 77–84.

Gil, D. (1998). *Confronting injustice and oppression. Concepts and strategies for social workers.* New York: Columbia University Press.

Gjone, H., & Stevenson, J. (1997). A longitudinal twin study of temperament and behavior problems: Common genetic or environmental influences? *Journal of the American Academy of Child and Adolescent Psychiatry, 36,* 1448–1456.

Gottfredson, M., & Hirschi, T. (1990). *A general theory of crime.* Stanford, CA: Stanford University Press.

Gray, H., & Foshee, V. (1997). Adolescent dating violence: Differences between one-sided and mutually violent profiles. *Journal of Interpersonal Violence, 12,* 126–141.

Henggeler, S., Schoenwald, S., Borduin, C., Rowland, M., & Cunningham, P. (1998). *Multisystemic treatment of antisocial behavior in children and adolescents.* New York: Guilford Press.

Herrenkohl, E., Herrenkohl, R., & Egolf, B. (1994). Resilient early school-aged children from maltreating homes: Outcomes in late adolescence. *American Journal of Orthopsychiatry, 64,* 301–309.

Hirschi, T. (1969). *Causes of delinquency.* Berkeley, CA: University of California Press.

Hotaling, G., Straus, M., & Lincoln, A. (1989). Intrafamily violence and violence and other crime outside the family. In L. Ohlin & M. Tonry (Eds.), *Family violence* (pp. 315–375). Chicago: University of Chicago Press.

Howell, J. C. (Ed.). (1995). *Guide for implementing the comprehensive strategy for serious, violent and chronic juvenile offenders.* Washington DC: U.S. Department of Justice, Office of Juvenile Justice and Delinquency Prevention.

Jonson-Reid, M. (1998). Youth violence and exposure to violence in childhood: An ecological review. *Aggression and Violent Behavior, 3,* 159–179.

Jonson-Reid, M., & Barth, R. (1998). *Pathways from child welfare to juvenile incarceration for serious and violent offenses.* Final report to the Office of Juvenile Justice and Delinquency Prevention (Grant #96-JN-FX-0008). Berkeley, CA: University of California at Berkeley, School of Social Welfare, Child Welfare Research Center.

Jonson-Reid, M., & Barth, R. (no date). *From maltreatment report to juvenile incarceration: Uncovering the role of child welfare services.* Unpublished manuscript.

Jonson-Reid, M., & Bivens, L. (in press). Foster youth and dating violence. *Journal of Interpersonal Violence.*

Kappeler, S. (1995). *The will to violence.* New York: Teachers College Press.

Karr-Morse, R., & Wiley, M. (1998). *Ghosts from the nursery: Tracing the roots of violence.* New York: Atlantic Monthly Press.

Kashani, J., & Allan, W. (1998). The impact of family violence on children and adolescents. *Developmental and Clinical Psychology and Psychiatry Series, 37.* Thousand Oaks, CA: Sage Publications.

Kazdin, A. (1994). Interventions for aggressive and antisocial children. In L. Eron, J. Gentry, & P. Schlegel (Eds.), *Reason to hope: A psychosocial perspective on violence and youth* (pp. 341–382). Washington, DC: American Psychological Association.

Kazdin, A., Siegel, T., & Bass, D. (1992). Cognitive problem-solving skills training and parent management training in the treatment of antisocial behavior in children. *Journal of Consulting and Clinical Psychology, 60,* 737–747.

Kennedy, J., & McCarthy, C. (1998). *Bridging worlds: Understanding and facilitating adolescent recovery from the trauma of abuse.* New York: Haworth Maltreatment and Trauma Press.

Kinard, E. M. (1998). Methodological issues in assessing resilience in maltreated children. *Child Abuse and Neglect, 22,* 669–680.

Knoblich, G., & King, R. (1992). Biological correlates of criminal behavior. In J. McCord (Ed.), *Facts, frameworks, and forecasts. Advances in criminological theory* (Vol. 3, pp. 1–22). New Brunswick, NJ: Transaction Publishers.

Lewis, D. O. (1992). From abuse to violence: Psychophysiological consequences of maltreatment. *Journal of the American Academy of Child and Adolescent Psychiatry, 31,* 383–391.

Lindsey, D. (1994). *The welfare of children.* New York: Oxford University Press.

Luthar, S., & Zigler, E. (1991). Vulnerability and competence: A review of research on resilience in childhood. *American Journal of Orthopsychiatry, 61,* 6–22.

Manly, J., Cicchetti, D., & Barnett, D. (1994). The impact of subtype, frequency, chronicity, and severity of child maltreatment on social competence and behavior problems. *Development and Psychopathology, 6,* 121–143.

Maxfield, M., & Widom, C. (1996). The cycle of violence: Revisited six years later. *Archives of Pediatric Adolescent Medicine, 150,* 390–395.

Moore, E., Armsden, G., & Gogerty, P. (1998). A twelve-year follow-up study of maltreated and at-risk children who received early therapeutic child care. *Child Maltreatment, 3,* 3–16.

Moore, K., Moretti, M., & Holland, R. (1998). A new perspective on youth care programs: Using attachment theory to guide interventions for troubled youth. *Residential Treatment for Children and Youth, 15,* 1–24.

Murphy, L., Pynoos, R., & James, C. B. (1997). The trauma/grief-focused group psychotherapy module of an elementary school-based violence prevention/intervention program. In J. Osofsky (Ed.), *Children in a violent society* (pp. 223–255). New York: Guilford Press.

Murray, J. P. (1997). Media violence and youth. In J. Osofsky (Ed.), *Children in a violent society* (pp. 72–96). New York: Guilford Press.

National Association of Social Workers. (1996). *Code of ethics.* Washington, DC: Author.

Ogbu, J. (1983). Minority status and schooling in plural societies. *Comparative Education Review, 27,* 168–190.

Ogbu, J. (1988). Cultural diversity and human development. *New Directions for Child Development, 42,* 11–28.

Osofsky, J., Wewers, S., Hann, D., & Fick, A. (1993). Chronic community violence: What is happening to our children? *Psychiatry, 56,* 36–45.

Otnow Lewis, D., Pincus, J., Bard, B., Richardson, E., Prichep, L., Feldman, M., & Yeager, C. (1988). Neuropsychiatric, psychoeducational, and family characteristics of 14 juveniles condemned to death in the United States. *American Journal of Psychiatry, 145,* 584–589.

Pakiz, B., Reinherz, H. Z., & Giaconia, R. M. (1997). Early risk factors for serious antisocial behavior at age 21: A longitudinal community study. *American Journal of Orthopsychiatry, 67,* 92–101.

Pearce, J. W., & Pezzot-Pearce, T. D. (1997). *Psychotherapy of abused and neglected children.* New York: Guilford Press.

Perry, B. (1997). Incubated in terror: Neurodevelopmental factors in the "cycle of violence." In J. Osofsky (Ed.), *Children in a violent society* (pp. 124–149). New York: Guilford Press.

Pettit, G., Bates, J., & Dodge, K. (1997). Supportive parenting, ecological context, and children's adjustment: A seven-year longitudinal study. *Child Development, 68,* 908–923.

Phillips, D., Schwean, V., & Saklofske, D. (1997). Treatment effect of a school based cognitive-behavioral program for aggressive children. *Canadian Journal of School Psychology, 13,* 60–67.

Pope, C., & Feyerherm, W. (1992). *Minorities in the juvenile justice system. Statistics summary.* Washington, DC: U.S. Department of Justice, Office of Juvenile Justice and Delinquency Prevention.

Price, J., & Landsverk, J. (1998). Social information-processing patterns as predictors of social adaptation and behavior problems among maltreated children in foster care. *Child Abuse and Neglect, 22,* 845–858.

Radke-Yarrow, M., & Brown, E. (1993). Resilience and vulnerability in children of multiple risk families. *Development and Psychopathology, 5,* 581–592.

Reiss Jr., A., & Roth, J. (Eds.). (1993). *Understanding and preventing violence.* Washington, DC: National Academy Press.

Rivera, B., & Widom, C. (1990). Childhood victimization and violent offending. *Violence and Victims, 5,* 19–34.

Runyan, D., & Gould, C. (1985). Foster care for child maltreatment: Impact on delinquent behavior. *Pediatrics, 75,* 562–568.

Rutter, M., & Rutter, M. (1993). Anxiety and aggression: Fears and delinquency. *Developing minds: Change and continuity across the lifespan.* London: Penguin Books Ltd.

Sadker, M., & Sadker, D. (1993, March). Fair and square? *Instructor,* 45–46, 67–68.

Sampson, R. J., & Laub, J. H. (1992). Crime and deviance in the life course. *Annual Review of Sociology, 18,* 63–84.

Schwartz, I., Rendon, J., & Hsieh, C. (1994). Is child maltreatment a leading cause of delinquency? *Child Welfare, 73,* 639–655.

Sedlak, A., & Broadhurst, D. (1996). *Third National Incidence Study of Child Abuse and Neglect*. Washington, DC: U.S. Department of Health and Human Services.

Shaw, C., & McKay, H. (1942). *Juvenile delinquency and urban areas*. Chicago: University of Chicago Press.

Silverman, A., Reinherz, H., & Giaconia, R. (1996). The long-term sequelae of child and adolescent abuse: A longitudinal community study. *Child Abuse and Neglect, 20,* 709–723.

Smith, C., & Thornberry, T. (1995). The relationship between childhood maltreatment and adolescent involvement in delinquency. *Criminology, 33,* 451–481.

Smith, J., & Williams, J. (1992). From abusive household to dating violence. *Journal of Family Violence, 7,* 153–165.

Steiner, H., Garcia, I., & Matthews, Z. (1997). Posttraumatic stress disorder in incarcerated juvenile delinquents. *Journal of the American Academy of Child and Adolescent Psychiatry, 36,* 357–365.

Stiffman, A., Dore, P., & Cunningham, R. (1996). Violent behaviors in adolescents and young adults: A person in environment model. *Journal of Child and Family Studies, 5,* 487–502.

Straus, M., & Gelles, R. (1992). *Physical violence in American families*. New Brunswick, NJ: Transaction Publishers.

Thornberry, T. (1994). *Violent families and youth violence. Fact Sheet #21*. Washington, DC: Office of Juvenile Justice and Delinquency Prevention.

Tremblay, R., Vitaro, F., Bertrand, L., LeBlanc, M., Beauchesne, H., Boileau, H., & David, L. (1992). Parent and child training to prevent the early onset of delinquency: The Montreal Longitudinal-Experimental Study. In J. McCord & R. E. Tremblay (Eds.), *Preventing antisocial behavior: Interventions from birth through adolescence* (p. 85). New York: Guilford Press.

Ulzen, T., & Hamilton, H. (1998). Psychiatric disorders in incarcerated youth. *Youth Update, 16,* 4–5.

U.S. Department of Health and Human Services. (1998). *Child maltreatment 1996: Reports from the states to the national child abuse and neglect data system*. Washington, DC: U.S. Government Printing Office.

Vega, W., Zimmerman, R., Warheit, G., Apospori, E., & Gil, A. (1993). Risk factors for early adolescent drug use in four ethnic and racial groups. *American Journal of Public Health, 83,* 185–189.

Vissing, Y., Straus, M., Gelles, R., & Harrop, J. (1991). Verbal aggression by parents and psychosocial problems of children. *Child Abuse and Neglect, 15,* 223–238.

Walker, S., Spohn, C., & DeLone, M. (1996). *The color of justice: Race, ethnicity and crime in America*. San Francisco: Wadsworth.

Werner, E. (1993). Risk, resilience and recovery: Perspectives from the Kauai longitudinal study. *Development and Psychopathology, 5,* 503–515.

Widom, C. (1989). Child abuse, neglect, and adult behavior: Research design and findings on criminality, violence, and child abuse. *American Journal of Orthopsychiatry, 59,* 355–367.

Widom, C. (1991). The role of placement experiences in mediating the criminal consequences of early childhood. *American Journal of Orthopsychiatry, 61,* 195–209.

Widom, C. (1996). *An update on the cycle of violence*. Washington, DC: National Institute of Justice.

Wolfe, D., & McGee, R. (1994). Dimensions of child maltreatment and their relationship to adolescent adjustment. *Development and Psychopathology, 6,* 165–181.

Zeanah, C., & Scheeringa, M. (1997). The experience and effects of violence in infancy. In J. Osofsky (Ed.), *Children in a violent society* (pp. 97–123). New York: Guilford Press.

Zingraff, M., Leiter, J., Myers, K., & Johnsen, M. (1993). Child maltreatment and youthful problem behavior. *Criminology, 31,* 173–202.

Chapter 5

Violence and Aggression in Girls

Cathryn C. Potter

W hy a chapter on violence and aggression in girls? Girls comprise only a small percentage of the delinquent population and an even smaller percentage of the violent juvenile offender population. Still, we see increased attention to female offenders among researchers, policymakers, and the popular media (Office of Juvenile Justice and Delinquency Prevention [OJJDP], 1998a).

The answer lies in the long-term trends in juvenile offending. At a point when rates of juvenile offending generally, and violent offending specifically, are decreasing, female juvenile offending, especially violent offending, is increasing (OJJDP, 1998a; Poe-Yamagata & Butts, 1996).

Because girls have historically comprised a small percentage (15 percent to 26 percent) of offenders (Poe-Yamagata & Butts, 1996; Snyder, 1997) and because most delinquency research has not included girls, much less is known about violent offending among girls than among boys. We know relatively little about the characteristics of violent girls, their pathways to and through delinquent activity, their use of service systems, and the intervention models effective for them. In this chapter we consider what is known about these girls and identify critical areas in which knowledge is lacking. Along the way we encounter multiple perspectives on female juvenile offenders, views that are grounded in the differing ways in which both delinquency researchers and juvenile justice systems have considered these young women.

There are two primary approaches to understanding female offenders. The first represents the mainstream of empirical research on juvenile delinquency, of which the literature regarding girls is a very small part. The second is a feminist critique of the juvenile justice system's response to female delinquents.

Most delinquency research concentrates exclusively on male offenders. The general delinquency literature focuses on understanding risk and protective factors for delinquent behavior, an emphasis that has crossed disciplinary lines (Jessor, 1992; Jessor, Bos, Vanderryn, Costa, & Turbin, 1995). Specifically, this research has united researchers from a sociological tradition with those interested in the developmental trajectory of youth violence. These studies are located in an ecological framework that calls attention to differing levels of risk and protective factors (for example, individual, family, neighborhood, and so forth) (Sommers & Baskin, 1994). As more is known about risk and protective factors, researchers are refining theory to better explain observed relationships and to support improved intervention models (Hawkins, 1998; Jessor et al., 1995).

This interdisciplinary approach holds promise for understanding female delinquency, providing common ground for divergent perspectives on female offending, and moving toward better understanding of effective intervention. Unfortunately, most of the research has focused on boys or has not adequately examined gender differences (Loeber & Hay, 1997). Moreover, to date the focus has been almost exclusively on identifying risk factors, with little examination of protective factors or discussion of the complexity of incorporating protective factors into models of delinquency (Jessor et al., 1995).

The second approach to understanding female offending is represented by numerous feminist critiques of both delinquency research and justice system responses to female offenders (Chesney-Lind, 1989; Daly, 1989; 1992; Pepi, 1998). Feminist authors argue that all empirical examination of female offending takes place in the context of a culture that encourages and condones violence *against* girls and women, but is profoundly uncomfortable with violence *by* girls and women (Daly, 1992). Examination of female juvenile offending is further clouded by ingrained assumptions about gender differences in normative behaviors and about the nature of justice system responses to nonnormative behaviors. Feminist writers, pointing to differences between boys and girls in their characteristics and life histories, their offenses, and justice system responses to their behaviors, make a case for differential treatment of female offenders (Albrecht, 1996; Chesney-Lind, 1989; Daly, 1989, 1992; Pepi, 1998).

Emerging from this body of literature is a growing call for a gender-specific theory of offending (Rhodes & Fischer, 1993), but proponents have not yet articulated a clear theoretical framework that responds to this call. Most of the discussion addresses the use of gender-specific developmental theory to inform intervention models (Albrecht, 1996), although there is also increasing reference to feminist intervention principles (Pepi, 1998; Potter & Molidor, 1998). The growing debate on the value of universal responses compared with gender-specific responses to female offending is not yet fully informed by a strong research tradition focusing on both risk and protective factors (Hoyt & Scherer, 1998); that is, there is relatively little integration of feminist critiques and the risk and protective factor literature.

Investigators representing these two schools of thought have not articulated strong, theory-based intervention models for girls. Mainstream delinquency approaches focused on treatment models for boys have assumed that the same etiological principles and intervention processes operate similarly for girls. Chesney-Lind (1989) refers to this as the "just add girls and stir" perspective. Such conceptualizations overlook gender differences by subsuming the small minority of girls into models dominated by male respondents.

On the other hand, feminist critiques often stop short of providing either explanatory or intervention models. Although some consensus is emerging on intervention principles, these are largely drawn from outside the delinquency literature (Albrecht, 1996; OJJDP, 1998b; Pepi, 1998). The danger here is that the tendency to reframe female delinquent behavior as mental illness may downplay the seriousness of delinquent behavior.

Juvenile justice systems face growing numbers of female offenders, many of whom are increasingly violent. A recent survey of state juvenile justice system administrators indicated that a majority clearly believed that reasons for entry, offense patterns, and service needs of boys and girls differ (Potter & Molidor, 1999). They had much less clarity about how they might respond to these differences and were eager for a more sophisticated discussion of the characteristics and treatment needs of female offenders.

This, then, is the context for our thinking about violent female offenders. Very little is known about these young women. What is known is grounded in approaches to understanding that are informed by differing perspectives: a traditional delinquency research perspective that has until recently largely ignored girls, and a feminist perspective that primarily critiques system performance. Meanwhile, in the real world of juvenile justice systems, professionals are asking for intervention programs that respond to their reality: more girls entering the system, and shifting patterns of female offending.

NATURE AND SCOPE OF FEMALE JUVENILE OFFENDING

Young females are far less likely than their male counterparts to violate the law and to enter the juvenile justice system. They also commit different types of offenses than males do. Girls are less likely than boys to commit violent crimes and more likely to come to official attention for status offenses (Poe-Yamagata & Butts, 1996). In recent years, however, the nature of female juvenile offending appears to be changing: Much of the change consists of increases in violent offending.

Female Juvenile Arrest Patterns

In 1996, 723,000 girls were arrested for juvenile offenses, a 106 percent increase over the 350,000 girls arrested in 1989 (Federal Bureau of Investigation, 1997). Girls represented 26 percent of all juveniles arrested in 1996 (Snyder, 1997). The record reflects a continuous rise in the proportion of juvenile offenders who are female: 11 percent in 1960, 15 percent in 1975, 19 percent in 1990, and 21 percent in 1992 (Poe-Yamagata & Butts, 1996; Snyder, 1997).

Between 1992 and 1996 the number of girls arrested for violent crimes increased by 25 percent, whereas arrests of boys remained constant (Budnick & Shields-Fletcher, 1998). Although the overall juvenile arrest rate for violent crime fell by 23 percent from 1994 to 1997, including decreases in all violent offense categories, these figures mask a disturbing trend in female violence. Between 1987 and 1996, the overall increase in the violent crime arrest rate was far greater for girls than for boys (111 percent compared with 63 percent), and the decrease from 1994 to 1996 was far smaller (12 percent compared with 23 percent) (OJJDP, 1998b). Much of the increase in violent crime rates among girls is accounted for by a large increase in the number of aggravated assaults. Female juvenile arrest rates for aggravated assault rose by 28 percent between 1992 and 1996, whereas the same rates declined 3 percent for male arrests (Poe-Yamagata & Butts, 1996; Snyder, 1997).

Arrests for juvenile property crimes involving girls also increased between 1989 and 1993, whereas the number of boys arrested declined (Poe-Yamagata & Butts, 1996). These increases in arrests were: 16 percent for burglary (down 6 percent for boys), 21 percent for larceny–theft (down 1 percent for boys), 28 percent for motor vehicle theft (down 8 percent for boys), and 53 percent for arson arrests (down 21 percent for boys) (Poe-Yamagata & Butts, 1996).

Girls are increasingly represented in arrests for forgery and counterfeiting (37 percent of all juvenile arrests), embezzlement (45 percent), prostitution and commercialized vice (52 percent), offenses against family and children (37 percent), and running away (57 percent). The greatest percentage increases in other crimes for girls between 1987 and 1996 are in the following categories: other assaults (100 percent), weapons violations (69 percent), drug-related violations (133 percent), gambling (213 percent), offenses against family and children (113 percent), disorderly conduct (93 percent), and curfew and loitering violations (113 percent) (Snyder, 1997). However, it is important to keep these trends in perspective: Male juvenile arrest rates continue to outpace female arrest rates by 6 to 1 (Poe-Yamagata & Butts, 1996).

Patterns in Court Filings and Dispositions

Delinquency offenses. "At all stages of juvenile court processing, delinquency cases involving female youths received less severe outcomes than cases involving males" (Poe-Yamagata & Butts, 1996, p. 10). In 1993, 20 percent of cases filed in juvenile court had female defendants, although 24 percent of the arrests were of girls. Girls were less likely to be formally processed with the filing of a delinquency petition (43 percent) than boys (56 percent) (Poe-Yamagata & Butts, 1996).

Table 5-1 presents the percentage of cases against delinquent girls by type of offense (Poe-Yamagata & Butts, 1996, p. 10). Relative to their overall proportion of delinquency cases, girls are overrepresented in the aggravated assault and simple assault categories and underrepresented in all other person offense categories. Among property offense categories, girls are overrepresented in the larceny theft and "other" property offense domains. In the public order category, girls are overrepresented in obstruction of justice, disorderly conduct, and liquor law violations.

Girls are less likely than boys to be placed in secure detention between filing and disposition (16 percent for girls compared with 22 percent for boys). Girls are also less likely than boys to be detained for most offense categories, with the exception of public order offenses (14 percent compared with 11 percent) and probation and parole violations (24 percent compared with 12 percent). However, the detention rate is increasing more rapidly for girls than for boys. Cases against girls are less likely to be adjudicated than are those against boys (53 percent compared with 59 percent). After adjudication, cases involving females are more likely than comparable male cases to result in probation (60 percent compared with 55 percent). Adjudicated girls are less likely to be ordered into an out-of-home placement than are boys (23 percent compared with 29 percent) (Poe-Yamagata & Butts, 1996).

Status offenses. Status offenses (for example, truancy, running away) are acts committed by youths that are law violations only for juveniles. Table 5-2 presents changes in status offense case rates between 1986 and 1995. Although status offense rates in many categories are comparable for boys and girls, girls are more likely to be petitioned for running away, whereas boys are more likely to be petitioned for liquor law violations.

Table 5-1. **Delinquency Cases by Most Serious Offense and Gender, 1993**

Most Serious Offense	Total		Number of Female Cases		Percent Female
Total Cases	1,489,700		297,400		20
Person Offense	318,800		70,400		22
Criminal homicide		2,800		200	8
Forcible rape		6,100		200	3
Robbery		35,600		3,200	9
Aggravated assault		77,500		16,200	21
Simple assault		166,400		46,300	28
Other violent sex offense		10,900		500	5
Other person offense		19,300		3,800	20
Property Offense	808,900		161,000		20
Burglary		149,700		13,300	9
Larceny-theft		353,700		102,800	29
Motor vehicle theft		61,100		10,200	17
Arson		8,200		1,000	12
Vandalism		117,100		12,200	10
Trespassing		60,500		10,000	16
Stolen property offense		27,400		3,000	11
Other property offense		31,300		8,500	27
Drug Law Violation	89,100		11,000		12
Public Order Offense	272,800		54,900		20
Obstruction of justice		96,000		22,100	23
Disorderly conduct		71,200		17,200	24
Weapons offense		47,200		4,300	9
Liquor law violation		13,200		3,500	27
Nonviolent sex offense		10,900		1,000	10
Other public order		34,400		6,800	20
Violent Crime Index	122,000		9,800		16
Property Crime Index	572,600		127,300		22

DATA SOURCE: Poe-Yamagata, E., & Butts, J. A. (1996). *Female offenders in the juvenile justice system*. Washington, DC: U.S. Department of Justice, Office of Juvenile Justice and Delinquency Prevention.

NOTE: National estimates of juvenile delinquency cases are generated annually for the *Juvenile Court Statistics* series. Detail may not add to totals because of rounding. Percentages are calculated on unrounded numbers.

The age profiles of status offenders differ by gender. For girls rates peak at age 15 and decline through age 17. For boys rates increase steadily between ages 10 and 17. This increase appears to reflect boys' greater activity in liquor law violations at older ages (Sickmund et al., 1998).

Boys and girls seem equally likely to be placed in detention for all types of status offenses (Sickmund et al., 1998). However, running away is the most likely offense to be punished by detention: Use of detention in cases of running away increased by 37 percent between 1991 and 1995 (Sickmund, 1998).

Table 5-2. **Percent Change in Petitioned Status Offense Case Rates by Gender, 1986–1995**

Most Serious Offense	Cases per 1,000 Youths at Risk			Percent Change	
	1986	1991	1995	1986–95	1991–95
Males	3.6	3.9	5.9	65	50
Running away	0.4	0.5	0.7	52	45
Truancy	0.8	1.0	1.4	66	33
Ungovernability	0.6	0.5	0.7	14	49
Liquor law violation	1.4	1.5	1.8	28	17
Miscellaneous	0.3	0.5	1.4	320	208
Females	2.7	2.9	4.4	60	51
Running away	0.7	0.7	1.0	43	51
Truancy	0.8	0.9	1.3	65	36
Ungovernability	0.6	0.4	0.6	–4	44
Liquor law violation	0.5	0.6	0.8	84	39
Miscellaneous	0.2	0.2	0.6	315	205

SOURCE: Sickmund, M., Stahl, A. L., Finnegan, T. A., Snyder, H. N., Poole, R. W., & Butts, J. A. (1998). *Juvenile court statistics 1995.* Washington, DC:. U.S. Department of Justice, Office of Juvenile Justice and Delinquency Prevention.

NOTE: Detail may not add to totals because of rounding. Percent change calculations are based on unrounded numbers.

The path from status to delinquency offenses for juvenile offenders has not been clearly mapped. However, there are indications that the paths may differ by gender. Girls are most likely to come to the attention of the juvenile court for status offenses, especially running away. They are more likely to receive probation than are boys (Sickmund et al., 1998). They are also more likely to have a delinquency petition filed with a charge of probation violation or violation of a court order (Snyder, 1997).

There has been ongoing discussion of the process of "bootstrapping"—charging juveniles who have not committed a criminal offense with delinquency for violation of a court order. Many argue that this practice is used more widely with female offenders (Chesney-Lind & Federele, 1992; OJJDP, 1998a).

A recent survey of juvenile justice administrators (Potter & Molidor, 1999) found that many administrators identified this practice as a significant entry route for girls into their systems. There is evidence that bootstrapping results in harsh and inequitable treatment for girls (Federele & Chesney-Lind, 1992). For example, a study of delinquency cases in Florida revealed that girls charged with contempt of court are more likely to be petitioned in court than either girls charged with other offenses or boys charged with contempt. Moreover, they are far more likely to be sentenced to detention: The probability of incarceration increases from 4.3 for all girls to 30 for girls with contempt charges (Bishop & Frazier, 1990).

Self-Report Data

Arrest and charge rates are influenced by a number of factors beyond the actual criminal behaviors of youths. They are as much a measure of the behaviors of law enforcement officers as of youths. What, then, can be learned from self-report data for juveniles? In general, self-report data indicate greater gender equality than arrest data do, particularly for less serious property crimes, status offenses, and substance use. The behaviors of boys and girls seem remarkably similar with regard to the most common forms of delinquency, although boys are much more likely to report violent crimes (Chesney-Lind & Shelden, 1992).

In 1986 OJJDP funded three coordinated longitudinal projects on the epidemiology, development, and risk and protective factors for serious delinquency, violence, and drug use (Kelly, Huizinga, Thornberry, & Loeber, 1997). Two sites (Denver and Rochester) included girls. In Denver, the sample of girls was roughly equal to that of boys. The Rochester sample was 25 percent female; however, the girls were chosen because they were thought to be at highest risk for problem behavior, whereas the boys were chosen to represent varying risk levels. These studies assess self-reported involvement in aggravated assault, robbery, rape, and gang fights.

In general, a greater percentage of boys reported involvement in serious violence. Girls' self-reports indicated that violence peaks for them at midadolescence (ages 13 to 15), when some 8 percent of Denver and 18 percent of Rochester girls reported recently committing violent acts. Girls in both samples showed a steady decline in reported violence during later adolescence.

In contrast, boys did not report a decrease in violent behavior during the later teen years; prevalence rates remained at 17 percent to 21 percent across ages 16 to 19. At every age level, girls engaged in far less serious violence than did boys. Even at age 13, when the girls in Rochester reported greater involvement in violence than did the boys (18 percent compared with 16 percent), the girls committed fewer than half as many serious violent offenses as the boys (Kelly, Huizinga, et al., 1997).

Clearly, violent behavior is not limited to boys. However, self-report data, mirroring official findings, indicate that girls engage less often in violence than boys and that girls' violence is less severe. Moreover, as Kelly, Huizinga, and colleagues (1997) observed, "It cannot be assumed that girls become involved in violence for precisely the same reasons as boys. Perhaps different risk factors may be influencing the onset and persistence of violent behavior in girls. Therefore, in terms of program initiatives, what works for boys is not necessarily effective for girls" (p. 9).

RISK FACTORS

Characteristics of Female Offenders

Girls differ from boys in abuse histories and mental health functioning. They are much more likely to have experienced abuse as children (Dembo, Williams, & Schmeidler, 1993; Kelly, Thornberry, & Smith, 1997; Thornberry, 1994; Widom, 1989). Reports of the prevalence of physical and sexual abuse histories for delinquent girls vary from a low of 40 percent to a high of 85 percent (Chesney-Lind & Shelden, 1992; Evans, Alber, Marcari, & Mason, 1996; Lake, 1993). Rates of sexual abuse are especially high: 61 percent of females entering one state's detention system reported sexual abuse (Dembo, Williams, & Schmeidler, 1993). Of those sexually abused girls, 81 percent had previous contact with the juvenile court for status offenses.

A history of child abuse increases the risk of later delinquency for both genders (Dembo, Williams, Wothke, Schmeidler, & Brown, 1992). For girls, it is strongly associated with running away from home (Chesney-Lind & Shelden, 1992). Widom (1989) found that child abuse and neglect increased the likelihood of a juvenile arrest by 53 percent, the likelihood of an adult arrest by 38 percent, and the likelihood of committing a violent crime by 38 percent. Girls who have been abused have a higher likelihood of arrest for delinquency, a significantly larger mean number of offenses, an earlier mean age at first offense, and a higher rate of chronicity than do matched controls. Thornberry (1994) found that boys and girls from families experiencing more than two types of violence are more than twice as likely to commit violent offenses as those from nonviolent families.

The mental health functioning of girls appears to differ from that of boys. Timmons-Mitchel and colleagues (1997) found that 84 percent of incarcerated girls in Ohio's juvenile justice facilities reported mental health symptoms in the clinical range of the Symptom Checklist (SCL-90-R), compared with just 27 percent of males. The results from the Millon Adolescent Clinical Inventory were similar, with females reporting significantly more problems with impulsivity, social insensitivity, propensity for delinquency, unruliness, and suicidal tendency than boys. Such girls also report significantly more suicide attempts than do boys (Dembo et al., 1993; Evans et al., 1996). The link between abuse histories and mental health functioning, especially suicidal ideation and suicide attempts, has been demonstrated for adolescents in general (Garland & Zigler, 1993) and for female adolescent offenders (Evans et al., 1996).

Serious and Violent Offending

With regard to the contemporaneous occurrence of violent behavior with other problem behaviors, analyses of the Causes and Correlates Studies have compared serious violent offenders to serious nonviolent offenders, minor offenders, and nondelinquent youths (Huizinga & Jakob-Chien, 1998). Many of these relationships have been examined comparatively for boys and girls.

For all youths, as the level of offending increases, so does substance use. However, the prevalence rates for marijuana, alcohol, and other drug use are all lower for girls than for boys. The relationship between type of offense and school grades is significant for both genders; however, girls of all offender types do better in school than do similar boys. For boys, truancy overlaps significantly with serious violent offending, but this pattern does not hold for girls. Whereas truancy is evenly distributed across offense types for boys, the vast majority of truant girls are nonoffenders or minor offenders. Dropping out of school is associated with more serious offending for boys but is evenly distributed across offense categories for girls.

For all youths, the highest levels of mental health problems are found in delinquents of all types compared with nondelinquents. For boys, the overlap between serious violent offending and mental health problems is exhibited most clearly in externalizing behaviors, such as violence and aggression. Female serious offenders, both violent and nonviolent, have significantly more internalizing problems, such as anxiety and depression, than do male offenders (Huizinga & Jakob-Chien, 1998).

What predicts violent behavior? Unfortunately, the literature gives only a few indications of potential differences between boys and girls. In a recent review of the literature on youth violence, Catalano and Hawkins (1998) identified 36 longitudinal studies, which in turn examined some 200 predictor variables. Many samples contained only boys, and the proportion of girls was not clearly specified in the remainder. Many predictors have been studied only for boys.

It is common for data analyses of mixed gender samples to control for gender when examining the relationships between predictor and outcome variables but to ignore the nature of the gender differences. That is, the effects of gender are removed before risk or protective factors are examined. The few studies that examine gender differences suggest that predictors may operate differently for boys and girls. Early aggression is a good predictor of later violence for boys but not for girls (Statin & Magnusson, 1989; White & Hansell, 1996). Positive beliefs about violence are predictive of later violent behavior for boys but are much less consistent predictors for girls (Williams, 1994). Parent–child involvement and interaction is inversely related to later violence for boys but not for girls (Williams, 1994). In short, we know very little about the predictors of serious, violent offending for girls.

Here is the paradox of the risk factor literature: Although authorities delineate clear differences in prevalence rates for boys and girls and contend that risk factors differ across gender, few have attempted to examine these factors for girls. Lack of attention to the etiology of violent female offending has limited current understanding of effective interventions with girls.

EFFECTIVE PREVENTION AND INTERVENTION

Given the lack of attention to gender differences in the etiology of serious violent offending, it is not surprising that a similar pattern emerges in the literature on prevention and intervention effectiveness. A recent examination of the effectiveness of prevention concluded that

> [the] manifestation and developmental sequencing of antisocial behavior may be very different for boys and girls. Overall, preventive interventions appear to have been designed with boys, and not girls, in mind; many programs have been applied only to boys; and in a number of cases, even when girls are included, there has been limited program effectiveness with girls. (Wasserman & Miller, 1998, p. 234)

Similarly, most interventions have been developed for use with boys, and their effectiveness tested with male samples. A recent analysis of 200 intervention studies (Lipsey & Wilson, 1998) noted that 94 percent of studies were conducted on predominantly or all-male samples. Of the studies that included females, few examined gender differences in effectiveness.

Most of those that did were in the context of Multi-Systemic Therapy (MST) evaluations (Henggeler & Borduin, 1990). MST is grounded in an ecological systems theory of behavior change. Although MST has much in common with traditional family therapy interventions, it broadens intervention to the multiple systems with which families and youths interact. MST therapists work intensively with families and youths to identify strengths and problems and target specific areas for behavior change, emphasizing changes in natural environments. They also emphasize equipping parents with the skills and resources they need to intervene with their children (Henggeler & Borduin, 1990).

MST has been evaluated in several random-assignment studies, all of which have used mixed gender samples (Borduin et al., 1995; Henggeler, Melton, & Smith, 1992; Henggeler, Melton, Smith, Schoenwald, & Hanley, 1993). Youths who have received MST have half as many arrests as control youths at 59 weeks after referral. MST families report more cohesion, and MST youths demonstrate decreased peer aggression (Henggeler et al., 1992). Differences in arrest rates persist up to four years after referral. Moreover,

MST youths who are arrested commit fewer and less serious crimes than do control group youths. No differential treatment effects based on gender or ethnicity have been found (Borduin et al., 1995).

Clearly, MST shows promise as an effective intervention for both boys and girls. Because MST is highly individualized, the foci of intervention are not fixed, and little information is available about how the intervention may or may not be operationalized differently for boys and girls. Increased examination of the micro-aspects of the intervention may inform our understanding of the most effective treatment components.

Except for MST, most delinquency interventions continue to target male offending and assume effectiveness with girls. Feminist observers argue that an examination of the political realities surrounding girls' experiences with juvenile justice systems and of a wider range of literature on adolescent girls should inform new programming for female offenders.

ENHANCING TREATMENT OUTCOMES FOR GIRLS: THE FEMINIST PERSPECTIVE

Feminist critiques of the juvenile justice system target differential and discriminatory treatment of female offenders (Belknap, 1996; Chesney-Lind, 1989; Chesney-Lind & Shelden, 1992; Daly, 1992; Federele & Chesney-Lind, 1992; Girls, Incorporated, 1996; Horrowitz & Pottieger, 1991; Pepi, 1998). Although the delinquency literature has largely ignored girls, at the practical level the justice system does intervene with female delinquents—often in ways that exercise maximum control.

We have noted that girls are more likely than boys to come into the juvenile justice system because of status offenses and sexual crimes, such as promiscuity, prostitution, and running away. The system has historically responded harshly to girls' sexual and unruly behavior. Controlling for offense and offense history, prostitution is more likely to result in adjudication than any other offense (Horrowitz & Pottieger, 1991). A history of status offenses increases the likelihood of a restrictive placement for girls after criminal adjudication. In addition, the role of families differs for girls, with more parents represented as the complaining party (Belknap, 1996).

Feminist critics argue that the juvenile justice system has operated as an enforcer of socially acceptable behavior for both boys and girls, but that the behavior sanctioned has differed by gender: "Problem behaviors of girls are judged more harshly because they represent a greater violation of gender expectations than the same behaviors in boys" (Albrecht, 1996, p. 62). Programming for girls has tended to reinforce female gender stereotypes, emphasize rules and control, and deemphasize educational and vocational opportunities (Belknap, 1996).

The passage of the Juvenile Justice and Delinquency Prevention Act of 1974, with its emphasis on separating status and delinquent offenders, decreased the number of girls who were committed to training schools. However, there was a parallel increase in the involuntary placement of girls in mental health and substance abuse residential centers (Schwartz, Jackson-Beeck, & Anderson, 1984). The trend makes these girls less visible to the formal juvenile justice system. An absence of formal attention to the needs of girls has masked a pervasive, systemic emphasis on controlling girls, especially in the relational aspects of their lives. Any examination of theory, intervention, and program development must consider the effects of past and present gender bias.

Many argue that it is important to reach beyond traditional delinquency theory and intervention models, developed primarily for boys, to address female adolescent development and feminist intervention models and ecological frameworks (Albrecht, 1996; Miller, Trapani, Mendoza-Fejes, Eggleston, & Dwiggins, 1995; Pepi, 1998; Potter & Molidor, 1998).

An Ecological Framework

An ecological framework focuses intervention on the multiple influences on the lives of individuals. The approach argues that simple explanatory theories that focus on, for example, individual personality attributes or societal variables are not sufficient to understand human behavior and to guide intervention. Whittaker, Schinke, and Gilchrist (1986) argued the clear intervention implications of an ecological framework, including an emphasis on developing competencies for multiple environments and social support.

These conclusions are consonant with recent meta-analysis of intervention research in juvenile justice in which the most powerful correlates of outcomes were those related to skill-oriented and multimodal interventions (Lipsey, 1992; Lipsey & Wilson, 1998). They are also consonant with MST (Henggeler et al., 1993). In a review of the effectiveness of treatment for violent juvenile offenders, Tate, Reppucci, and Mulvey (1995) concluded that "service provision should be re-conceptualized as an ongoing care model that emphasizes intervention in multiple spheres of an adolescent's life. The most promise lies in a comprehensive, long-term commitment, not in the development of any singular, more powerful approach" (p. 780).

Female Adolescent Development

The literature on female adolescent development offers some important guides to intervention. Here we will focus on qualitative studies of girls' experience of adolescence and the emerging literature on gender differences in aggression. Both have implications for intervention with violent female offenders.

Gilligan's (1993) and Gilligan and Mikel-Brown's (1992) studies of adolescent girls have prompted years of debate and research about gender differences in adolescent development. Gilligan's attention to *voice* and *relationship* as powerful themes for adolescent girls is widely cited in the literature on female adolescent offenders (Albrecht, 1996; Girls, Incorporated, 1996): "When I speak of voice, I mean something like what people mean when they speak of the core of their being. . . . To have a voice is to be human. To have something to say is to be a person. But speaking depends on listening and being heard; it is an intensely relational act" (Gilligan, 1993, p. xiv). With regard to relationship, Gilligan (1993) writes, "I reframe women's psychological development as centering on a struggle for connection rather than speaking about women in the way that psychologists have spoken about women—as having a problem in achieving separation" (p. xxii).

Research with adolescent girls describes a painful process of losing both voice and relationship (Gilligan & Mikel-Brown, 1992). For younger girls, voice is strong, and the power of relationship is intense. For older adolescent girls, the passage to adulthood involves the realization that their options are limited by their gender, that their voices are not equally heard in male-dominated social systems, and that their experiences may not be recognized as legitimate. Gilligan also notes that much traditional psychological theory posits that both boys and girls must separate from powerful women to mature, which for boys is theorized to occur in early childhood, and for girls in adolescence. In contrast, Gilligan argues that the social passage through adolescence requires that girls struggle to retain a connection to a community of women.

From this perspective, interventions must enhance rather than suppress girls' sense of authenticity of self and the ability for their voices to be heard in meaningful relationships with women and other girls. Thus, interventions should take place in the context of relationship; the power of relationship drives the intervention. Intervention, then, is not a technique, but a person. The desired outcome is not compliance but a personal sense of enhanced ability to act (self-efficacy).

Gender differences in aggressive behavior have long been observed among children, adolescents, and adults, with males exhibiting more aggressive behavior than females. Some reviews of this literature conclude that differences in aggression (commonly understood as overt, physical aggression) result from differences in both perceived and experienced consequences of aggressive behavior. Women and girls are more likely to perceive negative consequences and to experience anxiety about their aggressive behavior (Eagly & Steffen, 1986; Frodi, Macaulay, & Thome, 1977; Perry, Perry, & Weiss, 1989).

Much of the research on aggression among adolescents examines overt physical aggression, most often among boys (Rys & Bear, 1997). During the past decade, the perspective has widened to gender differences in multiple types of aggression, including physical, direct–verbal, and indirect or relational forms (Bjoerkqvist, 1994; Crick & Grotpeter, 1995). Bjoerkqvist, Osterman, and Kaukianen (1992) found that although direct verbal aggression was common among both genders, boys were more physically aggressive, whereas girls of all ages exhibited more indirect social aggression. They concluded that this difference is the result of earlier maturation and improved social intelligence among adolescent girls.

Crick and Grotpeter (1995) propose that children, especially girls, engage in *relational aggression,* which is characterized by the threat of withdrawal of relationship to control the behavior of others. They argue that physical and verbal aggression are more central to the social world of adolescent boys, whereas relational aggression is more central to the social world of girls. Although both boys and girls perceive relationally aggressive acts as hostile and harmful (Crick, Bigbee, & Howes, 1996), girls report significantly more distress in response to such situations (Crick, 1995). Moreover, girls are more likely to engage in relational aggression (Crick & Grotpeter, 1995) and to be relationally victimized (Crick & Bigbee, 1998). Friendships among relationally aggressive youths tend to be characterized by high levels of exclusivity or jealousy and high rates of relational aggression within the friendship. In contrast, friendships among physically aggressive youths are characterized by engagement in group acts of aggression toward others (Grotpeter & Crick, 1996).

Both forms of aggression are associated with poor psychosocial functioning and peer rejection, with relational aggression contributing uniquely to the prediction of future social functioning, especially among girls (Crick, 1996; Rys & Bear, 1997). Children who engage in gender-nonnormative forms of aggression (for example, physical aggression by girls and relational aggression by boys) have significantly more internalizing and externalizing problems than do peers who engage in gender-normative forms of aggression (Crick, 1997).

This literature is consonant with the previous discussion of the importance of relationship to adolescent girls. Relationally aggressive girls pay a price in terms of their own functioning and the quality of their relationships. For girls who engage in nonnormative physical aggression, the price is even higher.

Some have suggested that differences in aggression are caused in part by differences in the processing of social information (Crick & Dodge, 1996; Dodge & Crick, 1990). They suggest that interventions focused on the five steps of information processing (encoding social cues, interpreting social cues, response searches, response evaluation, and enactment) should be helpful. Interventions that build specific skills—both information processing and general prosocial skills—in the relational domain may help girls successfully navigate their social world.

Feminist Intervention Theory

Bricker-Jenkins and Hooyman (1986) describe some of the attributes of feminist helpers. Those involved in feminist interventions should

- bring forward the reality of patriarchy in our society and submit official versions of reality to feminist critique,
- reconceptualize power and commit to egalitarian relationships,
- value the nature of the process used to reach a desired outcome as strongly as they value the outcome itself,
- ground personal problems and conditions in political realities,
- seek communal solutions, not simply individual ones,
- value solidarity with other girls and women while celebrating diversity,
- value multiple perspectives on reality and acknowledge many "truths," and
- seek to increase understanding of women's condition and active involvement in social change.

Worell and Remer (1993) articulate similar principles in the context of therapeutic relationships, emphasizing (1) the importance of consciousness raising about the roles of women in society and the nature of gender power differences, (2) the importance of valuing women, relationships with women, and female perspectives, and (3) the importance of an egalitarian relationship between client and helper. Thus, a feminist perspective calls for viewing both the juvenile offender and the juvenile justice system through a feminist lens, a lens that highlights significant deficiencies in both justice and justice systems relative to girls.

A TALE OF TWO STORIES

At present, the literature on violent girls requires a choice between stories. Each story makes an argument grounded in existing information, but each is also missing significant information. Please refer to Rose's Story and consider the differing perspectives on her delinquent behavior.

ROSE'S STORY

Rose is 15 years old. She is currently in detention awaiting a hearing on a charge of aggravated assault stemming from a fight at Rose's group home in which she attacked a 16-year-old girl whom she suspected of stealing from her room. Rose beat the other girl with a pipe, causing a broken cheekbone, multiple contusions, and concussion. Rose had apparently found the pipe some weeks before and hidden it in her room. The staff member who restrained Rose described her as "totally out of control. I thought she might kill that girl."

Rose has two younger sisters. She has been known to the Juvenile Court since the age of eight, when a dependency and neglect petition was filed. Rose had disclosed to her teacher that her mother's boyfriend had been molesting her. She was placed in foster care for six months, during which time the perpetrator was arrested and disappeared while on bail. Rose's mother took part in a support group for mothers and regained custody of Rose. The social services case remained open for three years, because of the social worker's concern about the mother's use of physical discipline with her children. There have been no more live-in boyfriends, but the mother has recently begun a relationship that appears to be serious.

At age 12 Rose began dating a boy age 16 and soon began running away from home. Her mother sought help from the Department of Social Services and filed several status offense petitions. Rose was placed on probation and then, after running away several times, charged with violation of probation. Her mother was persistent in finding Rose, often discovering her at the apartments of young adult males. Rose describes moderate substance use and much sexual activity during these episodes. It is assumed that Rose traded sex for money and drugs. Rose was adjudicated delinquent on the violation of probation charge and entered the group home six months ago.

Rose describes herself as "strong," saying, "I don't need anyone. I can take care of myself." Of the assault, she says, "She deserved it. I wish I'd killed her." Rose is mildly flirtatious with male staff members, and alternately clingy and disdainful with female staff.

Rose has a quick mind and a sharp tongue; she seems to know just what to say to anger peers and staff alike. She has developed a wary alliance with her group leader, confessing that she has trouble sleeping and "feels worried all the time." Rose says that she needed the pipe "for protection." She describes episodes in which she "feels like I'm drifting. I hear my voice echoing—like in an empty room—but it's not coming from me."

Rose's mother is very angry with Rose, but is still engaged with her. She visits Rose each week, although the visits tend to be stormy. She has not allowed home visits, fearing Rose's influence on her 12-year-old sister. The mother's boyfriend takes a strong punitive role with Rose, feeling that she needs "a firm hand." Rose's mother says, "She's a pain in the butt. I hope they can keep her locked up until she's old enough to be safe."

As Rose's new case manager, you have been asked to make a recommendation to the court.

Questions:

What risk and protective factors do you identify for Rose?

What information will you gather to help you make decisions about Rose?

What would be the "ideal" program for Rose?

How will you tell her story?

The first story is about increasingly violent, out-of-control young women. These girls have significant histories of nondelinquent status offenses; have been out of control in their homes, schools, and communities; and eventually cross into violent behavior. They come from families where violence is prevalent. They have many co-occurring problems, such as substance abuse and mental health problems. Violent female offenders increasingly engage in assaultive behavior, in addition to delinquent acts that are thought of as "gender appropriate," such as prostitution, forgery, and embezzlement.

These young women are hard to serve. They are especially hard to "hold on to"; controlling their running away is essential. This is difficult because these girls receive more lenient treatment from the formal juvenile justice system in that they are less likely to have charges filed, to be adjudicated delinquent, and to be incarcerated. As their numbers increase, effective delinquency-focused interventions are needed.

Feminists offer a different perspective. Female juvenile offenders are first and foremost girls growing up in a patriarchal society. When they encounter the juvenile justice system, they encounter a male-dominated system designed to intervene with boys; a system that is very uncomfortable with their violation of gender-based norms of behavior. These girls are often victims of familial abuse, which leads to significant mental health problems and to significant levels of status offending. Protective behaviors, such as running away, are treated harshly by a system that seeks to control girls.

Many girls find their way into the juvenile justice system through court processes that favor detaining girls for relatively minor offenses. Thus, for many girls, behaviors that are caused by victimization are transformed into delinquency. When girls encounter a male-dominated justice system they receive harsher treatment for lesser offenses. More serious violent offenders represent extreme cases of this phenomenon. Their increased violence is caused by victimization in their own families and peer groups and by inappropriate systemic responses to their needs. Effective gender-specific, mental health–focused interventions are needed.

Without better information on these young women we are not able to tell a coherent story about their needs. What are the risk and protective factors associated with female offending generally and serious violent offending specifically? What are the diverse pathways to offending for different subgroups of girls? What systemic responses effectively alter these trajectories? Not only are the answers to these questions unclear, the questions are as yet largely unasked. Hoyt and Scherer (1998) speculate about possible answers:

> Clearly, female delinquency is a multivariate phenomenon with a variety of determinants and diverse etiological paths. It is quite likely that a subset of female delinquents manifest delinquent offenses that are every bit as serious and antisocial as male delinquents and acquire their behavioral problems through similar etiological processes. On the other hand, it is equally likely

that many female delinquents acquire their antisocial conduct through gender-specific developmental processes, gender-related socialization and a vulnerability to sexual abuse that are not a part of the pathway to male delinquency. In other words, female delinquents are both *similar to* male delinquents and *different than* male delinquents. (p. 102)

Figure 5-1. Practice Principles for Violent and Aggressive Girls

Program Context

- Be explicit about feminist considerations in the juvenile justice system.
- Be actively involved in action for change within the juvenile justice system.
- Be staffed by those who will commit to intensive relationships with individual girls and with groups of girls.
- Commit to empowerment approaches to management, supervision, and team decision making.

Assessment

- Conceptualize risk and protective factors in a multisystemic ecological framework.
- Assess both competencies and problems in critical domains of girls' lives.
- Avoid pathologizing adaptive behaviors (running away to escape familial abuse).
- Resist labeling all delinquent behavior as mental health symptoms.

Intervention

- Resist cultivating a victim status among girls.
- Take a skill-oriented approach to intervention.
- Focus on authenticity of self and a sense of genuine ability.
- Foster a focus on the future.
- Take an empowerment intervention approach to legitimate mental health needs.
- Target interventions to multiple systems in girls' lives.
- Engage families and informal support networks in treatment.
- Teach girls to create, use, and give social support.
- Focus on collectivity for mutual aid, that is, on developing a sense of collective identity among groups of girls and engaging those groups in purposive activity in the larger environment.
- Deal directly with power issues in girls' lives.
- Explicitly connect girls' subjective meanings of gender to their experiences with crime and with the criminal justice system.

Source: Adapted with permission from Potter, C., & Molidor, C. M. (1998). Female delinquency interventions: Is the just-add-girls-and-stir approach adequate? *National Social Science Perspectives Journal, 13,* 129–140.

TOWARD A FRAMEWORK TO GUIDE INTERVENTION

Potter and Molidor (1998) have argued that ecological, feminist, and female adolescent developmental principles can be integrated to guide programming with female adolescents. Figure 5-1 presents practice principles that can serve as a starting point for discussion among professionals and as a guide to intervention design. Largely derived from theoretical perspectives, these principles go well beyond the empirical understanding of female juvenile offending. How might they guide the development of specific intervention models? How should information on risk and protective factors be used to inform intervention design? Will these intervention models work to reduce recidivism and ameliorate related problems? These questions must be answered as programs are designed, implemented, and evaluated.

NEXT STEPS

Clearly the empirical literature on female offenders has significant gaps that are impeding our understanding of female juvenile offending and our ability to design effective programs. Four issues are of immediate importance.

Risk and Protective Factors

First, there is a need to examine the risk and protective factors for female offending. While there is evidence that boys and girls offend in different ways and to different degrees, as well as evidence that they experience different types of co-occurring problems, we know very little about the predictors of differing levels of offending. Existing longitudinal studies, such as the Denver and Rochester data sets, might be profitably examined with an eye to gender differences in predictive factors. In addition, it is important that new longitudinal studies be initiated, studies that incorporate variables that may shed light on the competing perspectives on female youth violence.

It is also important to initiate research into protective factors for both male and female offenders. There has been one examination of protective factors for the Rochester Causes and Correlates study (Smith, Lizotte, Thornberry & Krohn, 1995), but no examination of results by gender. Jessor and colleagues (1995) found that protective factors were among the strongest predictors of changes in problem behaviors among youths. In order to design effective interventions, more information is needed on the skills and supports that alter the life course of girls at risk of violent careers.

Developmental Pathways to Violence

Although there has been some attention to developing and testing models that describe differing pathways through male delinquency (Loeber & Hay,

1997; OJJDP, 1998c), there has been none for female delinquency. As Hoyt and Sherer (1998) suggest, both stories about female juvenile delinquency may well be rooted in reality. That is, there may be different pathways into the juvenile justice system for girls, pathways based on unique etiologies that require variations in treatment approach. Here again, reexamination of the few longitudinal studies involving girls with an eye to gender differences may be profitable, and new longitudinal research is needed.

Testing Intervention Models

It is not sufficient to simply call for better research on risk and protective factors and developmental trajectories. Juvenile justice systems, which are already intervening with female offenders, require guidance in program planning and evaluation. Many states are turning to the theoretical literature on gender-specific development and feminist intervention principles to help guide gender-specific programming for girls. It is imperative that these interventions be adequately described, reliably implemented, and rigorously evaluated so that the lessons learned can improve programming.

Examining Justice System Performance

There is ample evidence that the juvenile justice system responds differently to boys and girls under some circumstances (Federele & Chesney-Lind, 1992; Horrowitz & Pottieger, 1991). The aggregate national statistics, while providing some clues about system performance, are not likely to provide the level of information needed. Particular attention should be paid to the decision-making systems that operate within the juvenile justice system. What are the critical decision points for juveniles as they move through the justice system? What gender-specific assumptions about offending affect decision making? It is not sufficient to examine the trajectory of youths through our juvenile justice system without critical analysis of how the system guides those trajectories.

CONCLUSION

Female juvenile offenders have long been ignored in the delinquency literature and in juvenile justice programming. Today, their numbers are increasing, as is their involvement in serious, violent crime. This situation presents an opportunity to refocus attention on the needs of these young women. At present, we have relatively little empirical information on which to base improved programming. If effective interventions are to be crafted, we must increase our knowledge of the risk and protective factors and developmental trajectories of female offenders. We must also find a way to use information from the adolescent development and feminist intervention literatures to inform our understanding of the correlates of offending. Without an integration of these two perspectives, we are unlikely to tell a meaningful story about the possibilities for change that will resonate in the lives of these young women.

REFERENCES

Albrecht, L. (1996, Fall). Gender specific programming in juvenile detention and corrections. *Journal for Juvenile Justice and Detention Services, 55*–63.

Belknap, J. (1996). *The invisible woman: Gender, crime, and justice.* New York: Wadsworth Publishing.

Bishop, D., & Frazier, C. (1990, March). Gender bias in the juvenile justice system: Implications of the JJDP Act. Paper presented at the annual meeting of the Academy of Criminal Justice Sciences, Denver, CO.

Bjoerkqvist, K. (1994). Sex differences in physical, verbal, and indirect aggression: A review of recent research. *Sex Roles, 30,* 177–127.

Bjoerkqvist, K., Osterman, K., & Kaukianen, A. (1992). The development of direct and indirect aggressive strategies in males and females. In K. Bjoerkqvist & P. Niemela (Eds.), *Of mice and women: Aspects of female aggression* (pp. 51–64). San Diego: Academic Press.

Borduin, C. M., & Henggeler, S. W. (1990). A multisystemic approach to the treatment of serious delinquent behavior. In R. J. McMahon & R. D. Peter (Eds.), *Behavior disorders of adolescence* (pp. 63–80). New York: Plenum Press.

Borduin, C. M., Mann, B. J., Cone, L. T., Henggeler, S. W., Fucci, B. R., Blaske, D. B., & Williams, R. A. (1995). Multisystemic treatment of serious juvenile offenders: Long-term prevention of criminality and violence. *Journal of Consulting and Clinical Psychology, 63,* 569–578.

Bricker-Jenkins, M., & Hooyman, N. R. (1986). A feminist worldview: Ideological themes from the feminist movement. In M. Bricker-Jenkins & N. R. Hooyman (Eds.), *Not for women only: Social work practice for a feminist future* (pp. 3–21). Silver Spring, MD: National Association of Social Workers.

Budnick, K. J., & Shields-Fletcher, E., (1998, September). What about girls? *OJJDP Fact Sheet, 84.* Washington, DC: U.S. Department of Justice, Office of Juvenile Justice and Delinquency Prevention.

Catalano, R. F., & Hawkins, J. D. (1998). The social development model: A theory of antisocial behavior. In J. D. Hawkins (Ed.), *Delinquency and crime: Current theories* (pp. 149–197). New York: Cambridge University Press.

Chesney-Lind, M. (1989). Girls' crime and woman's place: Toward a feminist model of female delinquency. *Crime & Delinquency, 35,* 5–29.

Chesney-Lind, M., & Shelden, R. (1992). *Girls, delinquency and juvenile justice.* Pacific Grove, CA: Brooks/Cole.

Crick, N. R. (1995). Relational aggression: The role of intent attributions, feelings of distress and provocation type. *Development and Psychopathology, 7,* 313–322.

Crick, N. R. (1996). The role of overt aggression, relational aggression and prosocial behavior in the prediction of children's future social adjustment. *Child Development, 67*, 2317–2327.

Crick, N. R. (1997). Engagement in gender normative versus non-normative forms of aggression: Links to social-psychological adjustment. *Developmental Psychology, 33*, 610–617.

Crick, N. R., & Bigbee, M. A. (1998). Relational and overt forms of peer victimization: A multi-informant approach. *Journal of Consulting and Clinical Psychology, 66*, 337–347.

Crick, N. R., Bigbee, M. A., & Howes, C. (1996). Gender differences in children's normative beliefs about aggression: How do I hurt thee? Let me count the ways. *Child Development, 67*, 1003–1014.

Crick, N. R., & Dodge, K. A. (1996). Social information-processing mechanisms on reactive and proactive aggression. *Child Development, 67*, 993–1002.

Crick, N. R., & Grotpeter, J. K. (1995). Relational aggression, gender and social-psychological adjustment. *Child Development, 66*, 710–722.

Crick, N. R. & Grotpeter, J. K. (1996). Children's treatment by peers: Victims of relational and overt aggression. *Development and Psychopathology, 8*, 367–380.

Daly, K. (1989). Neither conflict nor labeling nor paternalism will suffice: Intersections of race, ethnicity, gender and family in criminal court decisions. *Crime & Delinquency, 35*, 136–168.

Daly, K. (1992). Women's pathways to felony court: Feminist theories of lawbreaking and problems of representation. *Review of Law and Women's Studies*, 11–51.

Dembo, R., Williams, L., & Schmeidler, J. (1993). Gender differences in mental health service needs among youths entering a juvenile detention center. *Journal of Prison & Jail Health, 12*, 73–101.

Dembo, R., Williams, L., Wothke, W., Schmeidler, J., & Brown, C. (1992). The role of family factors, physical abuse and sexual victimization experiences in high-risk youths' alcohol and other drug use and delinquency: A longitudinal model. *Violence & Victims, 7*, 245–266.

Dodge, K., & Crick, N. R. (1990). Social information-processing bases of aggressive behavior in children. *Personality & Social Psychology Bulletin, 16*, 8–22.

Eagly, A. H., & Steffen V. J. (1986). Gender and aggressive behavior: A meta-analytic review of the social psychological literature. *Psychological Bulletin, 100*, 309–330.

Evans, W., Alber, E., Marcari, D., & Mason, E. (1996). Suicide ideation, attempts and abuse among incarcerated gang and non-gang delinquents. *Child and Adolescent Social Work Journal, 13*, 115–127.

Federal Bureau of Investigation. (1997). *Crime in the United States: Uniform crime reports*. Washington, DC: Author.

Federele, K. H., & Chesney-Lind, M. (1992). Special issues in juvenile justice: Gender, race and ethnicity. In I. Schwartz, (Ed.), *Juvenile justice and public policy: Toward a national agenda* (pp. 165–195). New York: Macmillan.

Frodi, A., Macaulay, J., & Thome, P. R. (1977). Are women always less aggressive than men? A review of the experimental literature. *Psychological Bulletin, 84*, 634–660.

Garland, A. F., & Zigler, E. (1993). Adolescent suicide prevention: Current research and social policy implications. *American Psychologist, 48*, 169–182.

Gilligan, C. (1993). *In a different voice: Psychological theory and women's development*. Cambridge, MA: Harvard University Press.

Gilligan, C., & Mikel-Brown, L. (1992). *Meeting at the crossroads: Women's psychology and girls' development.* Cambridge, MA: Harvard University Press.

Girls Incorporated (1996). *Prevention and parity: Girls in juvenile justice.* Indianapolis: Author.

Grotpeter, J. K., & Crick, N. R. (1996). Relational aggression, overt aggression, and friendship. *Child Development, 67,* 2328–2338.

Hawkins, J. D. (Ed.). (1998). *Delinquency and crime: Current theories.* New York: Cambridge University Press.

Henggeler, S. W., & Borduin, C. M. (1990). *Family therapy and beyond: A multisystemic approach to treating the behavior problems of children and adolescents.* Pacific Grove, CA: Brooks/Cole.

Henggeler, S. W., Borduin, C. M., Melton, G. B., Mann, B. J., Smith, L. A., Hall, J. A., Cone, L., & Fucci, B. R. (1991). Effects of multisystemic therapy on drug use and abuse in serious juvenile offenders: A progress report from two outcome studies. *Family Dynamics of Addiction Quarterly, 1,* 40–51.

Henggeler, S. W., Melton, G. B., & Smith, L. A. (1992). Family preservation using multisystemic therapy: An effective alternative to incarcerating serious juvenile offenders. *Journal of Consulting and Clinical Psychology, 60,* 953–961.

Henggeler, S. W., Melton, G. B., Smith, L. A., Schoenwald, S. K., & Hanley, J. H. (1993). Family preservation using multisystemic treatment: Long-term follow-up to a clinical trial with serious juvenile offenders. *Journal of Child and Family Studies, 2,* 283–293.

Horrowitz, R., & Pottieger, A. E. (1991). Gender bias in juvenile justice handling of seriously crime-involved youths. *Journal of Research in Crime and Delinquency, 28,* 75–100.

Hoyt, S., & Scherer, D. G. (1998). Female juvenile delinquency: Misunderstood by the juvenile justice system, neglected by social science. *Law and Human Behavior, 22,* 81–107.

Huizinga, E., & Jakob-Chien, C. (1998). The contemporaneous co-occurrence of serious and violent juvenile offending and other problem behaviors. In R. Loeber & D. P. Farrington (Eds.), *Serious & violent juvenile offenders: Risk factors and successful interventions* (pp. 47–67). Thousand Oaks, CA: Sage Publications.

Jessor, R. (1992). Risk behavior in adolescence: A psychosocial framework for understanding and action. *Developmental Review, 12,* 374–390.

Jessor, R., Bos, J. V., Vanderryn, J., Costa, F. M., & Turbin, M. S. (1995). Protective factors in adolescent problem behavior: Moderator effects and developmental change. *Developmental Psychology, 31,* 923–933.

Kelly, B. T., Huizinga, D., Thornberry, T. P., & Loeber, R. (1997, June). Epidemiology of serious violence. *Juvenile Justice Bulletin.* Washington, DC: U.S. Department of Justice, Office of Justice Programs, Office of Juvenile Justice and Delinquency Prevention.

Kelly, B. T., Thornberry, T. P., & Smith, C. A. (1997). In the wake of childhood maltreatment. *Juvenile Justice Bulletin, August 1997.* Washington, DC: U.S. Department of Justice, Office of Justice Programs, Office of Juvenile Justice and Delinquency Prevention.

Lake, E. S. (1993). An exploration of the violent victim experiences of female offenders. *Violence and Victims, 8,* 41–51.

Lipsey, M. W. (1992). Juvenile delinquency treatment: A meta-analytic inquiry into the variability of effects. In T. Cook, H. Cooper, D. Cordray, H. Hartman, L. Hedges, R. Light, T. A. Lewis, & F. Mosteller (Eds.), *Meta-analysis for explanation: A casebook* (pp. 83–127). New York: Russell Sage Foundation.

Lipsey, M. W., & Wilson, D. B. (1998). Effective intervention for serious juvenile offenders: A synthesis of research. In R. Loeber & D. P. Farrington (Eds.), *Serious & violent juvenile offenders: Risk factors and successful interventions*. Thousand Oaks, CA: Sage Publications.

Loeber, R., & Farrington, D. P. (Eds.) (1998). *Serious & violent juvenile offenders: Risk factors and successful interventions*. Thousand Oaks, CA: Sage Publications.

Loeber, R., & Hay, D. F. (1997). Key issues in the development of aggression and violence from childhood to early adulthood. *American Review of Psychology, 48,* 371–410.

Miller, D., Trapani, C., Mendoza-Fejes, L., Eggleston, C., & Dwiggins, D. (1995). Adolescent female offenders: Unique considerations. *Adolescence, 30,* 429–435.

Office of Juvenile Justice and Delinquency Prevention. (1998a). *Juvenile Female Offenders: A Status of the States Report*. Washington, DC: U.S. Department of Justice.

Office of Juvenile Justice and Delinquency Prevention. (1998b). *Office of Justice Programs News, December 10, 1998*. Washington, DC: U.S. Department of Justice.

Office of Juvenile Justice and Delinquency Prevention. (1998c). Serious and violent juvenile offenders. *Juvenile Justice Bulletin, May, 1998*. Washington, DC: U.S. Department of Justice.

Pepi, C.L.O. (1998). Children without childhoods: A feminist intervention strategy utilizing systems theory and restorative justice in treating female adolescent offenders. *Women & Therapy, 20*(4), 85–101.

Perry, D. G., Perry, L. C., & Weiss, R. J. (1989). Sex differences in the consequences that children anticipate for aggression. *Developmental Psychology, 25,* 312–319.

Poe-Yamagata, E., & Butts, J. A. (1996). *Female offenders in the juvenile justice system*. Washington, DC: U.S. Department of Justice, Office of Justice Programs, Office of Juvenile Justice and Delinquency Prevention.

Potter, C., & Molidor, C. M. (1998). Female delinquency interventions: Is the just-add-girls-and-stir approach adequate? *National Social Science Perspectives Journal, 13,* 129–140.

Potter, C., & Molidor, C. M. (1999). *Female juvenile offenders: A view from the states*. Unpublished manuscript, University of Denver, Colorado.

Rhodes, J. E., & Fischer, K. (1993). Spanning the gender gap: Gender differences in delinquency among inner-city adolescents. *Adolescence, 28,* 879–889.

Rys, G. S., & Bear, G. G. (1997). Relational aggression and peer relations: Gender and developmental Issues. *Merrill-Palmer Quarterly, 43,* 87–106.

Schwartz, I. M., Jackson-Beeck, M., & Anderson, R. (1984). The "hidden" system of juvenile control. *Crime and Delinquency, 30,* 371–385.

Sickmund, M. (1998, April). Offenders in juvenile court, 1995. *Juvenile Justice Bulletin*. Washington, DC: U.S. Department of Justice, Office of Justice Programs, Office of Juvenile Justice and Delinquency Prevention.

Sickmund, M., Stahl, A. L., Finnegan, T. A., Snyder, H. N., Poole, R. W., & Butts, J. A. (1998). *Juvenile court statistics 1995*. Washington, DC:. U.S. Department of Justice, Office of Juvenile Justice and Delinquency Prevention.

Smith, C., Lizotte, A. J., Thornberry, T. P., & Krohn, M. D. (1995). Resilient youth: Identifying factors that prevent high-risk youth from engaging in delinquency and drug use. *Current Perspectives on Aging and the Life Cycle, 4,* 217–247.

Snyder, H. N. (1997). *Juvenile arrests 1996.* Bulletin. Washington, DC: U.S. Department of Justice, Office of Justice Programs, Office of Juvenile Justice and Delinquency Prevention.

Sommers, I., & Baskin, D. R. (1994). Factors related to female adolescent initiation into violent street crime. *Youth & Society, 25*(4), 468–489.

Statin, H., & Magnusson, D. (1989). The role of early aggressive behavior in the frequency, seriousness and types of later crime. *Journal of Consulting and Clinical Psychology, 57,* 710–718.

Tate, D. C., Reppucci, N. D., & Mulvey, E. P. (1995). Violent juvenile delinquents: Treatment effectiveness and implications for future action. *American Psychologist, 50,* 777–781.

Thornberry, T. P. (1994). *Violent families and youth violence.* Washington, DC: U.S. Department of Justice, Office of Justice Programs, Office of Juvenile Justice and Delinquency Prevention.

Timmons-Mitchel, J., Brown, D., Schulz, S. C., Webster, S., Underwood, L. A., & Semple, W. E. (1997). Comparing the mental health needs of female and male incarcerated juvenile delinquents. *Behavioral Sciences and the Law, 15,* 195–202.

U.S. Department of Justice. (1998). *Women in criminal justice: A twenty year update.* Washington, DC: U.S. Department of Justice.

Wasserman, G. A., & Miller, L. S. (1998). The prevention of serious and violent juvenile offending. In R. Loeber & D. P. Farrington (Eds.), *Serious & violent juvenile offenders: Risk factors and successful interventions.* Thousand Oaks, CA: Sage Publications.

White, H. R., & Hansell, S. (1996). The moderating effects of gender and hostility on the alcohol-aggression relationship. *Journal of Research in Crime and Delinquency, 33,* 450–470.

Whittaker, J. K., Schinke, S. P., & Gilchrist, L. D. (1986). The ecological paradigm in child, youth and family services: Implications for policy and practice. *Social Services Review, 60,* 483–503.

Widom, C. S. (1989). The cycle of violence. *Science, 244,* 160–166.

Williams, J. H. (1994). *Understanding substance use, delinquency involvement, and juvenile justice system involvement among African-American and European-American adolescents.* Unpublished dissertation, University of Washington, Seattle.

Worell, J., & Remer, P. (1993). *Feminist perspectives in therapy: An empowerment model for women.* New York: John Wiley & Sons.

Chapter 6

School Violence: Research, Theory, and Practice

Ron Avi Astor, Lorelei Atalie Vargas, Ronald O'Neal Pitner, and Heather Ann Meyer

O pinion surveys continually show that the general public perceives safety as the top problem facing U.S. schools (for example, Elam & Rose, 1995; Elam, Rose, & Gallup, 1994, 1996; Morrison, Furlong, & Morrison, 1997; Rose, Gallup, & Elam, 1997). Recent mass homicides on school grounds in Littleton, Colorado, and other American towns and cities have only intensified public concern over school violence (for example, Bragg, 1997; Brooke, 1999; Gegax, Adler, & Pedersen, 1998; Hays, 1998; Witkin, Tharp, Schrof, Toch, & Scattarella, 1998). In response to growing public concern, politicians, school officials, educational scholars, parents, teachers, law enforcement officers, and pupil personnel organizations initiated dialogue in an effort to find ways of addressing the school violence problem (for example, American Psychological Association, 1993; Dwyer, Osher, & Warger, 1998; Kaufman et al., 1998; National Education Goals Panel, 1995). School violence research and intervention literature has also shown a dramatic increase during the 1990s. Several professional and academic journals have devoted entire issues to this topic (for example, Beauboeuf, *Harvard Educational Review*, 1995; Freeman,

Sections of this chapter were adapted with permission of Sage Publications from Astor, Meyer, & Pitner (1999) and with permission of NASW Press from Astor, Behre, Wallace, & Fravil (1998). The chapter was supported by a fellowship awarded to the first author from the National Academy of Education/Spencer Foundation.

Social Work in Education, 1995; Fuller, *Psychology in the Schools,* 1998; Johnson, *Journal of Negro Education,* 1996; Meyer, *Journal of School Psychology,* 1998; Shapiro, *School Psychology Review,* 1994).

Clearly, school violence has become a major focus of research and practice with many new programs but conflicting evaluations as to their effectiveness. Consequently, the objectives of this chapter are to (1) provide a broad overview of the school violence problem, (2) discuss promising empirically based school violence programs, (3) highlight major conceptual problems pertaining to school violence research and interventions, (4) identify common components of successful school violence programs, and (5) detail a school violence mapping procedure designed to develop site-based interventions.

NATURE AND SCOPE OF SCHOOL VIOLENCE

School violence covers a wide array of intentional or reckless behaviors that include physical harm, psychological harm, and property damage. These behaviors vary in severity and frequency: murder (Bragg, 1997; Hays, 1998); carrying weapons (Pittel, 1998); sexual harassment (Stein, 1995), school fighting (Boulton, 1993; Schafer & Smith, 1996); bullying, verbal threats, and intimidation (Batsche & Knoff, 1994; Fraser, 1996; Olweus, 1993); corporal punishment (Youssef, Attia, & Kamel, 1998); gang violence (Kodluboy, 1997; Parks, 1995); rape (Page, 1997); hate crimes (Berrill, 1990); vandalism (Goldstein, 1996); and dating violence (Burcky, Reuterman, & Kopsky, 1988; Cano, Avery-Leaf, Cascardi, & O'Leary, 1998).

Estimates of violence in schools vary widely depending on who is asked what. Students tend to report higher rates of violence than do teachers or principals. This could be related to differences in awareness and contact; many fights or other violent events may not filter up to principals or teachers. For example, data from Kaufman and colleagues (1998) are based on reports from principals, although they are commonly cited as "percent of schools reporting." Also, in that particularly influential study, principals were asked to report only on violence that required a response from law enforcement agencies. Acts that occurred off school grounds or en route to and from school (aside from bus travel) were excluded. These restrictions could cause serious underestimation of violent events. Although they are valuable because they represent the perspective and awareness of principals, the disparity between principals, teachers, and students should be considered when interpreting national data.

This review, then, is an overview of specific types of violence based on recent national data, though recognizing their limitations. Since most surveys and studies of school violence do not address all forms of school violence, this review will focus on specific forms, rather than on the broad array of violence.

Low-level forms of aggression, for instance—"horseplay, rule violation, disruptiveness, and cursing"—are usually not included in reports on school violence (Goldstein & Conoley, 1997). One exception is the work of Furlong, Morrison, Bates, and Chung (1998), who reported that over a 30-day period 52 percent of the students studied reported that someone had made fun of them, 56 percent that someone had cursed at them, 23 percent that they had been grabbed or shoved, 12 percent that they had been hit with a rock or other object, and 31 percent that someone had tried to scare them with a look.

Student Victimization

School fights and lethal violence. Although the public, the mass media, and politicians tend to focus mainly on the most lethal forms of school violence (acts involving weapons that result in severe physical injury), recent data suggest that physical fights are common among children attending U.S. schools. For example, the Centers for Disease Control and Prevention (CDC) (1998) reported that in 1997 36.6 percent (±2 percent) of U.S. high school students (26.0 percent of females and 45.5 percent of males) had been in a physical fight during the previous 12-month period. For about 14.8 percent (±1.3 percent) (8.6 percent of females and 20 percent of males), these fights occurred on school property. The 12-month incidence of physical fighting per 100 students was 115.1 (±14) (69.4 for females and 153.1 for males). Many high school students, then, were having more than one fist fight a year.

Moreover, findings from the National Household Education Survey (Brick et al., 1994) suggest that 8 percent of students in grades 6 to 12 are chronic victims of bullies at school (Kaufman et al., 1998, p. 10, Figure 4.1). Accurate estimates of physical fighting among U.S. elementary and middle school students are not currently available. However, based on data from bully and victim studies, Olweus (1993) estimated that 15 percent of students were regularly either bullies or victims. If these estimates are remotely accurate, numerous physical fights must occur in the majority of U.S. elementary, middle, and high schools, and most students must be familiar with school fights as victims, witnesses, or perpetrators.

The National Crime Victimization Survey (Kaufman et al., 1998, p. 45) examined student reports of serious violence (rape, sexual assault, forced robbery, and aggravated assault) and nonlethal acts of violence, which included acts of serious violence plus simple assault or school fights. (Because the survey used a more conservative definition of violence than did the CDC [1998], its estimates tend to be somewhat lower than the CDC's.)

In 1996 students aged 12 to18 experienced an estimated 1.3 million events of nonfatal violence (both serious acts of violence and simple assault) (Kaufman et al., 1998). This translates to 49 incidents per 1,000 students (64 events for males versus 32 events for females). The rates of nonfatal violence occurring at school or going to or from school were virtually the same for urban (55 events per 1,000 students) and suburban (54 events per 1,000 students) schools. Furthermore, students reported that approximately 1.4 million violent events occurred off school grounds. This translates to 55 incidents per 1,000 students (66 for males and 43 for females). However, the rates for nonfatal violence occurring off school grounds in urban settings (69 per 1,000 students) were higher than those in suburban schools (52).

This means that whether in the city or the suburbs, students have almost the same rates of victimization at school and in the community, but students from urban settings are more likely than suburban students to be victimized away from the school grounds. If personal theft is considered a form of violence (some researchers do so), about 2.1 million high school students reported being victims of theft at school and 1.6 million off school grounds.

Overall, the data suggest that students are experiencing high levels of victimization both on and off school grounds. It is unclear from these and other national data the degree to which victimization off school grounds is related to issues of school violence (for example, conflicts arising in school that are fought off school grounds to avoid being caught).

Fatal student victimization. Homicide and suicide are not common on school grounds. Kachur and colleagues (1996) estimated that 76 students were murdered or committed suicide on school grounds between 1992 and 1994. However, given the recent mass homicides on school grounds (Bragg, 1997; Gegax et al., 1998; Hays, 1998; Witkin et al., 1998), the rates of fatal school-related victimization may be somewhat higher during the years 1997 through 1999 than during previous years.

The patterns of fatal student victimization differ among ethnic groups. This is true in our society generally (Ash, Kellermann, Fuqua-Whitley, & Johnson, 1996; Gray, 1991; Hammond & Yung, 1993; Issacs, 1992; Prothrow-Stith & Weissman, 1991) and on school grounds (Astor, Pitner, & Duncan, 1996; Kachur et al., 1996; Kaufman et al., 1998). Hispanic students were five times more likely and African American students nine times more likely than Caucasian students to suffer a school-related lethal event (Kaufman et al., 1998, p. 70).

The potential for lethal violence in high schools remains high due to the availability of weapons. In 1997, the CDC (1998) reported 18.3 percent of high school students carried a weapon (for example, a gun, knife, or club) during the 30 days preceding its survey (7 percent of females and. 27.7 percent of males). However, the data suggested that many students are careful not to bring their weapons onto school grounds. For example, only 8.5 percent of high school students (3.7 percent of females and 12.5 percent of males) reported bringing a weapon onto school grounds over the past 12 months. Approximately 7.4 percent of high school students (4 percent of females and 10.2 percent of males) reported being threatened or injured with a weapon on school grounds. The prevalence of weapons during or after school hours could influence the rate of severe and lethal forms of school violence.

Teacher and School Social Worker Victimization

According to the National Crime Victimization Survey (see Kaufman et al., 1998, p. 25), teachers are also the victims of both theft and violent crimes. Between the years of 1992 and 1996, the annual average rate of victimization (combining theft and physical violence) for teachers was 76 incidents per 1,000 teachers (Kaufman, et al., 1998). Middle and junior high school teachers were more vulnerable to violent victimization than were teachers in elementary and senior high schools. Also, men were more likely than women to report being the victim of serious violent acts (41 crimes per 1,000 teachers for men and 26 for women). Teachers in urban schools were much more likely than those in suburban and rural schools to report being the victim of violent acts (Kaufman et al., 1998). Within a 12-month period, national data suggest, approximately 15.8 percent of teachers (18.6 percent of males and 14.7 percent of females) were either threatened with physical injury or physically attacked by a student.

The setting of schools appears to influence teachers' victimization. A larger proportion of inner-city teachers report being threatened or attacked (20.7 percent) than suburban (14.7 percent) and rural (12.9 percent) teachers. We do not have national data indicating how many teachers are threatened or attacked by other adults such as parents or by school outsiders such as gang members. However, we do have such data on school social workers.

In a recent national study, 35 percent of school social workers reported being physically assaulted or physically threatened during the previous year (Astor, Behre, Fravil, & Wallace, 1997; Astor, Behre, Wallace, & Fravil, 1998). Of these, 77 percent identified the assailant as a student, 49 percent as a parent, and 11 percent as a student gang member (some social workers were attacked more than once and by more than one type of perpetrator, making the total greater than 100 percent). Not surprisingly, many school social workers feared for their personal safety. In fact, fully one-third of school social workers reported that they feared for their personal safety about once a month or more. However, there were differences in the proportion of social workers in each community setting who reported fear. Compared with social workers in urban (36 percent), suburban (37 percent), and rural (31 percent) schools, more social workers in inner-city schools (71 percent) feared for their personal safety.

Philosophical Discussions about School Violence

When does a school have a serious violence problem? How do researchers, teachers, administrators, other school personnel, and the public determine which schools have a violence problem? What is considered a safe school context, and what is considered an unsafe school context? Although these philosophical issues have not been clarified by the practice and research literature, they affect the way we interpret the scope of the school violence problem.

For more than 20 years, starting with the Safe School Study for the United States Congress (National Institute of Education, 1978), researchers have argued about the extent of school violence as a problem in the United States (Furlong & Morrison, 1994; Goldstein & Conoley, 1997; G. Gottfredson, 1985; Morrison et al., 1997). At the core of the debate are seemingly conflicting results from national studies. On the one hand, the empirical debate is supported by public opinion surveys that demonstrate great concern about school violence. On the other hand, multiple large-scale surveys suggest that very few (between 10 and 15 percent) students, teachers, and principals rate *their own schools* as unsafe. These conflicting data have often been interpreted as evidence supporting the position that schools are in fact very safe, and that the public hysteria is a result of media hyperbole combined with a handful of publicized but very rare lethal events (Dwyer et al., 1998; Kaufman et al., 1998; Lee & Croninger, 1995).

However, very little research has investigated how professionals and students decide when their school has a violence problem. For example, one can ask: How many violent events are necessary before a school is perceived to have a problem? Current research and conceptual discussions do not address this threshold issue. Even so, severity or frequency of violence does not necessarily address how safe or dangerous the school is perceived to be, or, even more important, how safety *should* be categorized.

How children, teachers, and the public judge the overall safety or extent of a problem in any particular school *as a whole* is not the same as judging a *particular behavioral event*. For example, students or teachers may be reluctant to categorize their school (as a whole) as having a violence problem even though they may be aware of multiple violent events. Furthermore, a school may be safe in some respects and unsafe in others. Classroom spaces during class time might be considered safe, while the cafeteria during lunch may be seen as dangerous. Some children may avoid unsafe areas entirely; others may be continually exposed to dangerous situations within the same school setting.

From the perspective of school constituents who were victims and parents whose children were victimized, it could be argued that one severe act of violence (such as a potentially lethal event) would qualify a school as having a violence problem. However, if the criteria are both severity and frequency, defining a "problem school" is harder. Is a school that had six potentially lethal events compared with a school that had ten during a given year a safer school? If frequency and severity are used, how many severe events (shootings, rapes, knifings, beatings, or fights that require medical attention) does a school need before school staff and students perceive the school as having a *serious* violence problem? The same questions can be asked for lower-level violent events, such as pushing, punching, and tripping.

Do educators or researchers have a sense of what the threshold is for a "big" problem when discussing the school as a whole? In our many contacts with principals and teachers, we have asked, "How many playground fights [per month or per year] would it take before you would be willing to say that your playground has a violence problem? 50? 200? 400? 1,000?" To date, we have found no administrators who are able to define frequency criteria. The questions of how many and what types of violence constitute a problem are difficult to answer because they have not yet been addressed on a philosophical level.

INTERVENTIONS TO PREVENT OR REDUCE SCHOOL VIOLENCE

Characteristics of Ineffective Interventions

A singular focus on the source of the problem. Most practitioners and researchers would agree that school violence is associated with a wide array of individual, family, community, and societal variables. Table 6-1 presents correlates often mentioned in the literature; these correlates are presented at different ecological levels. Given the number of variables associated with school violence, one would expect interventions to target multiple factors. Instead, most school violence interventions focus only on one or two variables or ecological levels (for example, either the child, the family, or the classroom), ignoring the complex interplay of variables. It is not surprising that programs which address only one variable tend not to be effective in reducing levels of school violence.

A psychological focus. The most popular school violence interventions are psychological and behavioral (for example, anger management, conflict mediation, peer counseling, curriculum-based programs). Historically, psychology has focused on identifying cognitive, emotional, and social-relational reasons why individual children become violent (American Psychological Association, 1993). Psychological interventions have been primarily geared toward individual children (or their families), with very little attention to the interplay between school violence and the social dynamics of normative contexts like schools (Hudley, Britsch, Wakefield, Demorat, & Cho, 1998). With few exceptions, social skills interventions, peer counseling or mediation, and other kinds of psychological interventions have proved ineffective in reducing levels of school violence and in some cases (for example, peer mediation groups and programs like DARE) may even increase aggression and violence

Table 6-1. **Selected Correlates of School Violence**

Risk Factor Level	Risk Factor	Sources
Community	Inner-city location	Kaufman et al., 1998; Heaviside et al., 1998
	Large minority population	Kaufman et al., 1998; Heaviside et al., 1998
	High rate of poverty	Kaufman et al., 1998; Heaviside et al., 1998
	High crime rate	Laub & Lauritsen, 1998; Heaviside et al., 1998
School and classroom	School structure	National Research Council, 1993
	Overcrowded schools	Hellman & Beaton, 1996; National Research Council, 1993; Walker & Gresham, 1997
	Weapons in schools	Harrington-Lueker, 1992
	Gang presence	Embry et al., 1996; Thompson & Jason, 1988; Walker, Colvin, & Ramsey, 1995
	Availability of drugs	D. Gottfredson, Fink, Skroban, & Gottfredson, in press
	Consistency and clarity of rule enforcement	Frude & Gault, 1984; D. Gottfredson et al., in press
Individual	Parental disengagement	Farrington, 1991; Loeber & Stouthamer-Loeber, 1986; Olweus, 1980
	Academic failure	Blumstein, 1995; Patterson, Reid, & Dishion, 1992
	Bullying	Fagan & Wilkinson, 1998
	Low verbal IQ	Farrington, 1991; Heusmann et al., 1984; Moffitt, 1993
	Peer pressure	Gottfredson, 1990; Toby, 1994
	High rate of truancy	Carins, Carins, & Neckerman, 1989
	Drug/alcohol use	Goldstein et al., 1985; Kaufman et al., 1998

in schools (see D. Gottfredson, 1997, and Samples & Aber, 1998, for detailed reviews of these programs). Psychological programs are effective only when used conjointly with other interventions that target the organizational or social system of the school (D. Gottfredson, 1997; Olweus, 1993).

Underuse of the school context. Many programs tend to be "add on" programs that do not take into account the normal components of the school social structure (Larson, 1998) or relate to the academic curriculum and social goals of the school. This situation is due in part to the fact that the social variables associated with school violence have not been clearly conceptualized (see Astor, 1998, for a discussion of these issues). For example, researchers have conducted very few studies of the social dynamics of hallway fistfights or sexual harassment on school grounds. Moreover, until very recently, researchers and practitioners have not carefully distinguished between the concepts of *school violence* and *youth violence* (Astor, 1998; Astor & Meyer, 1998)—though many youth violence studies have collected their data on school grounds using classroom peer and teacher rating scales. Although these "youth violence" studies may have been measuring the social dynamics or structure of violence within the school and classroom, they did not conceptualize the school as part of the theoretical paradigm beyond using academic achievement as an outcome. Instead, many analyses of youth violence are presented without context, with a strong implicit assumption that youths are the "carrier" of violent behavior and that the dynamics of settings play only a tangential role.

Deficits in children. Many school violence interventions are based on either formal or implicit theoretical assumptions of deficits in individual children or subpopulations of children. For example, most social skills programs are based on the assumption that because they lack social exposure and practice, aggressive children also lack the social-cognitive or the behavioral skills needed to deal with conflict appropriately. Without these more complex skills, it is believed, children naturally gravitate toward using aggression as a solution to social conflict. Consequently, these types of programs target specific deficits in cognitive and behavioral skills, whether in specific children or within entire schools.

Common Interventions and Programs

The scope of programs. Nationwide, approximately 78 percent of principals report that their schools currently have programs addressing violence in their schools (Kaufman et al., 1998). Of these, 11 percent had programs that lasted one day or less, 24 percent had only ongoing violence programs, and 43 percent had both ongoing and one-day programs. It is not clear what types of programs principals consider to be violence interventions. However, school social workers report a wide array of violence intervention programs and services, including counseling services, crisis intervention, skill training, peer programs for students, community programs, teacher-based programs, and security measures. Table 6-2 presents the percentage of social workers who reported that their school had provided programs or services, and the percentage active in the programs. Unfortunately, the vast majority of services, methods-based interventions (for example, counseling, crisis intervention, and home visits), and programs have not been extensively evaluated as violence reduction strategies. For example, Astor and colleagues (1998) reported that 91 percent of social workers endorsed home visits as an effective intervention for violent children and 82 percent said they personally conducted home visits to help reduce aggressive behaviors. Yet there are few data on the effectiveness of home visits.

Common interventions. Few evaluations have assessed the effectiveness of interventions normally used by schools, such as expulsion, suspension, referral to special education, sending the child to the principal's office, detention during and after school, parent conferences, and counseling. Yet expulsion, suspension, and school transfer are common responses to acts of school violence. During the 1996–97 school year, 39 percent of school principals said they expelled, suspended, or transferred a student for fighting; 27 percent expelled, suspended, or transferred students who carried a weapon on school grounds (Heaviside et al., 1998, p. 81, Table 18). Other common interventions such as contacting parents, parent–school meetings about aggressive behaviors, or school-based consequences—staying after school, better adult supervision in the school yard, better monitoring of the routes to and from school and within violence-prone school areas—all need greater evaluation. Data from Europe and Australia suggest that these types of interventions are easy to implement and may be highly effective in reducing some types of school violence such as "bullying" (Olweus, 1993; Sharp & Smith, 1994; Smith & Sharp, 1994).

Special education and violence. Another common response of schools to persistent and chronic aggression in individual children is special education referral, assessment, and placement. Unfortunately, the school violence literature has not closely examined the relationships between special education and violence reduction in schools. Nevertheless, it is likely that many children receive services for aggressive behavior through special education, whether counseling, parent training, contained classrooms, specialized curricula, and day-treatment facilities. It is possible that social workers, psychologists, counselors, and teachers may view the special education process as a preferred intervention with some aggressive children.

Promising Prevention and Intervention Programs

Table 6-3 presents school-based programs that have been evaluated or are widely used. We highlight a handful that show promise or have already demonstrated their effectiveness.

School-based bully and victim intervention programs. In the 1970s when surveys in Norway found that bullying was a problem for many students, a comprehensive nationwide anti-bullying program was conducted (Olweus, 1993). In an effort to reduce bully and victim problems, D. Olweus, professor of psychology at the University of Bergen, Norway, developed a nationwide program for children in grades 1 through 9. The program, which has many simple interventions, is aimed at students, teachers, and parents, in schools, classrooms, and individual settings.

Findings from 42 schools showed a 50 percent reduction in rates of bullying and victimization. Furthermore, the positive effects of the program

Table 6-2. **Percentage of School Social Workers[a] Reporting Specific Violence Programs and Services in Their Schools**

Type of Program or Service	Percentage of Schools with Program	Percentage of Social Workers Involved in Program
Counseling services		
Violence crisis intervention	50	40
Victim assistance and support services	30	24
Individual or family counseling	53	46
Posttraumatic stress groups for observers or victims	15	12
Services targeting ethnic, religious or racial conflicts	24	13
Child abuse education	58	41
Skills training		
Conflict management	63	43
Social skills training	66	53
Prosocial behavior curriculum	53	35
Skill streaming	35	25
Groups for aggressive children	54	43
Leadership training	41	19
Peer programs for students		
Positive peer culture	39	24
Friendship clubs	31	15
After school sports or clubs	75	15
Community programs		
Antigang program	22	8
Services that address community violence	15	6
Police antiviolence program	38	7
Parent support group	21	14
Church group or youth group	15	3
Teacher-based programs		
Teacher support groups or training on violence	26	14
Classroom management	60	34
Antibully campaign	14	9
Academic programs aimed at aggressors, victims, or witnesses	8	3
Physical plant changes		
Metal detectors	14	3
Security guards	37	6

Source: Adapted with permission from Astor, R., Behre, W., Wallace, J., & Fravil, K. (1998). School social workers and school violence: Personal safety, violence programs, and training. *Social Work, 43,* 223–232. Copyright 1998, NASW Press.
[a] *N* = 576.

Table 6-3. **Selected School-Based Prevention and Intervention Programs**

Program Name	Description of Intervention	Author(s)
Adolescent Anger Control: Cognitive–Behavioral Techniques	12-session group anger-control program for adolescents	Feindler & Ecton, 1986
Aggression Replacement Training: A Comprehensive Intervention for Aggressive Youth	Program combining anger-management, moral-education, and social–skills training for aggressive youths	Goldstein et al., 1985
Anger Coping Intervention with Aggressive Children	18 one-hour group sessions for boys in grades 4 through 6 exhibiting chronic patterns of aggressive behavior	Lochman et al., 1986
BrainPower Program	12-lesson attribution retraining intervention for grades 3 through 6	Hudley et al., 1998
FAST Track Program	Combines family, child, and school-based interventions in a multistage program for high-risk youths from grades 1 through middle school	Dodge, 1993
Peace Builders	Schoolwide program implemented by staff and students to foster positive school climate for students in grades K through 5	Embry et al., 1996; Flannery, 1996; Flaxman et al., 1998
Positive Adolescents Choices Training (P.A.C.T.)	20 one-hour weekly group sessions focusing on social–skills training, violence awareness, and anger management for African American youths	Yung & Hammond, 1998
Positive Youth Development Program	20-session curriculum for sixth and seventh graders emphasizing social competence	Caplan et al., 1992
Resolving Conflict Creatively Program	Curriculum-based program integrating conflict resolution and intergroup relationships for middle school youths	Aber et al., 1996; Coben et al., 1994
School-based Bully/Victim Intervention Program	Nationwide campaign integrating family, school, and community to reduce and prevent bully/victim problems	Olweus, 1993
School Transitional Environmental Program (STEP)	Curriculum-based program focusing on self-esteem development and anger-management training for children and adolescents	Larson, 1998; Yung & Hammond, 1998
Second Step: A Violence Prevention Curriculum	Curriculum-based direct classroom instruction for preschool through middle school	Committee for Children, 1992; Grossman et al., 1997
The Parents and Children Series: A Comprehensive Course Divided into Four Programs	Uses videotape program to train parents of children with conduct problems	Bierman et al., 1992

(Continued on next page)

Table 6-3. *(continued)*

Program Name	Description of Intervention	Author(s)
Viewpoints Training Program	Treatment-based program focused on altering the beliefs and attitudes of violent youths about the legitimacy of violence	Guerra & Panizzon, 1986
Violence Prevention Curriculum for Adolescents	Curriculum-based health education for high school students	Prothrow-Stith, 1987

increased over time, as did student satisfaction with school life (Olweus, 1993, 1996). Similar antibullying programs have been implemented in Great Britain (Sharp & Smith, 1994; Smith & Sharp, 1994) and Australia (Rigby, 1996). Evaluations of those programs also show significant reductions in aggressive behaviors and increases in student satisfaction with school life. Gottfredson (1997) suggested that such a systemic and broad approach could be successful in the United States.

Although large-scale antibullying programs have not been conducted in the United States, Gottfredson (1997) cites similar positive effects from American "capacity building programs" that focus on school improvement, staff development, and the creation of policies to deal with crime, violence, and discipline. These programs have many of the same school, classroom, and individual components as the Norwegian program. Specifically, they attempt to

- increase the clarity of rules
- promote consistency of rule enforcement
- increase student and staff sense of responsibility for discipline
- create a sense of ownership to solve the school violence problem
- focus on the entire school
- involve all staff and students in owning the rules and their consequences
- change the norms about school violence
- target many levels of the school system (student, teacher, parent, administrator, classroom, school site) for interventions.

High-quality early childhood education. A high-quality preschool education can be effective in reducing violence throughout the life span (Schweinhart, Barnes, & Weikart, 1993). In a longitudinal study of the Perry Preschool High Scope program, children who were randomly assigned to participate in a high-quality preschool program were far less likely to have been involved in criminal and violent activity through development than those who were assigned to a lower-quality preschool program.

These longitudinal data are important because they suggest that the effects carry into adulthood. By age 27, students who had been assigned to low-quality preschool programs were five times more likely than high-quality preschool students to have been arrested five or more times. In addition, children in the high-quality classes were significantly more likely than children in the low-quality classes to earn more money, own a house, and graduate from high school. They were significantly less likely to have used social services. A cost-benefit analysis suggested that participation in a high-quality preschool saved the general public $57,585 per child (in 1992 dollars) in costs related to crime and victimization alone. Researchers believe that a preschool focus on social responsibility, empowerment, decision making, and conflict resolution are important in reducing later violence (Schweinhart et al., 1993). Also, the High Scope/Perry preschool program emphasized parent education and teacher training in conflict and discipline. Schweinhart and colleagues (1993) believe that the tripartite focus on students, parents, and teachers accounts for the lower levels of violence.

Second Step. Based on the "habit of thought" model positing that violence can be unlearned, the Second Step program targets children in preschool through kindergarten, grades 1 to 3, and grades 4 and 5. Second Step is a curriculum-based approach that attempts to prevent aggressive behavior by increasing competence in peer interactions and in interpersonal conflict resolution skills. The curriculum, with an average of 50 to 60 lessons, is designed to help youths acquire empathy, impulse control, and problem-solving and anger-management skills and is administered twice a week.

A recent evaluation of a 30-lesson Second Step curriculum found that it decreased the amount of physical aggression and increased positive and prosocial behaviors on the playground and in the lunchroom (Grossman et al., 1997). In another report on training elementary and middle school teachers to use the curriculum, teachers and administrators reported considerable respect for the capacity of the curriculum (Milwaukee Board of School Directors, 1993).

Similar curriculum-based conflict resolution programs have not performed as well when intensively evaluated (Webster, 1993). For example, the Violence Prevention Curriculum for Adolescents (Prothrow-Stith, 1987) has few results showing that it actually reduces violence (Larson, 1998; Tolan & Guerra, 1994).

Peace Builders. The Peace Builders program is a schoolwide violence prevention program for students in grades K to 5 (Embry, Flannery, Vazsonyi, Powell, & Atha, 1996) that is currently operating in almost 400 schools in Arizona, California, Ohio, and Utah. Implemented by both staff and students, the program incorporates strategies to promote prosocial behavior among students and staff, enhancing social competence and reducing aggressive behavior. Children learn five principles:

1. Praise people.
2. Avoid put-downs.
3. Seek wise people as advisors and friends.
4. Notice and correct any hurts the children cause.
5. Right wrongs.

Teachers, administrators, and parents reinforce and model these behaviors.

Peace Builders differs from most school-based programs because it is not curriculum-based. Instead, it is described as "a way of life" (Flaxman, Schwartz, Weiler, & Lahey, 1998). The CDC is evaluating the program in a six-year study of process and outcome data; the initial results demonstrated a significant decrease in aggressive behavior and a significant increase in social competence (Flannery, 1996, 1998; Flannery & Vazsonyi, 1996).

Positive Adolescents Choices Training. The Positive Adolescents Choices Training (PACT) program was "designed to teach African American youth social skills to aid in prevention of violence" (Hammond & Yung, 1991, 1993; Yung & Hammond, 1998). PACT is unique in that it is culturally relevant and aimed at reducing aggression and victimization in high-risk youths. Program components include anger management, prosocial skills training, and violence risk education. The sessions are built around videotapes that demonstrate culturally sensitive social situations. Participants learn the skills needed to solve the situation peacefully.

Participants in the program improved an average of 33.5 percent in giving negative feedback, problem solving, and resisting peer pressure. Students perceived the greatest improvement in their ability to provide negative feedback; they felt they gained least in problem solving. Teachers observed significant improvement in the targeted skills of trained youths (30.4 percent) compared to untrained youths (–1.1 percent). Most importantly, students demonstrated a significant reduction in physical aggression at school, and a reduction in their overall aggressive behavior during the training was maintained when they graduated from the program (Yung & Hammond, 1998).

Based on our review, it appears that successful school intervention programs have these core characteristics:

• They raise the awareness and responsibility of students, teachers, and parents regarding the types of violence in their schools (for example, sexual harassment, fighting, weapon use) and create clear guidelines for the entire school.

- They clarify to the entire school community what procedures should be followed before, during, and after violent events.
- They get school staff, students, and parents involved.
- The interventions fit easily into the normal flow and mission of the school.
- They use faculty, staff, and parents in the school to plan, implement, and sustain the program.
- They increase monitoring and supervision in nonclassroom areas.

IN-DEPTH CLINICAL INTERVENTION: MAPPING SCHOOLS FOR VIOLENCE

Mapping Violence within Schools

We believe the process described next could contribute to the success of grassroots strategies. This procedure is designed to help practitioners better understand how violence within a school building interacts with locations, patterns of the school day, and social organizational variables (for example, teacher and student relationships, teachers' professional roles, and the school's organizational response to violence). An important goal of the procedure is to *allow students and teachers to convey their personal theories* about why specific locations and times in their schools are more dangerous. The approach assumes that students, teachers, school staff, and administrators have important information that should be the foundation for setting specific interventions.

This process is designed to document (1) the locations and times within each school where violence occurred for a given term, and 2) the perspectives of students, teachers, staff, and administrators on the school's responses (or nonresponses) to violent events in these locations. In particular, this assessment process is sensitive to areas that are "unowned" by adults in the school, that is, the times and places that are not perceived to be the responsibility of any adults. These unowned spaces appear to be the locations where most school violence occurs (Astor & Meyer, in press; Astor, Meyer, & Behre, 1999).

Use of Focus Groups

We recommend that students, teachers, and staff (for example, administrators, hall monitors, cafeteria workers) be interviewed in four or five separate one-hour focus groups about where violence has been committed and when the violence occurred. Groups should represent various constituencies of the school organization, as well as locations within the school. We recommend that administrators, teachers, staff, and students be interviewed in separate focus groups. Students may fear repercussions from teachers; teachers may not want to discuss issues openly in front of administrators. It is important that focus group members be assured anonymity, especially with regard to comments about the school's response to violence. To allow for thorough discussion, we recommend that there be six to eight individuals in each group. The ecology of violence within the school can thus be assessed in about six hours.

To ensure confidentiality the focus groups should be conducted in a room that affords privacy. Therefore, securing a room or unused classroom space is important for the success of this assessment strategy.

Composition of Focus Groups

Students. Clearly, the nature of the violence may suggest a specific composition for student focus groups. For example, in a school that has a problem with sexual assaults, some groups could be made up of only girls and others only of boys. However, for most schools, we suggest a mixed gender group. In the past, we have organized students into older (11th and 12th graders) and younger (ninth and 10th graders) groups with an equal number of boys and girls in each. However, depending on the nature of the violence within the school, groups could be organized by gender, age, or any other relevant characteristic.

Teachers and staff. Teachers, administrators, and other important school staff members (security guards, vice principals, hall monitors) are almost never included in research or interventions related to school violence. These individuals often have valuable knowledge about where and when violence occurs that may be critical to structuring interventions. Nevertheless, it is not necessary to interview large numbers of school personnel to understand where, when, and why violence occurs. Interviews with four or five teachers per school are sufficient to gain a fairly accurate range of teachers' perspectives. Only a handful of cafeteria workers, yard aides, bus drivers, and security guards need to be interviewed to learn how school personnel are responding to student aggression.

Practitioners can anticipate themes that include a sense of "being caught in the middle." Some teachers who express a desire to prevent violence may not possess the skills needed to intervene effectively. Many staff members are also unclear about their professional role in nonclassroom locations (see Astor et al., 1999, for more detail about what themes can be anticipated in each group).

In our interviews, nonteaching staff suggested very specific interventions associated with their areas. For example, cafeteria workers in one school revealed that only two or three adults were expected to supervise over 1,000 children during the lunch period. In several schools secretaries had very clear suggestions for interventions regarding children who were sent to the office for fighting during less supervised periods (recess, lunch, or transitions between classes).

Materials and Procedure

Obtaining school maps. The first step in this assessment procedure is to obtain a map of the school. A detailed blueprint is not necessary. Usually, the school office has a small (8" × 11") map of the school, as required by fire marshals. Ideally, the map should contain all internal school territory plus areas surrounding the school and playground facilities. Schools with several floors may require two or more pages. In some communities where the routes to and from school are dangerous, a simple map of the surrounding neighborhood may be added.

The maps are an essential part of the interviewing process. They help to anchor discussions to places and times in ways that interviews about issues alone cannot. Two sets of the school maps should be photocopied for each participant in the focus groups, one marked A and the other marked B at the upper corner. Each interviewee should also be given a pencil or pen and eight circular colored stickers (about an eighth of an inch in diameter). The circular stickers will be used to mark violent events on the map (described in the following section). These materials can be found in most schools or agencies or bought for a few dollars.

Maps procedure. The focus groups begin with the facilitator distributing two sets of maps to each individual, orienting the group to the different areas of the school as they are represented on the map. Participants should be asked not to identify by name any individual who may have been involved in violence. The purpose of the discussion is to identify locations, not individuals. (Some groups may need several gentle reminders.) We have found that talking about places rather than people provides the freedom to discuss events without fear of repercussions or revealing personal information about friends or colleagues.

Map A: Three most violent events. The first map is used to determine the location of the most violent events. Using the stickers, participants are asked to identify on the maps the locations of up to three of the most violent events that occurred within the past academic year. In some schools the most violent event may be a lethal shooting, in others it may be a fight. Each participant is free to interpret "most violent" subjectively. Students and school personnel take this task seriously, tending to report fairly severe events.

Next to each event (marked by a sticker) participants are then asked to write directly on the map (1) the general time of the event (before school, after school, morning period, afternoon period, evening sports event, between classes, etc.); (2) the grade and gender of those involved in the violence; and (3) what they know about any organizational response to the event (nothing, participants sent to principal's office, suspended, sent to peer counselor, etc.). During the first part of the interview participants should be encouraged to work from their own recollections, without discussing locations and times.

Map B: Dangerous areas in and around school. Once the first set of maps is completed, participants can then be given the second map. On this map, using a pencil or pen, participants should be asked to circle areas or territories that they perceive to be "unsafe" or potentially dangerous. Asking about unsafe places reveals different information than would asking about events alone. This second map provides information about areas within the school that participants avoid even though no particular violent event occurred there. Participants should then be asked to explain in a few sentences on the second set of maps *why* they believe this particular area or time is prone to violence or should be avoided.

Completing both sets of maps consumes approximately 10 minutes of focus group time. When group members are finished, the facilitator begins the discussion portion of the interview. The interviews should be tape-recorded so that the practitioner can listen for themes later. In the past, we have transcribed the interviews for ease of reference, as this allows staff members who are interested in school violence to read and discuss the interviews.

Discussion of violent events and areas. The first part of the discussion centers on the specific violent events and areas marked as unsafe or dangerous on the maps. We have asked questions such as: "Are there times when those places you've marked on the maps are less safe?" "Is there a particular group of students that is more likely to get hurt there?" and "Why do you think that area has so many violent events?" Locations marked on both maps are particularly helpful in identifying areas and times that are prone to violence.

The purpose of the group interviews is to explore not just where and when but also why violence is occurring. Consequently, the interviews should gather information on organizational responses to the event ("What happened to the two students who fought?" or "Did the hall monitors intervene when they saw the fight?"), procedures ("What happens when someone is sent to the office after a fight?"), follow-up ("Do the teachers, hall monitors, or administrators follow up on any consequences given to the students?" or

"Did anyone check on the welfare of the victim?"), and clarity of procedures ("Does it matter who stops the fight?"—for example, a volunteer, security guard, teacher, or principal).

Interviewers should also explore participants' ideas for solutions to specific problems ("Can you think of ways to avoid this type of violence in that place?" or "If you were the principal, what would you do to make that place safer?"). The interviewer should also probe for any obstacles participants foresee with implementation ("Do you think that type of plan is realistic?", "Has that been tried before? What happened?", or "Do you think that plan would work?"). Such obstacles might relate to roles ("It's not my job to monitor students during lunch"), discipline policy, or personal safety ("I don't want to intervene because I may get hurt").

In schools that already have programs to address school violence, specific questions should be asked about how effective they are, why they do or do not work, and what could be done to make them more effective. We recommend that the interviewer ask both subjective questions ("Do you like the conflict management program?") and specific questions about reducing violence (for example, "Do you believe the conflict management program has reduced the number of fights on the playground? Why or Why not?").

Assembling the Data

Maps. The information from individual maps should be transferred to an enlarged poster-size map. Enlarging the map is relatively inexpensive and can be done fairly quickly at most photocopy stores. The poster is a powerful representation that helps school personnel to identify areas where violence most often occurs. Figure 6-1 shows how information from individual maps was coded and then transferred onto one combined map.

The events were coded on the poster map by time, age, and gender of participants. This visual depiction of violence as it clusters allows school staff to better create specific interventions. Unsafe areas from the second maps were identified by areas marked by crosshatching.

Transferring all the reported events onto one large map of the school enables students and staff to locate specific "hot spots" for violence and dangerous time periods. For the high school shown in Figure 6-1, events for older students (11th and 12th graders) were clustered in the parking lot outside the auxiliary gym immediately after school; for younger students (ninth and 10th graders) events clustered in the lunchroom and hallways during transition periods. For this school, the map suggests that interventions be geared towards older students directly after school by the main entrance and in the parking lot. Students and teachers agreed that increasing the visible presence of staff in and around the parking lot for the 20 minutes after school had great potential for preventing many violent events. Increased

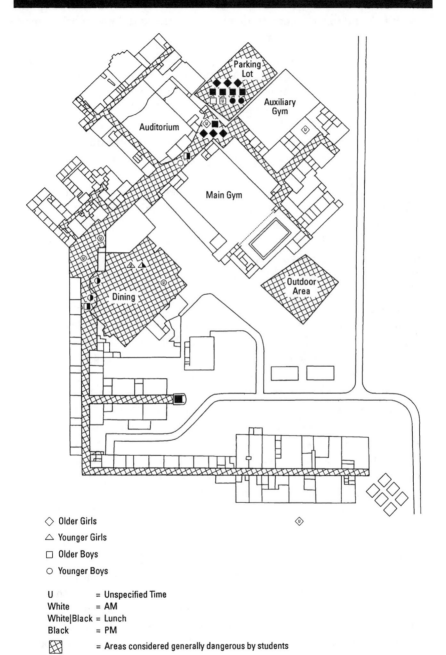

Figure 6-1. Violent Events Marked by Location, Time, Gender, and Age

◇ Older Girls

△ Younger Girls

□ Older Boys

○ Younger Boys

U	= Unspecified Time
White	= AM
White|Black	= Lunch
Black	= PM
▨	= Areas considered generally dangerous by students

supervision was also the consensus solution for younger students who were experiencing violence near the cafeteria immediately before, during, and after lunch and for the many students who expressed feelings of being unsafe between classes in the hallways.

Interview data. Compiling all the suggestions into a readable table is an important step in creating context-relevant interventions. Students, teachers, and administrators may have differing viewpoints about the organizational response of the school when violence happened. Table 6-4 represents the different opinions of students, teachers, and administrators. Relaying the diversity of responses to students, teachers, and administrators can provide an opportunity for reflection and may generate ways to remedy violence in certain situations.

This type of format also provides an interesting way to exemplify the different perspectives of students, staff, and administrators on how to deal with violent events. The responses in Table 6-4 pointed to ambivalence about whose role it was to intervene when violence occurred. These contrasting anonymous viewpoints can function as a vehicle for communication between the various subsystems of the school and inform the direction of relevant interventions.

Organizing the interventions suggested by participants into a table is also recommended. For example, Table 6-5 shows that students had clear opinions about how to make these areas safer. Depending on the important themes, comments by the students, teachers, and administrators could be organized like those presented in Table 6-4. We recommend creating tables for each important theme for the particular school. In the past we have organized comments related to race, gender, poverty, community, and religious conflict when it was perceived that these variables were contributing to violence within a school. In schools that already have measures to prevent violence, we recommend compiling tables for those interventions (for example, metal detectors, security guards, electronic and video monitoring, suspension and expulsion policies). Table 6-6 represents another example of how various views can be presented—in this case opinions on the use of suspension or expulsion to deter violence.

Together, the poster-sized map of violent events, the interview data organized by themes, and the information on potential obstacles can generate concrete intervention strategies to reduce violence in school communities. At a minimum, the organized data provide a formal opportunity for school subsystems to discuss these issues. Because most unsafe areas usually have few adults, the dialogue among the various school subsystems should include realistic ways to reclaim unowned territory and time. This assessment process is powerful because the information presented back to the constituents emerged

Table 6-4. **Core Student, Teacher, and Administrator Comments on Organizational Response**

Domain	Students	Teachers	Administrators
Organizational Response	"I wouldn't actually jump in there either because these, like, goons up here they don't care about a teacher and they fight and they not concerned about the teacher. If the teacher gets hit, most likely they going to say they shouldn't be in the way. So it's not they job to break up fights."	"Two young ladies were going at it outside of my door, and I went to pull one off. She started punching me . . . and she was swearing. We ended up on the floor. I'll never forget. I looked up and two male teachers were standing there, not doing anything."	"We've told the teachers they can take any level of activity they feel comfortable taking. They can intervene physically if they feel they have to. And I've had some teachers do that."
	"Because I've seen a lot of people who get suspended and, you know, you see them a few weeks later getting in-school suspension. I mean what's the difference?"	"I have a call button . . . they don't answer, they don't respond. I have to run next door and tell my department head. She would pick up the phone and try to locate security . . . the kid would be back in my class in three days."	"If you're in the immediate area, you've got to break that fight up. You're to do what you can . . . state law requires teachers to be responsible in that situation."
	"[And] she told me to go to the hallway. We went to the hall. . . . The girl came out into the hall. . . . Then you know the teacher is still in the classroom, but she knows all this time that we are arguing and it is going to be a conflict. Why didn't she stop us when we were having words?"	"I can remember a few years back, we had a convicted rapist who was in classes at this school. The teachers were not told that this student was convicted of rape . . . he was scheduled with a number of young women teachers . . . and the principal never said a word. . . ."	"There's a liability issue here. It's something that a lot of teachers don't seem to understand . . . it means that they must at least give a verbal command to stop."
	"That's like when the tuition office got held up. Don't you know, I was walking down the hall and I didn't even know what happened. Can you imagine how I felt? I could have got shot for no reason. . . . I think they should let us leave at least when the police came. Evacuated out one of these doors."	"I think that some teachers probably would not like to get involved. In fact, I saw one [a fight] about nine months ago where the teacher walked away from it and didn't want to get involved."	"And, many times we would just transfer a student who had one fight. You could say anyone who fights in this building is gone."

from them, in contrast to assessment approaches where outside "experts" determine what the problem is and what the intervention should be.

Some schools may want to create an ongoing "hot spot" map to track unsafe places and times monthly. The technique has been used by urban

Table 6-5. **Student-Reported Violent Events and Suggested Interventions**

Location of Event	Nature of Violent Event	Suggested Interventions by Students
Hallway	• pushing • fighting • gun pulled • gang fights • assault	"There's so many people that you can understand that the hallways are crowded. That's our number one problem—the hallways are too crowded." "Have a rule that if you surround a fight you're helping . . . so you would get the same punishment as the people fighting, because you're helping people fight." "They [security] should know what is going on in their hallway instead of like two or three of them going down the same way."
Parking lot	• physical fights • weapons • shooting • stabbing • physical threats • racially motivated fights	"Well, where there's not supervision [parking lot] there's always going to be trouble. . . . The principal, he should be out there."
Abandoned or unmonitored spaces	• physical fights or assault • sexual assault or rape • strangers entering • weapons • robbery	"Maybe if we had regular security guards, like they had a 70-year-old man security guard, and like that guy can't even move." "People walk in at like 7 o'clock. No guards anywhere. It's just quiet—nobody anywhere." "When we have a weapon search, they supposed to check you. There's some people they don't check." "More lights . . . or have a monitor. Have somebody down there." "I mean lock the school doors . . . the back door is always open and people come in." "I think we need to have IDs to show . . . and then like a speaker at the door."
Cafeteria	• physical fights • food fights • throwing chairs • gang scuffles	"They should have at least five teachers in there . . . a minimum of five teachers. Because now there's only two teachers." "It's too crowded . . . our lunch hour is only 25 minutes." "I think you should go basically anywhere during lunch, as long as you clean up after yourself, because keeping a lot of people together kind of generates fights."

planners, criminologists, and law enforcement agencies to reduce crime in a variety of settings. The recent reduction in violent crime in many U.S. cities has been partially attributed to the use of this method. Interventions designed to increase the safety of housing projects have relied on similar mapping techniques.

Table 6-6. **Comments by Students, Teachers, and Administrators on Suspension and Expulsion**

Intervention	Students	Teachers	Administrators
Suspension/ Expulsion	"No [not useful], because I've seen a lot of people who will get suspended and, you know, you see them a few weeks later getting in-school suspension. I mean, what's the difference?"	"We have kids who are threats. They don't last long around here. They threaten a teacher and they're done. They're gone."	"If you are caught with a weapon in school, or if you're caught selling drugs, it's expulsion. There's not even a let's reconsider."
	"Suspend everyone. You know, they just, whoever was standing around, just suspend them . . . teachers just come and grab a handful of people who you see standing around who look like they were doing something. . . . You're all suspended."	"There are no exceptions to the policy. There is no exception. Would I change it? I don't know. Should a kid who is caught with a gun in his locker be kicked out or be allowed to come back into this school? . . . You are going to kick him out of here and throw him out in society? Who's going to care for him then?"	"If you're caught fighting, then you go home and you're suspended. It's either three or five days. If it's a fistfight, they can be suspended to another school."
	"I disagree with the administrators. How sometimes like when people are doing good stuff, they may get involved with something bad and they just feel like eliminating them will be the best thing, but they don't look at their good qualities, and stuff like that."	"Part of our fear is our knowing that no one gets rid of these kids. They just move from school to school. So, in the middle of the semester when you get a new kid all of a sudden, you know that kid has probably been put out of some other school for carrying a weapon."	"If we catch a kid with a weapon . . . we've expelled since I've been the principal here. We've expelled or there has been an expulsion pending on five kids."
	"You have to see each individual case and how it affects their lives. You can't just go out and rule for them."	"So, in other words, if you're hit in the face and your initial reaction as a 16-year-old is to smack this person back, you both will be suspended for 10 days."	"Possession of a weapon, using a weapon, you don't get a second chance."

Case Example

The main advantage of the mapping procedure is that the school can focus on site-specific issues. It also helps clarify why certain problems persist and what the roles of various constituents in reducing violence should be.

SCHOOL A

An elementary school with some 500 students, School A had implemented several conflict management programs; however, the principal and teachers felt that violence was still a chronic problem. After mapping and interviews it became clear that the vast majority of violent events were occurring immediately before and after school on the playground and just outside the school fence.

The school decided to track events every day for a month. It had an average of about 42 fights a week, 92 percent of them occurring in those hot spot locations and times. The ratio of adults to children at these locations ranged from 0:300 to 1:500. Teachers, parents, administrators, and students all agreed that these were areas where school violence problems existed.

This led to very heated discussions about whose role it was to supervise the children. Some teachers felt that parents were dropping their children off 30 or more minutes early and not ensuring that children were going home promptly (many children stayed on or near school grounds 30 minutes or longer). Other teachers felt that their jobs did not entail supervising students before and after school. Some teachers invoked the union contract, which specifically stated the hours, times, and roles of the teachers; they felt that such supervision competed with preparation time.

Over a period of several months the administrator and a small group of teachers and parents devised a system whereby all parties contributed to solve the problem. At a policy level, school staff required parents to drop their children off no earlier than 15 minutes before school started and to pick them up no later than 15 minutes after school ended. Teachers were asked to rotate supervision during those times and were compensated with an equal amount of preparatory time during the school day (this required negotiation with the union). Through the PTA, a group of parents and grandparents volunteered to support the teachers by sending two additional adults to help supervise and engage the children. Events that occurred immediately before and after school were to be dealt with by the child's teacher and school staff just as staff dealt with aggression during school hours.

At the procedural level, School A clarified how to follow up after a violent event. For example, the teachers were to notify parents after a violent event in school. Students were notified of the new policies through formal weekly class discussions with their teachers about violence and through an all-school assembly designed to bring attention to the issue. Students were also encouraged to use the same procedures before and after school as were used during school. Each day a small group of fifth and sixth graders helped in "hot spot" areas before and after school.

The school assembled a list of local afterschool youth programs and encouraged parents not to leave their children unsupervised for long periods of time. Eventually, the school invited a local youth organization to operate an afterschool sports program with school groups. In follow-up assessments, the maps showed that the areas and times had become more secure and the overall average of violent events during a month-long period fell by the end of the school year to 11 fights per week, a reduction of 84 percent.

CONCLUSION

Violence prevention efforts should be directed at the entire school setting. We have suggested an alternative school violence procedure that integrates maps to locate violent "hot spots" in the school and focus groups with students, teachers, school staff, and administrators to identify why violence is occurring in certain places and what to do about it. Information obtained through the mapping process can (1) increase the dialogue between students, teachers, and staff, on school violence; (2) serve to evaluate school violence interventions already in use in a school; and (3) increase school involvement in violence interventions.

A long history of failed school violence interventions points to the hard fact that programs in schools do not work if school staff, teachers, and students are not invested in the intervention. The mapping and interviewing process creates opportunities to generate grassroots interventions to secure the safety of children at school.

REFERENCES

Aber, J. L., Brown, J. L., Chaudry, N., Jones, S., & Samples, F. (1996). The evaluation of the Resolving Conflict Creatively Program: An overview. *American Journal of Preventive Medicine, 12,* 82–90.

American Psychological Association. (1993). *Violence and youth: Psychology's response* (Vol. 1). Washington, DC: Author.

Ash, P., Kellermann, A., Fuqua-Whitley, D., & Johnson, A. (1996). Gun acquisition and use by juvenile offenders. *JAMA, 275,* 1754–1758.

Astor, R. (1998). Moral reasoning about school violence: Informational assumptions about harm within school subcontexts. *Educational Psychologist, 33,* 207–221.

Astor, R., Behre, W., Fravil, K., & Wallace, J. (1997). Perceptions of school violence as a problem and reports of violent events: A national survey of school social workers. *Social Work, 42,* 1–20.

Astor, R., Behre, W., Wallace, J., & Fravil, K. (1998). School social workers and school violence: Personal safety, violence programs, and training. *Social Work, 43,* 223–232.

Astor, R., & Meyer, H. (1998, April). *Making schools safe: A first prerequisite for learning.* Paper presented at the annual meeting of the American Educational Research Association, San Diego.

Astor, R., & Meyer, H. (in press). Where girls and women won't go: Female students', teachers', and school social workers' views of school safety. *Social Work in Education.*

Astor, R., Meyer, H., & Behre, W. (1999). Unowned places and times: Maps and inter-views about violence in high schools. *American Educational Research Journal, 36*, 3–42.

Astor, R. A., Meyer, A., & Pitner, R. (1999). Mapping school violence with students, teachers, and administrators. In L. Davis (Ed.), *African American males: A practice guide* (pp. 129–144). Thousand Oaks, CA: Sage Publications.

Astor, R., Pitner, R., & Duncan, B. (1996). Ecological approaches to mental health con-sultation with teachers on issues related to youth and school violence. *Journal of Negro Education, 65*, 336–355.

Batsche, G., & Knoff, A. (1994). Bullies and their victims: Understanding a pervasive problem in the schools. *School Psychology Review, 23*, 165–174.

Beauboeuf, T. (Ed.). (1995). Violence and youth [Special issue]. *Harvard Educational Review, 65*.

Berrill, K. (1990). Anti-gay violence and victimization in the U.S.: An overview [Special issue, *Violence Against Lesbians and Gay Men: Issues for Research, Practice, and Policy*]. *Journal of Interpersonal Violence, 5*, 274–294.

Bierman, K., Cole, J., Dodge, K., Greenberg, M., Lochman, J., & McMahon, R. (1992). A developmental and clinical model for the prevention of conduct disorder: The FAST Track Program. *Development and Psychopathology, 4*, 509–527.

Blumstein, A. (1995, August). Violence by young people: Why the deadly nexus? *National Institute of Justice Journal, 2*–9.

Boulton, M. (1993). Aggressive fighting in British middle school children. *Educational Studies, 19*, 19–39.

Bragg, R. (1997, December 3). Forgiveness, after 3 die in Kentucky shooting; M. Carneal opens fire on fellow students at Heath High School in West Paducah. *New York Times*, p. A16.

Brick, J., Collins, M., Nolin, P., Ha, M., Levinsohn, M., & Chandler, K. (1994). *National Household Education Survey of 1993, School Safety and Discipline Data File User's Manual* (NCES 94–193). Washington, DC: U.S. Government Printing Office.

Brooke, J. (1999, April 21). Two youths in Colorado school said to gun down as many as 23 and kill themselves in a siege. *New York Times*, p. A1.

Burcky, W., Reuterman, N., & Kopsky, S. (1988). Dating violence among high school students. *School Counselor, 35*, 353–358.

Cano, A., Avery-Leaf, S., Cascardi, M., & O'Leary, K. (1998). Dating violence in two high school samples: Discriminating variables. *Journal of Primary Prevention, 18*, 431–446.

Caplan, M., Weissburg, R. P., Grober, J. S., Sivo, P. J., Grady, K., & Jacoby, C. (1992). Social competence promotion with inner city and suburban young adolescents: Effects on social adjustment and alcohol use. *Journal of Consulting and Clinical Psychology, 60*, 56–63.

Carins, R., Carins, B., & Neckerman, H. (1989). Early school dropout: Configurations and determinants. *Child Development, 60*, 1437–1452.

Centers for Disease Control and Prevention. (1998). Youth risk behavior surveillance— United States, 1997. *Morbidity and Mortality Weekly Report, 47*. SS-3. U.S. Department of Health and Human Services, Washington, DC: Author.

Coben, J., Weiss, H. B., & Mulvey, E. P. (1994). A primer on school violence preven-tion. *Journal of School Health, 64*, 309–313.

Committee for Children. (1992). *Second step: A violence prevention curriculum (preschool-kindergarten teacher's guide).* Seattle: Author.

Dodge, K. (1993, March). *Effects of intervention on children at high risk for conduct problems.* Paper presented at the meeting of the Society for Research in Child Development, New Orleans.

Dwyer, K., Osher, D., & Warger, C. (1998). *Early warning, timely response: A guide to safe schools.* Washington, DC: U.S. Department of Education.

Earls, F. (1994). Violence and today's youth. *Critical Issues for Children and Youth, 4,* 4–23.

Elam, S., & Rose, L. (1995). The 27th annual Phi Delta Kappa/Gallup poll of the public's attitudes toward the public schools. *Phi Delta Kappan, 77,* 41–56.

Elam, S., Rose, L., & Gallup, A. (1994). The 26th annual Phi Delta Kappa/Gallup poll of the public's attitudes toward the public schools. *Phi Delta Kappan, 76,* 41–56.

Elam, S., Rose, L., & Gallup, A. (1996). The 28th annual Phi Delta Kappa/Gallup poll of the public's attitudes toward the public schools. *Phi Delta Kappan, 78,* 41–59.

Embry, D., Flannery, D., Vazsonyi, A., Powell, K., & Atha, H. (1996). Peace Builders: A theoretically driven, school-based model for early violence prevention. *American Journal of Preventive Medicine, 12,* 91–100.

Fagan, J., & Wilkinson, D. L. (1998). Social contexts and functions of adolescent violence. In D. S. Elliot, B. Hamburg, & K. R. William (Eds.), *Violence in American schools: A new perspective* (pp. 55–93). New York: Cambridge University Press.

Farrington, D. (1991). Childhood aggression and adult violence: Early precursors and later life outcomes. In D. Pepler & K. Rubins (Eds.), *The development and treatment of childhood aggression* (pp. 5–31). Hillsdale, NJ: Lawrence Erlbaum.

Feindler, E., & Ecton, R. (1986). *Adolescent anger control: Cognitive-behavioral techniques.* New York: Pergamon Press.

Felner, R., & Adan, A. (1988). The school transitional environment project: An ecological intervention and evaluation. In R. Price, E. Cowen, R. Lorion, & J. Ramos-McKay (Eds.), *14 ounces of prevention: A casebook for practitioners* (pp. 111–122). Washington, DC: American Psychological Association.

Flannery, D. (1996). *Longitudinal follow up of PeaceBuilders.* Atlanta: Centers for Disease Control and Prevention.

Flannery, D. (1998). *Improving school violence prevention programs through meaningful evaluation.* New York: ERIC Clearinghouse on Urban Education, Institute for Urban and Minority Education, Teachers College, Columbia University.

Flannery, D. & Vazsonyi, A. (1996). *PeaceBuilders: A school-based model for early violence prevention.* Chicago: American Society of Criminology.

Flaxman, E., Schwartz, W., Weiler, J., & Lahey, M. (1998). *Trends and issues in urban education, 1998* [Online]. (Available: http://eric-web.tc.columbia.edu/monographs/ti20)

Fraser, M. (1996). Aggressive behavior in childhood and early adolescence: An ecological developmental perspective on youth violence. *Social Work, 41,* 347–361.

Freeman, E. (Ed.). (1995). Violence in schools [Special ed.]. *Social Work in Education, 17*(2).

Frude, N., & Gault, H. (1984). *Disruptive behavior in the schools.* Chichester, NY: Wiley.

Fuller, G. (Ed.). (1998). Addressing youth anger and aggression in school settings [Special issue]. *Psychology in the Schools, 35*(3).

Furlong, M., & Morrison, G. (1994). Introduction to mini-series: School violence and safety in perspective. *School Psychology Review, 23,* 139–150.

Furlong, M., Morrison, R., Bates, M., & Chung, A. (1998). School violence victimization among secondary students in California: Grade, gender, and racial-ethnic group incidence patterns. *California School Psychologist, 3,* 71–87.

Gegax, T., Adler, J., & Pedersen, D. (1998, April 6). The boys behind the ambush. *Newsweek, 131,* 21–24.

Goldstein, A. (1996). *The psychology of vandalism.* New York: Plenum Press.

Goldstein, A., & Conoley, J. (Eds.). (1997). *School violence intervention: A practical handbook.* New York: Guilford Press.

Goldstein, A., Glick, B., Reiner, S., Zimmerman, D., & Coultry, T. (1985). *Aggression replacement training: A comprehensive intervention for aggressive youth.* Champaign, IL: Research Press.

Gottfredson, G. (1985). *Victimization in schools.* New York: Plenum Press.

Gottfredson, D. (1990). Changing school structures to benefit high-risk youths. In P. E. Leone (Ed.), *Understanding troubled and troubling youth* (pp. 246–271). Newbury Park, CA: Sage Publications.

Gottfredson, D. (1997). School based crime prevention. In L. Sherman, D. Gottfredson, D. MacKenzie, J. Eck, P. Reuter, & S. Bushway (Eds.), *Preventing crime: What works, what doesn't, what's promising: A report to the United States Congress.* Washington, DC: U.S. Department of Justice.

Gottfredson, D., Fink, C., Skroban, S., & Gottfredson, G. (in press). Making prevention work. In R. P. Weissburg (Ed.), *Issues in Children's and Families' Lives (Volume 4): Healthy Children 2010: School- and Community-based Strategies to Enhance Social, Emotional and Physical Wellness.*

Gray, D. (1991). *The plight of the African American male: An executive summary of a legislative hearing.* Detroit: Council President Pro Tem Gil, the Detroit City Council Youth Advisory Commission.

Grossman, D., Neckerman, H., Koespell, T., Liu, P., Asher, K., Beland, K., Frey, K., & Rivara, F. (1997). Effectiveness of a violence prevention curriculum among children in elementary school. *JAMA, 277,* 1605–1611.

Guerra, N., & Panizzon, A. (1986). *Viewpoints training program.* Santa Barbara, CA: Center for Law-Related Education.

Hammond, R., & Yung, B. (1991). Preventing violence in at-risk African American youth. *Journal of Health Care for the Poor and Underserved, 2,* 358–372.

Hammond, R., & Yung, B. (1993). Psychology's role in the public health response to assaultive violence among young African-American men. *American Psychologist, 48,* 142–154.

Harrington-Lueker, D. (1992). Blown away. *American School Board Journal, 179,* 20–26.

Hays, K. (1998, April 26). Boy held in teacher's killing. *Detroit News & Free Press,* p. 5A.

Heaviside, S., Rowand, C., Williams, C., & Farris, E. (1998). *Violence and discipline problems in U. S. public schools: 1996–1997* (NCES 98-030). Washington, DC: U.S. Department of Education, National Center for Educational Statistics.

Hellman, D. A., & Beaton, S. (1986). The pattern of violence in urban public schools: The influence of school and community. *Journal of Research in Crime and Delinquency, 23,* 102–107.

Hudley, C., Britsch, B., Wakefield, T., Demorat, M., & Cho, S. (1998). An attribution retraining program to reduce aggression in elementary school students. *Psychology in the Schools, 35,* 271–282.

Huesmann, L., Eron, L., Lefkowitz, M., & Walder, L. (1984). Stability of aggression over time and generations. *Developmental Psychology, 20,* 1120–1134.

Issacs, M. (1992). *Violence: The impact of community violence on African-American children and families: Collaborative approaches to prevention and intervention.* Arlington, VA: National Center for Education in Maternal and Child Health.

Johnson, S. (Ed.). (1996). A Howard University quarterly review of issues incident to the education of Black people: Educating children in a violent society, Part 1 [Special issue]. *Journal of Negro Education, 65*(3).

Kachur, P., Stennies, G., Powell, K., Modzeleski, W., Stephens, R., Murphy, R., Kresnow, M., Sleet, D., & Lowry, R. (1996). School-associated violent deaths in the United States, 1992 to 1994. *JAMA, 275,* 1729–1733.

Kaufman, P., Chen, X., Choy, S., Chandler, K., Chapman, C., Rand, M., & Ringel, C. (1998). *Indicators of school crime and safety, 1998.* NCES 98-251/NCJ-172215. Washington, DC: U.S. Departments of Education and Justice.

Kodluboy, D. (1997). Gang-oriented interventions. In A. Goldstein (Ed.), *School violence intervention: A practical handbook* (pp. 189–214). New York: Guilford Press.

Larson, J. (1998). Managing student aggression in high schools: Implications for practice. *Psychology in the Schools, 35,* 283–295.

Laub, J., & Lauritsen, J. (1998). The interdependence of school violence with neighborhood and family conditions. In D. S. Elliott, B. Hamburg, & K. R. Williams (Eds.), *Violence in American schools: A new perspective* (pp. 127–155). New York: Cambridge University Press.

Lee, V., & Croninger, R. (1995, December). *The social organization of safe high schools.* Paper presented at the Goals 2000, Reauthorization of the Elementary and Secondary Education Act, and the School-to-Work Opportunities Act Conference, Palm Beach, FL.

Lochman, J., Lampron, L., Gemmer, T., & Harris, S. (1986). Anger coping intervention with aggressive children: A guide to implementation in school settings. In P. Keller & S. Heyman (Eds.), *Innovations in clinical practice: A source book* (Vol. 6, pp. 339–356). Sarasota, FL: Professional Resources Exchange.

Loeber, R., & Stouthamer-Loeber, M. (1986). Family factors as correlates and predictors of juvenile conduct problems and delinquency. In N. Morris & M. Tonry (Eds.), *Crime and justice: An annual review of research* (Vol. 7, pp. 9–149). Chicago: University of Chicago Press.

Metropolitan Life Insurance Company & Harris Poll. (1993–1994). *The Metropolitan Life Survey of the American teacher 1993–1994.* New York: Authors.

Meyers, J. (Ed.). (1996). School violence [Special issue]. *Journal of School Psychology, 36* (1).

Milwaukee Board of School Directors. (1993). *An evaluation of the Second Step Violence Prevention Curriculum for elementary students.* Milwaukee: Author.

Moffitt, T. (1993). Life-course-persistent and adolescent-limited antisocial behavior: A developmental taxonomy. *Psychological Review, 100,* 674–701.

Morrison, G., Furlong, M., & Morrison, R. (1997). In A. Goldstein & J. Conoley (Eds.), *School violence intervention: A practical handbook* (pp. 236–264). New York: Guilford Press.

National Education Goals Panel. (1995). *The National Education Goals Report: Volume I: National Data: Volume II: State Data.* Washington, DC: U.S. Government Printing Office.

National Institute of Education & U.S. Department of Health, Education and Welfare. (1978). *Violent schools—safe schools: The Safe School Study report to Congress* (No. 1). Washington, DC: U.S. Government Printing Office.

National Research Council. (1993). *Understanding and preventing violence.* Washington, DC: National Academy Press.

Olweus, D. (1980). Familial and temperamental determinants of aggressive behavior in adolescent boys: A causal analysis. *Developmental Psychology, 16,* 644–660.

Olweus, D. (1993). *Bullying at school.* Oxford, England: Blackwell.

Olweus, D. (1996). Bully/victim problems at school: Facts and effective intervention. *Reclaiming Children and Youth: Journal of Emotional and Behavioral Problems, 5,* 15–22.

Page, R. (1997). Helping adolescents avoid date rape: The role of secondary education. *High School Journal, 80,* 75–80.

Parks, C. (1995). Gang behavior in the schools: Reality or myth? *Educational Psychology Review, 7,* 41–68.

Patterson, G., Reid, J., & Dishion, T. (1992). *Antisocial boys.* Eugene, OR: Castilla.

Pittel, E. (1998). How to take a weapons history: Interviewing children at risk for violence at school. *Journal of the American Academy of Child & Adolescent Psychiatry, 37,* 1100–1102.

Prothrow-Stith, D. (1987). *Violence prevention curriculum for adolescents.* Newton, MA: Education Development Center, Inc.

Prothrow-Stith, D., & Weissman, M. (1991). *Deadly consequences.* New York: HarperCollins.

Rigby, K. (1996). *Bullying in schools: And what to do about it.* Melbourne, Australia: Australian Council for Educational Research.

Rose, L., Gallup, A., & Elam, S. (1997). The 29th annual Phi Delta Kappa/Gallup poll of the public's attitudes toward the public schools. *Phi Delta Kappan, 79,* 41–56.

Samples, F., & Aber, L. (1998). Evaluations of school-based violence prevention programs. In D. S. Elliott, B. Hamburg, & K. Williams (Eds.), *Violence in American schools: A new perspective* (pp. 217–252). New York: Cambridge University Press.

Schafer, M., & Smith, P. (1996). Teacher's perceptions of play fighting and real fighting in primary school. *Educational Research, 38,* 173–181.

Schweinhart, L., Barnes, H., & Weikart, D. (1993). Significant benefits of the High/Scope Perry preschool study through age 27. *Monographs of the High/Scope Educational Research Foundation* (No. 10).

Shapiro, E. (Ed.). (1994). School violence [Special issue miniseries]. *School Psychology Review, 23*(2).

Sharp, S., & Smith, P. (1994). *Tackling bullying in your school: A practical handbook for teachers.* London: Routledge.

Smith, P., & Sharp, S. (1994). *School bullying.* London: Routledge.

Stein, N. (1995). Sexual harassment in the school: The public performance of gendered violence. *Harvard Educational Review, 65,* 145–162.

Thompson, D., & Jason, L. (1988). Street gangs and preventive intervention. *Criminal Justice and Behavior, 15,* 323–333.

Toby, J. (1994). Everyday school violence: How disorder fuels it. *American Educator, 17,* 44–48.

Tolan, P., & Guerra, N. (1994). Prevention of delinquency: Current status and issues. *Applied and Preventive Psychology, 3,* 251–273.

Walker, H. M., Colvin, G., & Ramsey, E. (1995). *Anti-social behavior in school: Strategies and best practices.* Pacific Grove, CA: Brooks/Cole.

Walker, H. M., & Gresham, F. M. (1997). Making schools safer and violence free. *Intervention in School and Clinic, 32,* 199–204.

Webster, D. (1993). The unconvincing case for school based conflict resolution programs for adolescents. *Health Affairs, 4,* 126–141.

Witkin, G., Tharp, M., Schrof, J., Toch, T., & Scattarella, C. (1998, June 1). Again. In Springfield, a familiar school scene: Bloody kids, grieving parents, a teen accused of murder. *U.S. News & World Report, 124,* 16–21.

Youssef, R., Attia, M., & Kamel, M. (1998). Children experiencing violence II: Prevalence and determinants of corporal punishment in schools. *Child Abuse & Neglect, 22,* 975–985.

Yung, B., & Hammond, R. (1998). Breaking the cycle: A culturally sensitive violence prevention program for African-American children. In L. Lutzker (Ed.), *Handbook of child abuse research and treatments* (pp. 319–340). New York: Plenum Press.

Chapter 7

Adolescent Substance Abuse and Youth Violence

James R. Moran and Jeffrey M. Jenson

E xamples of violent youth behavior involving alcohol or illicit drug use are numerous in American society. A recent celebration following a major sporting event illustrates the complexity of the combination of alcohol or drug use and violence among the nation's youths. After the 1999 Super Bowl victory by the Denver Broncos, television viewers were greeted with scenes of armed police officers marching in formation down the city streets of Denver. After the big game the streets had filled with young people celebrating the victory. Newspaper stands were tipped over in the streets and the papers used as fuel for bonfires. Clouds of tear gas swirled around the police as they attempted to disperse a crowd of several hundred excited youths. Violence erupted, causing broken shop windows and overturned cars. The newscast ended with video clips of youths in gas masks hurling tear gas containers at police officers.

What were the components of the event? First, the crowd was composed of young people, mostly male. Second, many people had been drinking, and some were intoxicated. Third, the crowd turned violent when confronted by police. Finally, some members of the crowd had had the forethought to bring gas masks to the celebration. The newsclips also vividly demonstrate the image that much of the public has of this issue, namely, that drinking and drug use leads to or causes youth violence.

In this chapter we examine the relationship between substance use and violence. After a brief review of the prevalence of adolescent substance use and violent conduct, we identify substance abuse factors related to violence among adolescents and discuss how the relationship between substance abuse and violence is interpreted. We identify common risk factors for substance abuse and violence and explore appropriate interventions. A case example illustrates clinical issues in treating drug-abusing violent youths, and promising prevention and treatment approaches are identified.

PREVALENCE OF ADOLESCENT SUBSTANCE ABUSE AND YOUTH VIOLENCE

Substance abuse and violence among youths are serious public health problems in the United States. Despite a minimum legal drinking age of 21, many American children and adolescents use alcohol and illicit drugs. For some, drug use leads to involvement in serious delinquency and violence.

Violence

Recent trends in the prevalence of violent conduct in children and adolescents are reviewed in chapter 1. To summarize, rates of self- and police-reported violence among youths increased significantly in the late 1980s and early 1990s (Elliott, 1994). After more than a decade of stability, juvenile violent crime arrest rates increased 71 percent between 1987 and 1994 (Snyder, 1997). The number of homicides committed by juveniles tripled between 1983 and the early 1990s (Coordinating Council on Juvenile Justice and Delinquency Prevention, 1996). An increase in juvenile gangs and in drug-related crime has been suggested as the reason for the jump (Howell, Krisberg, & Jones, 1995).

Recent Federal Bureau of Investigation arrest statistics provide some basis for optimism concerning juvenile violence, however. Juvenile arrests for violent crimes decreased 4 percent in 1995, and similar declines have been reported each year since (U.S. Department of Justice, 1997). However, despite these recent decreases, rates of violence among American youths remain unacceptably high.

Substance Abuse

One important source of knowledge about the prevalence of adolescent substance use is the annual Monitoring the Future Study conducted at the University of Michigan (Johnston, O'Malley, & Bachman, 1997). Johnston and colleagues have assessed current (30-day), annual, and lifetime alcohol and illicit drug use among representative samples of American junior and senior high school youths each year since 1975.

Illicit drugs include marijuana, inhalants, hallucinogens, cocaine or crack, heroin or other opiates, and nonprescription barbiturates, stimulants, or tranquilizers. Some 50,000 students in 422 public and private schools were surveyed in 1998: 18,700 eighth graders, 15,400 10th graders, and 15,800 12th graders (Johnston, O'Malley, & Bachman, 1998).

There are limitations to the survey methods employed by Johnston and colleagues (1997). First, the survey relies on self-reports by adolescents. Although self-reported data may result in more sensitive, direct, and complete information about adolescent substance abuse, respondents may not remember events that included substance use, or they may conceal or exaggerate their substance use. Second, because the study sample consists of currently enrolled students, it misses adolescents who have dropped out of school, who have been found to use alcohol and illicit drugs at higher levels than enrolled students. Finally, estimates of drug and alcohol use among minority groups may also be affected because more American Indians and Hispanics drop out of school than African Americans, Asian Americans, or Caucasians (Wallace & Bachman, 1991).

Twelfth-grade students. Lifetime illicit drug use peaked among seniors in 1981, when 66 percent of 12th graders reported having used an illicit drug at least once in their lives, and 43 percent reported having used an illicit drug other than marijuana. Lifetime use of illicit drugs reached its lowest point in 1992: 41 percent of seniors had used an illicit drug, and 25 percent had used an illicit drug other than marijuana. In 1993 seniors reversed a decade-long pattern of declining illicit drug use: 43 percent had used an illicit drug, and 27 percent had used an illicit drug other than marijuana. Lifetime illicit drug use then increased each year between 1993 and 1997, when 54 percent of seniors reported using an illicit drug, and 29 percent reported using an illicit drug other than marijuana. Rates of illicit drug use fell slightly in 1998 (from 54.3 percent in 1997 to 54.1 percent in 1998). Figure 7-1 shows the lifetime prevalence of illicit drug use for 12th graders between 1975 and 1998.

Lifetime alcohol use by seniors peaked in the late 1970s and early 1980s. Approximately 93 percent of seniors reported lifetime alcohol use in annual assessments between 1977 and 1984. Lifetime prevalence of alcohol use decreased between 1985 and 1993, when 87 percent of seniors had used alcohol. Because the question assessing lifetime alcohol use was changed in 1994 to indicate that experimentation with alcohol meant "more than a few sips" (Johnston et al., 1998), comparisons of lifetime alcohol prevalence rates before and after 1993 must be interpreted cautiously. As measured by the new question, lifetime alcohol use for seniors has remained between 80 percent and 81 percent since 1994.

In 1998, 52 percent of seniors reported drinking alcohol, 23 percent reported using marijuana, and 4 percent reported using hallucinogens during

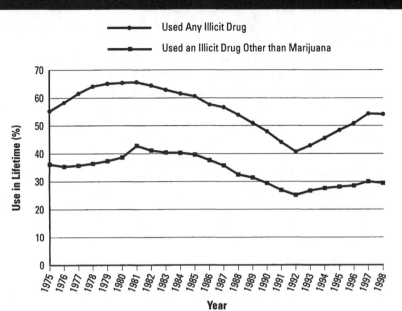

Figure 7-1. **Lifetime Prevalence of Illicit Drug Use by Twelfth Graders, 1975–1998**

the previous month; 4 percent of high school seniors reported using alcohol and 6 percent reported using marijuana daily in 1998.

Eighth-grade students. Drug use prevalence among younger students is important because alcohol and drug use by young adolescents may be a precursor of drug use trends among future high school students. Awareness of drug use prevalence among eighth graders may also inform the content and direction of prevention and treatment programs.

In 1998, 53 percent of adolescents had used alcohol by the eighth grade, 25 percent had been drunk at least once, 20 percent had tried inhalants, and 22 percent had smoked marijuana. Lifetime prevalence of marijuana use increased significantly between 1993 and 1998, whereas alcohol use decreased (Figure 7-2). In 1998, 10 percent of eighth graders had used marijuana during the previous month, 5 percent had used inhalants, and 23 percent had drunk alcohol.

These data suggest that use of alcohol, inhalants, and marijuana is common among the nation's 13- and 14-year-olds. Longitudinal studies of drug use among youths indicate that many who experiment with these drugs proceed to drugs such as hallucinogens, cocaine, amphetamines, and heroin

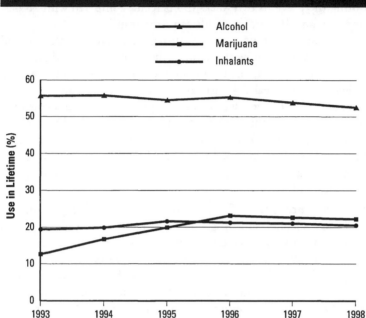

Figure 7-2.   **Lifetime Prevalence of Use of Alcohol, Marijuana, and Inhalants by Eighth Graders, 1993–1998**

(Dielman, 1995; Grant & Dawson, 1997; Kandel, Simcha-Fagan, & Davies, 1986; Loeber, 1990). Thus, a substantial number of eighth graders may be at risk for continued drug use.

Differences by gender and ethnicity. Earlier studies indicated that substance use was more prevalent among adolescent males than among females (Johnston, O'Malley, & Bachman, 1985). Recent results from Monitoring the Future surveys show a decrease in gender differences. Female high school seniors are more likely than male high school seniors to use amphetamines, and they use alcohol and marijuana at nearly the same rates as male seniors. Males continue to be more involved in heavy drinking and drunk driving than females (Johnston et al., 1998).

Alcohol and drug use apparently is more prevalent among Caucasian than African American or Hispanic high school seniors (Johnston et al., 1998). In 1997 the annual prevalence of marijuana use was 30 percent for African Americans, 36 percent for Hispanics, and 39 percent for Caucasians. Caucasians also had the highest annual prevalence of alcohol use (78 percent, compared with 73 percent for Hispanics and 60 percent for African Americans). Caucasians were also more likely to have had five or more drinks in a row during the previous two weeks (35 percent, compared with 28 percent of Hispanics and 13 percent of African Americans).

Differences among ethnic groups with regard to rates of alcohol and drug use should be interpreted with caution. African American and Hispanic inner-city youths, particularly males, are often underrepresented in national surveys. Other sources reveal that African American men account for one-third of admissions to emergency rooms for drug-related episodes (Institute of Medicine, 1990) and that substance abuse rates are highest among Hispanic men (Anthony, 1991). Evidence also indicates that American Indian youths, a group not included in annual Monitoring the Future surveys, consume more alcohol and use more drugs than any other racial or ethnic group (Institute of Medicine, 1990).

Summary of prevalence studies. These research results reflect important patterns in adolescent alcohol and drug use. First, national surveys of youths enrolled in school showed a decrease in the prevalence of most drug use between 1981 and 1992, suggesting that prevention efforts and social norms favoring drug abstinence during the 1980s may have had positive effects on reducing adolescent alcohol and drug use. Second, increases in illicit drug use between 1993 and 1997 reverse a decade-long pattern of decreasing substance use among the nation's youths. Despite the improvements of the 1980s, U.S. secondary school students in the 1990s use drugs more than students in any other industrialized nation (Johnston et al., 1998). Third, disparities in alcohol and drug use between males and females have decreased. Finally, substance use appears to be more prevalent among Caucasians and American Indians than among Hispanics and African Americans.

SUBSTANCE ABUSE AND VIOLENT BEHAVIOR

Investigations targeting adults suggest that violent offenses are often committed when an offender or a victim has been drinking alcohol or using illicit drugs. Alcohol use is present in one-third to three-fourths of all sexual assaults (Collins & Messerschmidt, 1993) and in one-fourth to one-half of all reported incidents of domestic violence (Leonard, 1993). In a national study of adult violent offenders, Goldstein (1989) reported that approximately 10 percent of homicides and assaults were the result of drug use. H. R. White (1997) found that approximately one-half of prison inmates had committed a property or violent crime under the influence of alcohol, drugs, or both.

A similar association of substance abuse and violence is evident among adolescents. Adolescent alcohol and drug use and seriousness of antisocial behavior have been shown to be positively related: As the frequency of drug use increases, so does the seriousness of antisocial conduct (see, for example, Elliott, Huizinga, & Menard, 1989; Fagan, Weis, & Chang, 1990; Johnson, Wish, Schmeidler, & Huizinga, 1991). Recent results from the Office of Juvenile Justice and Delinquency Prevention Program of Research on Causes and Correlates of Delinquency corroborate such findings. Violent youths in study samples in Rochester, Pittsburgh, and Denver were significantly more likely than other serious delinquents to abuse alcohol and marijuana (Huizinga & Jakob-Chien, 1998; Loeber, Van Kammen, Krohn, & Huizinga, 1991; Thornberry, Huizinga, & Loeber, 1995).

What is not clear from such studies, however, is *how* substance use and violence are related. What is the relationship between substance use and violence? Examining this question may inform the direction of interventions with adolescents displaying drug-using and violent behaviors.

Reciprocal Nature of Substance Use and Violence

Several interpretations have been forwarded to explain the relationship between drug use and crime. Some investigators (Akers, 1984; Blumstein, 1995) have suggested that participation in one behavior directly leads to participation in the other. In other words, the use of drugs or alcohol may lead to violent behavior or, conversely, violent behavior may lead to drug or alcohol use. This explanation also allows for the possibility of a reciprocal relationship between the two behaviors, with substance abuse and violent behavior mutually reinforcing one another.

H. R. White (1997) argued that the psychological and physical effects of alcohol directly contribute to aggressive tendencies, while acknowledging that the violent conditions characterizing the illegal drug market can lead to aggression and violence among drug users.

Goldstein (1985) thought that drug use and violence can be explained by economic and broad systemic motivational factors. His economic motivation model assumes that drug users engage in violent crime to generate income to buy illicit drugs. In his systemic model, Goldstein (1985) proposed that illicit drug distribution—characterized by organizational and territorial conflicts and by crimes such as robbery—leads directly to violent behavior. Fagan and Chin (1990) agreed that a systemic explanation of drug use and crime may account for a significant portion of drug-related violence among inner-city youths. However, most research addressing economic and systemic explanations of drug use and crime has been based on adult heroin addicts (for example, Chaiken & Chaiken, 1990). Only a small percentage of youths use heroin, and economic and systematic explanatory models may not apply to many adolescents.

Other investigators (for example, Pernanen, 1991; Phil & Peterson, 1993) have contended that effects of substance abuse and intoxication—

such as cognitive–behavioral distortions, poor judgment, attention deficits, and neurochemical changes—cause aggressive behavior. There is empirical support for this view, particularly for alcohol use. Investigators have found that consuming alcohol limits or distorts the processing of cues that normally direct behavior. For example, Pernanen (1991) found that alcohol's adverse effects on speech, eye movement, facial expressions, and motor coordination caused impairments in information processing and communication that often led to interpersonal misunderstandings and aggressive behavior. Alcohol has also been shown to reduce fear of retaliation, increase arousal, distort judgment, and reduce capacity to pay attention (Phil & Peterson, 1993).

Such psychopharmacological explanations help us understand at least part of the relationship between adolescent substance abuse and aggression (see, for example, Pernanen, 1991). For example, one accepted consequence of substance use is disinhibition, the idea that when one is intoxicated the factors that normally inhibit one from violating norms of society—norms that include not engaging in violent behavior—are suspended. MacAndrew and Edgerton (1969) refer to this as a *time out* period. Many people in the United States concur with the belief that alcohol and other drug use leads to aggressive behavior and that being drunk reduces one's degree of personal accountability (Lang, 1993). However, this proposition has not been adequately tested with adolescents.

Social norms relating to substance use and violent behavior have also been considered important explanatory factors in the causal relationship between drugs and crime. Fagan (1990) describes cultures in which heavy drinking almost always results in violent behavior (for example, the Lapps of Finland) and cultures where heavy drinking seldom leads to violence (for example, the Camba tribe of Bolivia). He suggests that the relationship between substance abuse and violence is mediated by culture and environment and questions the ability of existing pharmacological models to adequately explain the relationship between heavy drinking and violence in the absence of cultural factors.

The temporal order of substance use and violence must also be considered. One might logically assume that if substance abuse leads to or causes violent behavior, it must occur before the violence. Analyses examining these temporal relationships require longitudinal research methodologies that measure onset and frequency of each behavior over time. Unfortunately, longitudinal studies that have examined substance abuse and youth violence have produced somewhat inconsistent results. Using data from the National Longitudinal Youth Survey, Windle (1990) found that early substance use predicted later adolescent substance abuse and alcohol-related aggression. He also found that antisocial behaviors, including fighting, threatening to hit someone, and physically attacking someone during early adolescence, predicted alcohol and drug use during later adolescence. Thus, Windle's analyses (1990) suggested that for some youths, violent behavior occurred before substance abuse.

In a longitudinal study of incarcerated youths in Florida, Dembo, Williams, Fagan, and Schmeidler (1993) found results different from those reported by Windle (1990). Interviewing juvenile detainees at the time of their admission to a detention center and again 11 to 14 months later, Dembo and colleagues (1993) found that early alcohol use was the only significant predictor of later violent behavior. Yet in a longitudinal study of high-risk youths at ages 12, 15, and 18, H. R. White, Brick, and Hansell (1993) found that early violent behavior led to increases in alcohol use, whereas early alcohol use had no influence on later violence.

In general, then, investigations of the priority of substance abuse or violent behavior partially support the explanation that one behavior leads to the other. However, which behavior comes first varies across studies. Osgood (1994) suggested that social policies addressing drug use and crime in the United States have historically been based on a belief that drug use leads directly to involvement in crime. He stated, "Americans widely share the belief that drugs are a destructive force that generates other problems, with violence prominent among them" (p. 1). Although this belief is appealing in its simplicity and reinforced by events such as the street riot after the 1999 Super Bowl, our review indicates that the relationship between drug use and violence is far more complex.

A second interpretation of the relationship between drug use and violence suggests that both behaviors stem from common causal factors. In other words, rather than one behavior causing the other, substance abuse and violence may be the result of a shared set of causes. Evidence supporting this proposition is reviewed next.

Common Risk Factors for Substance Abuse and Violence

In earlier research, Johnston, O'Malley, and Eveland (1978) and Elliott, Huizinga, and Ageton (1985) concluded that common predictors such as drug-using peers and parental involvement in antisocial behavior explained the onset of and the relationship between delinquency and illicit drug use. Jessor and Jessor (1977) and Donovan and Jessor (1985) proposed that these and other similar variables explained a wide range of adolescent deviant behaviors, including substance abuse and violence. Similarly, Hirschi's (1969) proposition that the absence of prosocial bonds leads to antisocial behavior acknowledged the contribution of shared risk factors to a variety of deviant behaviors. In a more recent investigation, Osgood (1994) used a concept called the *generality of delinquency* to explain a variety of outcomes, including substance abuse and violence, among youths interviewed in the

Monitoring the Future studies (Johnston et al., 1998). He concluded that substance abuse and violent behavior were part of a set of deviant behaviors, all of which had common causes.

A preponderance of evidence suggests that substance abuse and violence share many common risk factors. There is also evidence that the greater the number of risk factors present, the greater the likelihood of substance use or violence (Ellis, 1998). Several investigators have summarized shared risk factors for substance use and delinquency; readers are encouraged to examine these reports for more comprehensive reviews (Dahlberg, 1998; Dryfoos, 1990; Earls, 1994; Elliott et al., 1985; Fagan, 1990; Hawkins, Arthur, & Olson, 1997; Hawkins, Catalano, & Miller, 1992; Hawkins et al., 1998; Hawkins, Jenson, Catalano, & Lishner, 1988; Jenson, 1997; Johnston et al., 1978; Newcomb & Bentler, 1988). Table 7-1 provides a summary of common risk factors for substance abuse by individual, family, school, peer group, and community domains.

CLINICAL ISSUES IN TREATING VIOLENT AND DRUG-ABUSING YOUTHS

Risk factors provide important clues for the design of effective interventions to combat substance use and violence. However, knowledge of risk factors alone does not address the many clinical issues associated with treating these behaviors. Challenges in assessing and treating violent youths who use drugs are discussed below, along with promising treatments.

Table 7-1. **Common Risk Factors for Substance Abuse and Violence among Adolescents by Domain**

Individual	Family	School	Peer Group	Community
• Low birth weight • Prenatal drug exposure • Hyperactivity • Lack of impulse control • Sensation seeking • Rebelliousness • Early initiation of antisocial behavior • Favorable attitudes toward delinquency and drug use	• Lack of supervision • Harsh or inconsistent discipline • Low family attachment • Family conflict • Family history of antisocial behavior • Favorable parental attitudes toward substance use and violence	• Early and persistent antisocial behavior • Academic failure • Low commitment to school	• Association with peers who engage in substance use, delinquency, and violence	• Neighborhood social disorganization • High rates of mobility • Economic deprivation • Availability of drugs or firearms • Permissive laws • Lax enforcement of laws • Norms favorable to antisocial behavior

Assessment of Substance Abuse and Youth Violence

The co-occurrence of substance abuse and violence poses unique assessment challenges. Chapter 3 identifies valuable tools for assessing violent tendencies among adolescents. However, practitioners may need additional assessment tools as they strive to understand the relationship between substance abuse and violent behavior in adolescent clients. Several instruments are considered below (see also Martin and Winters, 1998, for a more comprehensive review of assessment tools).

Assessment instruments. An understanding of the severity of a client's substance use is critical for practitioners working with drug-involved and violent youths. Fortunately, a variety of diagnostic tools is available to assess substance use among adolescents. Martin and Winters (1998) suggest that all assessments should include an evaluation of both lifetime and recent drug use, age at onset of drug use, persistence of use, and related problems such as family, peer, and school experiences.

Several diagnostic instruments are reliable indicators of drug and alcohol problems among youths (Martin & Winters, 1998). The Personal Experience Screening Questionnaire (PESQ), used to assess problem severity of alcohol and drug use, contains recommended cutoff scores for further assessment (Winters, 1992). The PESQ has been validated among juvenile offenders, suggesting that it may be particularly appropriate for youths with both drug use and violent tendencies. The Substance Abuse Subtle Screening Inventory (SASSI) is widely used in juvenile justice settings to assess alcohol and drug use among adolescent offenders (Miller, 1985). The SASSI produces clinical scores for alcohol and drug problems, one of them a score for the tendency of clients to deny problems associated with substance use.

Assessment tools for adolescents typically focus on single problems, such as substance use, aggression, or mental health functioning. However, the Problem Oriented Screening Instrument for Teenagers (POSIT) (Rahdert, 1991) was developed to assess 10 adolescent behaviors, including substance use, family relations, mental health, delinquency, and aggressive behavior. The POSIT establishes clinical criteria for each of the 10 problem areas and has been successfully implemented in juvenile justice programs (for example, Dembo, Schmeidler, Borden, Chin Sue, & Manning, 1997). Scales assessing aggression, delinquency, and drug use make this a useful instrument for practitioners working with substance abusing and violent youths.

Selecting Treatments for Multiple-Problem Youths: A Case Study

Assessment instruments are important tools, but they provide only part of a comprehensive clinical strategy for treating adolescents with multiple problems. The story of Joey illustrates additional clinical issues in treating adolescents.

JOEY'S STORY

Joey, a 16-year-old boy, was recently referred to a secure juvenile correctional facility. Joey displayed aggressive behaviors in the early grades of elementary school He had little parental support; his parents used marijuana and other drugs and often left Joey unsupervised for extended periods of time. As a young adolescent, Joey committed numerous property offenses and several acts of aggression, including an assault against a teacher. When he turned 14, Joey joined a gang. His aggressive and violent tendencies escalated considerably as his involvement in gang activities increased. Coinciding with Joey's increase in aggression was an intense interest in marijuana and crack cocaine. By age 15, Joey was using marijuana daily and regularly engaging in acts of gang-related violence. He was placed in secure care for assaulting a rival gang member and for carrying an illegal handgun. He was under the influence of crack cocaine at the time of his arrest.

Joey's prognosis on arrival was poor. He had a long history of aggressive behavior; his history of substance abuse, although short, was intense. Joey was behind in school, with little family support and few positive role models. Therapists at the correctional facility chose the following assessment procedures for Joey:

1. Use the PESQ to conduct a thorough assessment of Joey's substance use.
2. Use the POSIT to assess related problems, including family relations and aggressive conduct.
3. Administer the Diagnostic Interview Schedule for Children and Adolescents (DICA) (Reich, Shayka, & Taibleson, 1996).

Joey's therapists hoped that the structured psychiatric interview DICA would shed light on mental health problems that might be contributing to his violent tendencies.

The assessment confirmed many of the beliefs of the therapy team. Joey had significant substance abuse problems. His scores on the POSIT and DICA revealed high levels of aggression and anxiety, as well as inappropriate anger control. His therapists recommended that Joey be placed in a specialized drug and alcohol treatment cottage at the facility and that he participate in anger-management skills training and in a victim awareness group with other violent offenders.

Promising Treatment Approaches

The treatments afforded Joey are typical of those provided to hundreds of violent young offenders with drug problems in the United States. How effective are they? The drug treatment, skills training, and victim awareness interventions provided to youths like Joey have been found successful in reducing substance abuse and violence while youths are in community-based or secure programs (Lipsey & Wilson, 1998). Skills training, particularly anger management training, can be effective in helping adolescents control emotions that lead to inappropriate displays of anger in high-risk situations (see, for example, Glick & Goldstein, 1987; Hawkins, Jenson, Catalano, & Wells, 1991). Victim awareness and victim–offender mediation efforts with violent offenders can reduce insensitive attitudes toward victims (see, for example, Umbreit & Coates, 1992).

Unfortunately, longitudinal studies of drug treatment, skills training, victim awareness, and similar interventions for youths with multiple problems have found only moderate effects on substance use and violent conduct *after* youths are released from treatment programs or secure settings (for example, Lipsey & Wilson, 1998; McBride, Vander Waal, Van Buren, & Terry, 1997). Many of the gains made by adolescents during treatment seem to erode in the months after release. To combat this, investigators (Dryfoos, 1998; Krisberg, Currie, Onek, & Wiebush, 1995) suggest that treatment for youths with multiple problems address as many aspects of a youth's life as possible with multiple weekly contacts, build on a youth's strengths, and be of sufficient duration and intensity to affect the long-standing nature of problems. Several promising programs are reviewed below.

The Florida Environmental Institute (FEI) serves serious, violent, and drug offenders in a secure program in a remote part of the state. Adolescents, many with extensive substance abuse histories, participate for a minimum of one year in a structured program that emphasizes hard work and educational and vocational training. They progress through levels of treatment and supervision and are placed in a community-based program after treatment is completed. One evaluation of the program revealed significantly lower recidivism rates among FEI participants than among similar youths placed in other secure programs in Florida (Krisberg et al., 1995). Additional studies of the program's effects on drug use and violent conduct are needed.

Elliott (1998) identified 10 violence intervention programs that have been effective in reducing violence and other adolescent problem behaviors, including substance abuse. Model programs were selected on the basis of rigorous research design, replicability, and ability to produce sustained effects in deterring delinquency, drug use, and violence. Whereas most of these model programs seek to prevent violence, several of them target adolescents with demonstrated substance abuse and aggression problems.

One of these, Functional Family Therapy (FFT), provides structured family treatment for adolescents between ages 11 and 18 (Alexander et al., 1998). FFT employs probation officers, mental health specialists, and paraprofessionals in a variety of activities in home and agency settings. The phases of the intervention are engagement, motivation, assessment, behavior change, and generalization. Communication skills training, parent training, and case management are part of the intervention. FFT has produced significant reductions in participants' alcohol and drug use and violent conduct (Alexander et al., 1998).

Multidimensional Treatment Foster Care (MTFC) is an intensive intervention designed for chronic delinquents and emotionally disturbed youths (Chamberlain & Mihalic, 1998). The program offers behavior management training to youths, family therapy to their biological or adoptive families, and case management. MTFC participants spent 60 percent fewer days incarcerated and had significantly fewer arrests than similar youths in a control group (Chamberlain & Mihalic, 1998). They also had significantly less hard drug use than control subjects at 12-month follow-up.

A third program identified by Elliott (1998) is Multisystemic Therapy (MST) (Henggeler, Mihalic, Rone, Thomas, & Timmons-Mitchell, 1998). MST is an intensive family and community-based treatment program for juvenile offenders with substance abuse problems. The program is home-based and delivered by trained therapists who teach parents effective ways to address the difficulties experienced by their teenagers. MST also helps parents and adolescents access human services and drug treatment. MST has been extensively evaluated (see, for example, Henggeler et al., 1993; Henggeler, Melton, & Smith, 1992); recent results found reductions of 47 percent to 64 percent in out-of-home placements, improvements in family functioning, and reductions in substance abuse and mental health problems among participating youths and parents (Henggeler et al., 1998).

Such programs offer promise in treating adolescent substance abuse and violent conduct. However, the complexity of cases such as Joey's and the poor outcomes reported by many treatment programs illustrate the need for enhanced prevention efforts targeting drug use and violent conduct. Individual, family, and community interventions that seek to prevent or treat substance use and violence among youths are reviewed below.

PROMISING PREVENTION APPROACHES

Individual Approaches

Individual-level prevention efforts seek to increase appropriate social behaviors and cognitive skills of children who exhibit substance use and aggressive behavior. One strategy attempts to give youths accurate information about actual rates of substance use and correct negative stereotypes related to substance use. Moran (1995, 1999) uses this strategy, referred to as a normative belief approach, in his work with urban American Indian children in Denver to counteract negative stereotypes. The program challenges the common assumption that American Indians are genetically predisposed to alcoholism and that to be American Indian means it is *normal* to drink. Moran (1995) has suggested that if American Indian children accept that and similar beliefs, they are more likely to use alcohol. Epidemiological data showing that the rate of abstinence is actually higher among American Indians than among the general population are among the facts shared with American Indian children and their parents (May & Moran, 1995).

A second individual-level prevention approach teaches high-risk children structured systems for organizing information and making good decisions (Hanson, 1993). In these programs, decision making is normally taught through cognitive interpersonal skills training that teaches children and youths how to generate alternative solutions to high-risk situations involving drug use or violent behavior (see, for example, Jenson & Howard, 1990; Jenson, Howard, & Yaffe, 1995). The approach is often combined with behavioral practice in resisting antisocial peer pressure. One example is the Seventh Generation Program, a prevention program for urban American Indian children in Denver (Moran, 1999). In this program, fourth- through seventh-grade children are taught to use a structured problem-solving model in making decisions. The model, called STARS, has the following steps: Stop, Think, Act, Reflect, and Self-praise. The steps are related to traditional stories about the origin of the universe as a way to anchor the intervention in cultural values. As soon as the children learn this model, they role-play skits that allow them to use the STARS approach to resist peer pressure to engage in drug use and antisocial behavior. A recent evaluation of the STARS program found significant changes between pretest and posttest measures of Indian identity, locus of control, perceived social support, and alcohol expectancies among participants (Moran, 1999).

Botvin and colleagues have created a school-based program called Life Skills Training (LST) in an effort to prevent drug use and conduct problems in young children (Botvin & Botvin, 1992; Botvin & Eng, 1982; Botvin, Schinke, Epstein, & Diaz, 1994). LST was designed to reduce positive substance use–related expectancies, teach skills for resisting social influences to use substances, and promote personal self-management and social skills. The program consists of 15 45-minute class periods. Although the program has been successfully conducted by health professionals, the logical and preferred leader is the classroom teacher.

LST uses traditional didactic teaching methods, group discussion, classroom demonstrations, and cognitive–behavioral skills training. The first segment of the program—personal self-management skills—focuses on (1) decision making and problem solving; (2) skills for identifying, analyzing, interpreting, and resisting media messages about substance use; (3) self-control skills for coping with anxiety, anger, and frustration; and (4) goal setting, self-monitoring, and self-reinforcement. The skills-training component is designed to help students improve communication and social skills, such as initiating social interactions and engaging in conversation, as well as skills related to boy–girl relationships and verbal and nonverbal assertiveness. The final part of the program, information and skills related to substance use, concentrates on knowledge and attitudes, normative expectations, and skills for resisting pro-substance-use messages from the media and from peers.

A rigorous evaluation of the program was conducted in a randomized prevention trial with 5,000 seventh-grade students from 56 schools in New York state (Botvin, Baker, Dusenbury, Tortu, & Botvin, 1990). The sample was predominantly Caucasian (91 percent) and approximately equally divided by gender. Schools were randomly assigned to the LST or control (routine educational programs) group. At 28- and 40-month follow-up, students in the experimental group used significantly less marijuana and were significantly less likely to engage in problem drinking than those in the control group.

Family Approaches

Family-based programs include one or both parents in intervention efforts. Family approaches typically work to change parenting practices, increase parent–child bonding, reduce family conflict, and encourage appropriate parental attitudes toward substance use and violence. One particularly promising approach concentrates on working with families to prevent oppositional, defiant, aggressive, and noncompliant behavior in young children. This is important because early onset of such problems predicts substance abuse and aggression during adolescence (Campbell, Breaux, Ewing, Szumowski, & Pierce, 1986; J. White, Moffit, Earls, & Robbins, 1990). The program, Strengthening Parenting Competencies, was created by Webster-Stratton (1998) for mothers and teachers of Head Start children. It begins by teaching mothers positive discipline strategies and effective parenting skills. They also learn how to enhance their children's social skills and prosocial behaviors. Videotapes of parenting skills are followed by group discussions of parent–child interaction patterns. Therapists teach mothers how to play with their children, demonstrating ways they can help children learn to solve problems. Mothers are also taught to use praise, encouragement, and limit setting with their children.

Next the program trains teachers and teacher aides to modify their classroom management to be consistent with the skills being learned by the mothers. Teachers are trained in a two-day workshop during which they watch the same videotapes as the mothers and discuss how they can reinforce mothers' efforts. The teacher training also addresses effective ways to handle child misbehavior and promote social competence through clear rules, positive feedback, social skills, and problem-solving and self-control strategies, as well as ways to increase parents' involvement in their children's preschool education.

Webster-Stratton (1998) has evaluated the effects of the program on parenting competencies, level of parental involvement in school, and children's social competencies and conduct problems. Based on both self-reported data and observations, mothers significantly increased their ability to discipline and praise their children and significantly decreased their use of harsh and critical behavior, commands, and negative affect after participating in the program. Teachers reported significant increases in parents' involvement in their children's education and in contact with school officials. Children in the program had significantly reduced their deviant and noncompliant behaviors, negative affect, misbehavior, and antisocial conduct at 12- and 18-month follow-up.

A second family-based intervention that has received much attention is the Strengthening Families Program (SFP) developed by Kumpfer, Molgaard, and Spoth (1996). SFP is designed to reduce the risk of future substance abuse and delinquency among elementary school children who have substance-abusing family members. The program offers parent training and children's skill building. Parents are trained to enhance positive child behaviors by increasing attention and reinforcement, setting behavioral goals, and teaching differential attention, communication, problem-solving, and limit-setting skills. The parent program also includes alcohol and drug education. Children are trained to understand their feelings and increase their skills of behavior, communication, problem solving, resisting peer pressure, compliance, and anger management. Families participate in a structured play therapy session monitored by a trainer who provides feedback and support both to parents and to children. Parents practice interacting with their children in a nonpunitive, noncontrolling, and positive way.

A revised SFP was tested in a clinical research trial with middle school children and their families in 19 economically disadvantaged counties in rural Iowa (Kumpfer et al., 1996). In the revised program, the separate parent and child sessions, which are followed by family sessions, were modified to include more content on resiliency factors related to drug use and delinquency. The redesigned program puts greater emphasis on resilient traits such as optimism, empathy, insight, intellectual competence, self-esteem, purpose in life, and perseverance. The content of the youth sessions was expanded to strengthening prosocial goals for the future, dealing with stress and strong emotions, empathizing with and showing appreciation for parents and elders, increasing motivation for responsible behaviors, and building skills to deal with peer pressure. Parent sessions now emphasize understanding youth developmental characteristics, providing nurturance and support, setting appropriate limits, using respectful and reasonable consequences, and sharing expectations about alcohol and drug use. Family sessions use skill-building activities, videotapes, games, and family meetings to increase problem-solving skills and to identify family strengths and values. Evaluations reveal significant improvements in children's problem-solving ability, emotional status, and prosocial skills and significant reductions in family conflicts among participants (Kumpfer et al., 1996).

Community Approaches

Comprehensive community interventions include (1) intensive and sustained programs targeting youths with demonstrated antisocial behavior, (2) specific but less intensive services directed at high-risk youth populations, and (3) universal prevention interventions aimed at the whole community (Mrazek & Haggerty, 1994).

One universal community-level substance abuse prevention program is the Midwestern Prevention Project (Pentz et al., 1989). Program components include (1) school-based resistance-skills training for sixth and seventh graders, (2) homework requiring role playing with parents and family members, (3) a parent organization that reviews school prevention policy and trains parents in positive parent–child communication skills, (4) training sessions for community leaders in drug abuse prevention, and (5) mass media coverage.

The program has been evaluated in 40 Kansas City schools and 57 Indianapolis schools (Johnson et al., 1990; Pentz et al., 1989). Intervention schools received all four components, whereas comparison schools received only community leader training and mass media coverage (Johnson et al., 1990). The media and school-based components were introduced in the first year of the project, and the parent education, community organizing, and policy change components were implemented in the second year.

After the first year of the project, cigarette, alcohol, and marijuana use were significantly lower among youths in the intervention group than among youths in the comparison group. After three years, rates of cigarette and marijuana use were significantly lower for the intervention group than for the comparison group. A separate analysis examining only high-risk youths—those already using alcohol or other drugs at sixth or seventh grade—revealed significant reductions in cigarette and alcohol use (Chou et al., 1998). Unfortunately, the design of this study did not allow for separate assessment of the impact of each of the four components.

An intervention that combines classroom, parent, and community-based approaches is Project Northland (Williams & Perry, 1998), a program implemented in several small communities in northeastern Minnesota that were targeted because of a high prevalence of alcohol-related problems. Twenty-four school districts were randomly assigned to either intervention or delayed intervention groups. The study followed the same group of 2,351 students from sixth grade to high school graduation.

The first phase of the project was three years of behavioral curricula, peer leadership, parent involvement, and community task forces to initiate community-level changes. At the end of this phase the intervention group demonstrated statistically significant reductions in onset and prevalence of drinking. These effects were attributed to changes in peer norms concerning the acceptability of underage drinking, parent–child communication that reinforced nondrinking, increased perceptions of the adverse consequences of drinking, and increased resistance skills (Williams & Perry, 1998).

The second phase of Project Northland, which is still in progress, emphasizes changing community norms about adolescent alcohol use and reducing the availability of alcohol to high school students. Local action teams work to reduce underage access to alcohol, circulating petitions about alcohol abuse at community festivals and adopting community policies that provide discounts from local businesses to students who pledge to remain free of alcohol and drugs. Student teams organize alcohol-free events, sponsor activities that emphasize the negative consequences of drinking, and work to change local policies to reduce underage access to alcohol. A final component of the second phase is a campaign to increase newspaper coverage of the problems associated with underage drinking. Media kits emphasizing antidrinking messages are distributed to a wide variety of media outlets, including organization and community newsletters.

Although results of the second phase are not yet available, Project Northland already demonstrates the feasibility of a multilevel community prevention approach. Preliminary results indicate that action teams in several Minnesota communities have been successful in initiating curfew laws, mandatory server training, and laws prohibiting loud parties (Williams & Perry, 1998).

Hawkins and Catalano (1992) have produced a program that incorporates community involvement into the developmental phases of prevention. The Communities That Care (CTC) program is a comprehensive intervention with three phases:

1. Community leaders take part in an intensive orientation that introduces them to risk factors for substance abuse and violence. They become part of an oversight body for the program and are encouraged to use their knowledge of the community to establish a prevention board.

2. Prevention board members are trained to assess community risks and resources. After the assessment, board members design prevention strategies based on a menu of approaches shown to be effective in preventing substance abuse.

3. The prevention strategy is implemented and evaluated by community task forces.

This model has undergone both pilot testing and implementation in several communities. CTC seems to work best when there is proactive technical assistance during the early stages of community mobilization (Hawkins et al., 1997). Evaluations have shown positive community involvement across all three phases (Manger, Hawkins, Haggerty, & Catalano, 1992); for example, in Oregon, 31 of 35 community task forces completed all three phases of the CTC process, implementing a prevention program (Harachi, Ayers, Hawkins, Catalano, & Cushing, 1996).

All three of these multilevel approaches have shown positive results. Thus, if communities are to substantially reduce levels of adolescent substance abuse and violence, they must systematically address their own major risk factors. Longitudinal investigations of such prevention efforts are needed to determine long-term impacts on substance use and violence.

CONCLUSION

Adolescents who abuse drugs and engage in violence are often well entrenched in a deviant lifestyle in which such behavior is normative. Motivation to change is often lacking, making the assessment and treatment process difficult. Our review suggests that there is no single solution to ameliorating co-occurring substance abuse and violent conduct among adolescents. The best available evidence suggests that highly structured, intensive efforts that include family members in treatment are most effective.

Additional research and practice steps should be taken to better understand the relationship between violence and substance abuse.

• Practitioners should incorporate indicators of violence and substance abuse in routine assessments with adolescent clients.

• Practitioners should use assessment data systematically to match clients to appropriate treatments, thereby maximizing the likelihood of positive change in youths with multiple problems.

• Practitioners should analyze assessment results and treatment outcome data to unlock the complex causal relationships between youth violence and substance abuse.

• Practitioners and researchers should undertake longitudinal studies of youths exhibiting substance abuse and violent behavior to understand the temporal order of onset and persistence of violence and substance use. Gender and ethnic differences in violence and substance abuse should be examined in these studies.

Practitioners working with youths with multiple problems are in a unique position to improve knowledge of persistent problems such as violence and substance abuse. The application of these steps may do much to advance the etiological and practice knowledge about youths with multiple problems.

REFERENCES

Akers, R. L. (1984). Delinquent behavior, drugs and alcohol: What is the relationship? *Today's Delinquent, 3,* 19–48.

Alexander, J., Barton, C., Gordon, D., Grotpeter, J., Hansson, K., Harrison, R., Mears, S., Mihalic, S., Parsons, B., Pugh, C., Schulman, S., Waldron, H., & Sexton, T. (1998). *Blueprints for violence prevention, Book 3: Functional family therapy.* Boulder: Center for the Study and Prevention of Violence, University of Colorado.

Anthony, J. C. (1991). The epidemiology of drug addiction. In N. S. Miller (Ed.), *Comprehensive handbook of drug and alcohol addiction* (pp. 55–86). New York: Marcel Dekker.

Blumstein, A. (1995). Youth violence, guns, and the illicit-drug industry. *Journal of Criminal Law and Criminology, 86,* 10–36.

Botvin, G. J., Baker, E., Dusenbury, L., Tortu, S., & Botvin, E. M. (1990). Preventing adolescent drug abuse through a multimodal cognitive–behavioral approach: Results of a three-year study. *Journal of Consulting and Clinical Psychology, 58,* 437–446.

Botvin, G. J., & Botvin, E. M. (1992). Adolescent tobacco, alcohol, and drug abuse: Prevention strategies, empirical findings, and assessment issues. *Journal of Developmental and Behavioral Pediatrics, 13,* 290–301.

Botvin, G. J., & Eng, A. (1982). The efficacy of a multicomponent approach to the prevention of cigarette smoking. *Preventive Medicine, 11,* 199–211.

Botvin, G. J., Schinke, S. P., Epstein, J. A., & Diaz, T. (1994). The effectiveness of culturally-focused and generic skills training approaches to alcohol and drug abuse prevention among minority youth. *Psychology of Addictive Behavior, 8,* 116–127.

Campbell, S. B., Breaux, A. M., Ewing, L. J., Szumowski, E. K., & Pierce, E. W. (1986). Patient-identified problem preschoolers: Mother–child interaction during play at intake and 1-year follow-up. *Journal of Abnormal Child Psychology, 14,* 425–440.

Chaiken, J., & Chaiken, M. (1990). Drugs and predatory crime. In M. Tonry & J. Q. Wilson (Eds.), *Drugs and crime* (Vol. 13; pp. 203-239). Chicago: University of Chicago Press.

Chamberlain, P., & Mihalic, S. F. (1998). *Blueprints for violence prevention, Book 8: Multidimensional treatment foster care.* Boulder: Center for the Study and Prevention of Violence, University of Colorado.

Chou, C., Montgomery, S., Pentz, M. A., Rohrbach, L. A., Johnson, A., Flay, B. R., & MacKinnon, D. P. (1998). Effects of a community-based prevention program on decreasing drug use in high-risk adolescents. *American Journal of Public Health, 88,* 944–948.

Collins, J. J., & Messerschmidt, P. M. (1993). Epidemiology of alcohol related violence. *Alcohol Health and Research World, 17,* 93–100.

Coordinating Council on Juvenile Justice and Delinquency Prevention. (1996). *Combating violence and delinquency: The national juvenile justice action plan.* Washington, DC: Author.

Dahlberg, L. L. (1998). Youth violence in the United States: Major trends, risk factors, and prevention approaches. *American Journal of Preventive Medicine, 14,* 259–272.

Dembo, R., Schmeidler, J., Borden, P., Chin Sue, C., & Manning, D. (1997). Use of the POSIT among arrested youths entering a juvenile assessment center: A replication and update. *Journal of Child and Adolescent Substance Abuse, 6,* 19–42.

Dembo, R., Williams, L., Fagan, J., & Schmeidler, J. (1993). The relationships of substance abuse and other delinquency over time in a sample of juvenile detainees. *Criminal Behavior and Mental Health, 3,* 158–179.

Dielman, T. E. (1995). School-based research on the prevention of adolescent alcohol use and misuse: Methodological issues and advances. In G. M. Boyd, J. Howard, & R. A. Zucker (Eds.), *Alcohol problems among adolescents: Current directions in prevention research* (pp. 125–146). Hillsdale, NJ: Lawrence Earlbaum.

Donovan, J. E., & Jessor, R. (1985). Structure of problem behavior in adolescence and young adulthood. *Journal of Consulting Clinical Psychology, 53,* 200–216.

Dryfoos, J. G. (1990). *Adolescents at risk: Prevalence and prevention.* New York: Oxford University Press.

Dryfoos, J. G. (1998). *Safe passage.* New York: Oxford University Press.

Earls, F. J. (1994). Violence and today's youth. *Critical Health Issues for Children and Youth, 4,* 4–23.

Elliott, D. S. (1994). Serious violent offenders: Onset, developmental course, and termination. *Criminology, 32,* 1–21.

Elliott, D. S. (1998). *Blueprints for violence prevention.* Boulder: Center for the Study and Prevention of Violence, University of Colorado.

Elliott, D. S., Huizinga, D., & Ageton, S. (1985). *Explaining delinquency and drug abuse.* Beverly Hills, CA: Sage Publications.

Elliott, D. S., Huizinga, D., & Menard, S. (1989). *Multiple problem youth: Delinquency, substance use, and mental health problems.* New York: Springer.

Ellis, R. A. (1998). Filling the prevention gap: Multi-factor, multi-system, multi-level intervention. *Journal of Primary Prevention, 19,* 57–71.

Fagan, J. (1990). Intoxication and aggression. In M. Tonry & J. Q. Wilson (Eds.), *Drugs and crime* (Vol. 13; pp. 241–320). Chicago: University of Chicago Press.

Fagan, J., & Chin, K. (1990). Violence as regulation and social control in the distribution of crack. In M. de la Rosa, E. Lambert, & B. Gropper (Eds.), *Drugs and violence* (NIDA Monograph No. 103) (pp. 8–43). Rockville, MD: National Institutes of Health.

Fagan, J., Weis, J. G., & Chang, Y. (1990). Delinquency and drug use among inner city students. *Journal of Drug Issues, 20,* 351–402.

Glick, B., & Goldstein, A. P. (1987). Aggression replacement training. *Journal of Counseling and Development, 65,* 356–362.

Goldstein, P. J. (1985). The drugs/violence nexus: A tripartite conceptual framework. *Journal of Drug Issues, 15,* 493–506.

Goldstein, P. J. (1989). Drugs and violent crime. In N. A. Weiner & M. E. Wolfgang (Eds.), *Pathways to criminal violence* (pp. 16–48). Beverly Hills, CA: Sage Publications.

Grant, B. F., & Dawson, D. A. (1997). Age at onset of alcohol use and its association with DSM-IV alcohol abuse and dependence: Results from the National Longitudinal Alcohol Epidemiologic Survey. *Journal of Substance Abuse, 9,* 103–110.

Hanson, W. B. (1993). School-based alcohol prevention programs. *Alcohol World Health and Research, 17,* 54–60.

Harachi, T. W., Ayers, C. D., Hawkins, J. D., Catalano, R. F., & Cushing, J. (1996). Empowering communities to prevent adolescent substance abuse: Process evaluation results from a risk- and protective-focused community mobilization effort. *Journal of Primary Prevention, 16,* 233–254.

Hawkins, J. D., Arthur, M. W., & Olson, J. J. (1997). Community interventions to reduce risks and enhance protection against antisocial behavior. In D. M. Stoff, J. Breiling, & J. D. Maser (Eds.), *Handbook of antisocial behavior* (pp. 365-374). New York: John Wiley & Sons.

Hawkins, J. D., & Catalano, R. F. (1992). *Communities that care: Action for drug abuse prevention.* San Francisco: Jossey-Bass.

Hawkins, J. D., Catalano, R. F., & Miller, J. Y. (1992). Risk and protective factors for alcohol and drug problems in adolescence and early adulthood: Implications for substance abuse prevention. *Psychological Bulletin, 112,* 64–105.

Hawkins, J. D., Herrenkohl, T., Farrington, D. P., Brewer, D., Catalano, R. F., & Harachi, T. W. (1998). A review of predictors of youth violence. In R. Loeber & D. P. Farrington (Eds.), *Serious & violent juvenile offenders: Risk factors and successful interventions* (pp. 106–145). Thousand Oaks, CA: Sage Publications.

Hawkins, J. D., Jenson, J. M., Catalano, R. F., & Lishner, D. M. (1988). Delinquency and drug abuse: Implications for social services. *Social Service Review, 62,* 259–284.

Hawkins, J. D., Jenson, J. M., Catalano, R. F., & Wells, E. A. (1991). Effects of skills training intervention with juvenile delinquents. *Research on Social Work Practice, 1,* 107–121.

Henggeler, S., Borduin, C., Melton, G., Mann, B., Smith, D., Schoenwald, S., & Hall, J. (1993). Family preservation using multisystemic treatment: Long-term follow-up to a clinical trial with serious juvenile offenders. *Journal of Child and Family Studies, 2,* 283–293.

Henggeler, S., Melton, G., & Smith, L. (1992). Family preservation using multisystemic therapy: An effective alternative to incarcerating serious juvenile offenders. *Journal of Consulting and Clinical Psychology, 6,* 953–961.

Henggeler, S. W., Mihalic, S. F., Rone, L., Thomas, C., & Timmons-Mitchell, J. (1998). *Blueprints for violence prevention, Book 6: Multisystemic therapy.* Boulder: Center for the Study and Prevention of Violence, University of Colorado.

Hirschi, T. (1969). *Causes of delinquency.* Berkeley, CA: University of California Press.

Howell, J. C., Krisberg, B., & Jones, M. (1995). Trends in juvenile crime and youth violence. In J. C. Howell, B. Krisberg, J. D. Hawkins, & J. J. Wilson (Eds.), *A sourcebook: Serious, violent, and chronic juvenile offenders* (pp. 1–35). Thousand Oaks, CA: Sage Publications.

Huizinga, D., & Jakob-Chien, C. (1998). The contemporaneous co-occurrence of serious and violent juvenile offending and other problem behaviors. In R. Loeber & D. P. Farrington, (Eds.), *Serious & violent juvenile offenders: Risk factors and successful interventions* (pp. 47–67). Thousand Oaks, CA: Sage Publications.

Institute of Medicine. (1990). *Broadening the base of treatment for alcohol problems.* Washington, DC: National Academy Press.

Jenson, J. M. (1997). Risk and protective factors for alcohol and other drug use in childhood and adolescence. In M. W. Fraser (Ed.), *Risk and resilience in childhood: An ecological perspective* (pp. 117–139). Washington, DC: NASW Press.

Jenson, J. M., & Howard, M. O. (1990). Skills deficits, skills training, and delinquency. *Children and Youth Services Review, 12,* 213–238.

Jenson, J. M., Howard, M. O., & Yaffe, J. (1995). Treatment of adolescent substance abusers: Issues for practice and research. *Social Work in Health Care, 21,* 1–18.

Jessor, R., & Jessor, S. (1977). *Problem behavior and psychological development: A longitudinal study of youth.* New York: Academic Press.

Johnson, A., Pentz, M. A., Weber, M. D., Dwyer, D. W., Baer, N., MacKinnon, W. P., Hansen, W. B., & Flay, B. R. (1990). Relative effectiveness of comprehensive community programming for drug abuse prevention with high-risk and low-risk adolescents. *Journal of Consulting and Clinical Psychology, 58,* 447–456.

Johnson, B. D., Wish, E. D., Schmeidler, J., & Huizinga, D. (1991). Concentration of delinquent offending: Serious drug involvement and high delinquency rates. *Journal of Drug Issues, 21,* 205–291.

Johnston, L. D., O'Malley, P. M., & Bachman, J. G. (1985). *Drug use, drinking, and smoking: National survey results from high school, college, and young adult populations.* Washington, DC: U.S. Government Printing Office.

Johnston, L. D., O'Malley, P. M., & Bachman, J. G. (1997). *National survey results on drug use from the Monitoring the Future study, 1975–1995.* Rockville, MD: National Institute on Drug Abuse.

Johnston, L. D., O'Malley, P. M., & Bachman, J. G. (1998, December 18). *Monitoring the Future study press release.* (Available: *www.isr.umich.edu/scr/mtf/mtnar98*)

Johnston, L. D., O'Malley, P. M., & Eveland, L. K. (1978). Drugs and delinquency: A search for causal connections. In D. Kandel (Ed.), *Longitudinal research on drug use* (pp. 178-191). New York: John Wiley & Sons.

Kandel, D., Simcha-Fagan, O., & Davies, M. (1986). Risk factors for delinquency and illicit drug use from adolescence to young adulthood. *Journal of Drug Issues, 60*(1), 67–90.

Krisberg, B., Currie, E., Onek, D., & Wiebush, R. G. (1995). Graduated sanctions for serious, violent, and chronic juvenile offenders. In J. C. Howell, B. Krisberg, J. D. Hawkins, & J. J. Wilson (Eds.), *Sourcebook on serious, violent, and chronic juvenile offenders* (pp. 142–170). Thousand Oaks, CA: Sage Publications.

Kumpfer, K., Molgaard, V., & Spoth, R. (1996). The Strengthening Families program for the prevention of delinquency and drug abuse. In R. Peters & R. McMahon (Eds.), *Preventing childhood disorders, substance abuse, and delinquency* (pp. 241–267). Thousand Oaks, CA: Sage Publications.

Lang, A. R. (1993). Alcohol-related violence: Psychological perspectives. In S. E. Martin (Ed.), *Alcohol and interpersonal violence: Fostering multidisciplinary perspectives* (NIAAA Research Monograph No. 24) (pp. 121–147). Rockville, MD: National Institutes of Health.

Leonard, K. E. (1993). Drinking patterns and intoxication in marital violence: Review, critique, and future directions for research. In S. E. Martin (Ed.), *Alcohol and interpersonal violence: Fostering multidisciplinary perspectives* (NIAAA Research Monograph No. 24) (pp. 253–280). Rockville, MD: National Institutes of Health.

Lipsey, M. W., & Wilson, D. B. (1998). Effective intervention for serious juvenile offenders: A synthesis of research. In R. Loeber & D. P. Farrington (Eds.), *Serious & violent juvenile offenders: Risk factors and successful interventions* (pp. 313–345). Thousand Oaks, CA: Sage Publications.

Loeber, R. (1990). Development and risk factors of juvenile antisocial behavior and delinquency. *Clinical Psychology Review, 10,* 1–41.

Loeber, R., Van Kammen, W. B., Krohn, M. D., & Huizinga, D. (1991). The crime–substance use nexus in young people. In D. Huizinga, R. Loeber, & T. P. Thornberry (Eds.), *Urban delinquency and substance abuse.* Washington, DC: U.S. Department of Justice, Office of Juvenile Justice and Delinquency Prevention.

MacAndrew, C. R., & Edgerton, R. B. (1969). *Drunken comportment: A social explanation.* Chicago: Aldine.

Manger, T. H., Hawkins, J. D., Haggerty, K. P., & Catalano, R. F. (1992). Mobilizing communities to reduce risks for drug abuse: Lessons on research to guide prevention practice. *Journal of Primary Prevention, 13,* 3–22.

Martin, C. S., & Winters, K. C. (1998). Diagnosis and assessment of alcohol use disorders among adolescents. *Alcohol, Health, and Research World, 22,* 95–105.

May, P. A., & Moran, J. (1995). Prevention of alcohol misuse: A review of health promotion efforts among American Indians. *American Journal of Health Promotion, 9,* 288–299.

McBride, D., Vander Waal, C., Van Buren, H., & Terry, Y. (1997). *Breaking the cycle of drug use among juvenile offenders.* Washington, DC: National Institute of Justice.

Miller, G. (1985). *The Substance Abuse Subtle Screening Inventory.* Bloomington, IN: SASSI Institute.

Moran, J. (1995). Cultural sensitivity in alcohol prevention research in ethnic communities. In P. Langton (Ed.), *The challenge for participatory research in the prevention of alcohol related problems in ethnic communities* (Special Collaborative CSAP/NIAAA Monograph, 3) (pp. 43–56). Washington, DC: U.S. Department of Health and Human Services, Center for Substance Abuse Prevention Cultural Competence Series.

Moran, J. (1999). Preventing alcohol use among urban American Indian youth: The Seventh Generation Program. *Journal of Human Behavior in the Social Environment, 2,* 51–68.

Mrazek, P. J., & Haggerty, R. J. (1994). *Reducing risks for mental disorders: Frontiers for prevention intervention.* Washington, DC: National Academy Press.

Newcomb, M. D., & Bentler, P. M. (1988). *Consequences of adolescent drug use.* Newbury Park, CA: Sage Publications.

Osgood, D. W. (1994). *Drugs, alcohol, and adolescent violence* (Center Paper 002). Boulder: Center for the Study and Prevention of Violence, University of Colorado.

Pentz, M. A., Dwyer, J. H., MacKinnon, D. P., Flay, B. R., Hansen, W. B., Wang, E. Y., & Johnson, A. (1989). A multicommunity trial for primary prevention of adolescent drug abuse: Effects on drug use prevalence. *JAMA, 261,* 3259–3266.

Pernanen, K. (1991). *Alcohol in human violence.* New York: Guilford.

Phil, R. O., & Peterson, J. B. (1993). Alcohol, serotonin, and aggression. *Alcohol Health & Research World, 17,* 113–116.

Rahdert, E. R. (1991). *The adolescent assessment/referral system manual.* Washington, DC: Alcohol, Drug Abuse, and Mental Health Administration.

Reich, W., Shayka, J. J., & Taibleson, C. (1992). *The Diagnostic Interview for Children and Adolescents, Revised.* St. Louis: Washington University.

Snyder, H. N. (1997). *Juvenile arrests, 1995.* Washington, DC: U.S. Department of Justice, Office of Juvenile Justice and Delinquency Prevention.

Thornberry, T. P., Huizinga, D., & Loeber, R. (1995). The prevention of serious delinquency and violence: Implications from the program of research on the causes and correlates of delinquency. In J. C. Howell, B. Krisberg, J. D. Hawkins, & J. J. Wilson (Eds.), *Sourcebook on serious, violent, and chronic juvenile offenders* (pp. 213–237). Thousand Oaks, CA: Sage Publications.

Umbreit, M., & Coates, R. B. (1992). The impact of mediating victim–offender conflict: An analysis of programs in three states. *Juvenile and Family Court Journal, 43,* 28–43.

U.S. Department of Justice. (1997). *Crime in the United States, 1996.* Washington, DC: Author.

Wallace, J. M., & Bachman, J. G. (1991). Explaining racial/ethnic differences in adolescent drug use: The impact of background and lifestyle. *Social Problems, 38,* 333–357.

Webster-Stratton, C. (1998). Preventing conduct problems in Head Start children: Strengthening parenting competencies. *Journal of Consulting and Clinical Psychology, 66,* 715–730.

White, H. R. (1997). Alcohol, illicit drugs, and violence. In D. M. Stoff, J. Breiling, & J. D. Maser (Eds.), *Handbook of antisocial behavior* (pp. 511–523). New York: John Wiley & Sons.

White, H. R., Brick, J., & Hansell, S. (1993). A longitudinal investigation of alcohol use and aggression in adolescence. *Journal of Studies on Alcohol* (Suppl. 11), 62–77.

White, J., Moffit, T., Earls, F., & Robbins, L. (1990). Preschool predictors of persistent conduct disorder and delinquency. *Criminology, 28,* 443–454.

Williams, C. L., & Perry, C. L. (1998). Lessons from Project Northland. *Alcohol Health & Research World, 22,* 107–116.

Windle, M. (1990). A longitudinal study of antisocial behaviors in early adolescence as predictors of late adolescent substance use: Gender and ethnic differences. *Journal of Abnormal Psychology, 99,* 86–91.

Winters, K. C. (1992). Development of an adolescent alcohol and other drug abuse screening scale: Personal experience screening questionnaire. *Addictive Behaviors, 17,* 479–490.

Chapter 8

Delinquency, Gangs, and Youth Violence

James Herbert Williams and Richard A. Van Dorn

J uvenile delinquency, gang activity, and violent behavior continue to belea-
guer the United States. Gangs identified by officials nationwide are universally credited with disrupting life in areas where they gather.

There is considerable variation in youth crime, violence, and gang
membership and in the social contexts in which they thrive. Although preventing and treating violent youth crime is not easy, knowledge of causal factors and of effective prevention and treatment approaches is rapidly expanding.

Risk-based models explaining delinquency and gang violence suggest
that certain individual and social characteristics are associated with a higher
probability of delinquency, violence, and gang activity. Risk factors for delinquency, gang activity, and violent behavior exist in all domains of a youth's
life, including family, school, community, and peer groups. This chapter (1)
reviews the literature on risk factors for delinquency, violence, and gang
activities; (2) considers observations about violence made by researchers and
practitioners; (3) reviews studies of gang membership and gang activities;
and (4) discusses promising intervention efforts targeting violent delinquency
and gang involvement.

After defining delinquency, violence, and youth gangs, the chapter
reviews national incidence and prevalence trends. Risk factors for violent
behaviors and gang involvement are identified by domain. A case exemplifies
the issues associated with the prevention and treatment of violent behavior

and gang activities. The chapter finally reviews programs that show promise in preventing and treating delinquency, gang involvement, and violent behavior and suggests the implications for social work research and practice.

SCOPE OF THE PROBLEM

Delinquency and Violence

Juvenile delinquency is the commission of illegal acts by people younger than age 18. The term also includes behaviors that, if committed by people age 18 or older, would be legal, namely, status offenses (Williams, Ayers, & Arthur, 1997). The Federal Bureau of Investigation (1993) classifies delinquent acts into three categories based on the severity of the offense. The most serious are violent index crimes: forcible rape, robbery, aggravated assault, murder, and nonnegligent manslaughter. Property index crimes include such offenses as burglary, larceny-theft, motor vehicle theft, and arson. All other delinquent acts, the least serious, are categorized as nonindex offenses, which include forgery, vandalism, gambling, driving under the influence, drunkenness, disorderly conduct, vagrancy, and status offenses such as running away and curfew violations. This chapter addresses violent offenses committed by adolescents, with particular emphasis on gang activity.

Gangs

Some consensus about the nature of juvenile gangs has emerged in recent literature. First, gangs cannot be stereotyped. Some gangs are simply a source of social support and entertainment for members, others serve as drug distribution organizations, and still others do both. Gang members may commit a significant number of crimes, but crime is often not their primary, and certainly not their only, focus. Second, youths often join gangs to achieve goals that they perceive as difficult or impossible to achieve without gang support. However, members differ in their motivations for joining and their degree of commitment to gang life. Third, it is rare for entire gangs to organize their activities exclusively around the sale of drugs. Finally, communities with gangs differ in some respects, but generally all are struggling with social problems such as poverty, racism, mobility, and demographic changes.

Despite unanimous agreement that gangs exist, there is little consensus about how to define a gang (Spergel, 1990). The following definitions demonstrate how little consensus there is.

- A gang is an organized social system that is both quasi-private and quasi-secretive and one whose size and goals have necessitated that social interaction be governed by a leadership structure that has defined roles; where the authority associated with these roles has been legitimized to the extent that social codes are operational to regulate the behavior of both leadership and rank and file; that plans and provides not only for the social and economic services of its members, but also for its own maintenance as an organization; that pursues such goals irrespective of whether the action is legal or not; and that lacks a bureaucracy. (Jankowski, 1991, p. 29)

- A gang is a group of individuals who have symbols of membership, permanence, and criminal involvement. A gang member is a person who acknowledges membership in the gang and is regarded as a gang member by other members. (Decker & Curry, 1999, p. 247)

- A gang has the following characteristics: a denotable group comprised primarily of males who are committed to delinquent (including criminal) behavior or values and call forth a consistent negative response from the community such that the community comes to see them as qualitatively different from other groups. (Klein, 1995)

- A gang is a well-defined group of youths between 10 and 22 years old. Most research on youth gangs in the United States has concluded that the most typical age range of gang members has been approximately 14 to 24, although researchers have identified gang members as young as 10 and in some areas researchers have found several generations in the same family who are gang members. (Huff, 1998)

Definitions are important in choosing prevention and intervention strategies. This chapter focuses on gangs that can be defined as groups of youths who are engaged in sufficient levels of antisocial activities to warrant the involvement of the criminal justice system.

Most street gangs are located in low socioeconomic communities. Although gangs are more prevalent in urban settings, they also exist in suburban and rural areas (Curry, Ball, & Decker, 1996; Office of Juvenile Justice and Delinquency Prevention [OJJDP], 1997). Most gang members are adolescent or young adult males, although research is beginning to examine the growing numbers of female gang members (Chesney-Lind & Shelden, 1998). Although female gangs continue to be few, they represent a serious concern.

PREVALENCE OF VIOLENT DELINQUENCY AND GANGS

Delinquency and Violence

In 1995 law enforcement agencies made more than 2.7 million arrests of people under age 18 (Sickmund, Snyder, & Poe-Yamagata, 1997). More than 147,000 (5.4 percent) of these arrests were for violent index crimes.

Juveniles under age 13 were involved in only 9 percent of all juvenile arrests (Sickmund et al., 1997). In 1995 individuals under age 18 accounted for 15 percent of all homicide, 16 percent of all rape, 15 percent of all aggravated assault, and 32 percent of all robbery arrests (Zimring, 1998).

Data from self-report studies have yielded mixed findings about racial differences in offending behaviors. For example, data from the National Youth Survey showed no racial differences in offending levels between African Americans and Caucasians (Huizinga, Loeber, & Thornberry, 1993). In the Pittsburgh Youth Study, no differences were found between African American and Caucasian boys at age 10, but differences gradually developed, with the prevalence of serious delinquency at age 16 reaching 27 percent for African American boys and 19 percent for Caucasian boys (Browning & Loeber, 1999).

Studies based on arrest data indicate that African American adolescents have higher rates of certain types of delinquent behavior than Caucasians (Sickmund et al., 1997; Uniform Crime Reports, 1993). African American youths constituted 15 percent of the juvenile population in 1995 and were involved in 28 percent of all juvenile arrests (Sickmund et al., 1997). The statistics show that African American males are disproportionately involved in the juvenile justice system. The rate of referrals to the juvenile courts for African Americans in 1991 was 108 per 1,000 children, more than double the rate of referrals for Caucasians (42 per 1,000) (Maguire, Pastore, & Flanagan, 1993).

Regardless of whether official arrest or self-reported data are used, boys have a much higher prevalence of criminal involvement than girls (Chesney-Lind & Shelden, 1998). In 1992 boys comprised 88 percent of all violent crime and 74 percent of all property crime arrests (U.S. Department of Justice [USDOJ], Federal Bureau of Investigation, 1993). However, criminal propensities are not confined to boys. The 10-year period from 1983 to 1992 witnessed a 15 percent increase in arrests of boys and a 25 percent increase for girls. Violent crime arrest rates increased 82 percent for girls during this same period (Chesney-Lind & Shelden, 1998; USDOJ, 1992).

The concentration of violent crime among males is a familiar narrative. The homicide arrest rate of boys under age 18 is 15 times that of girls. The male-to-female ratio for youths involved in robbery is also significantly higher than the ratio for adults (Reiss & Roth, 1993; Zimring, 1998). One plausible hypothesis for the overrepresentation of younger males in official arrest data is that sociocultural forces that push male rates to high levels do not operate in the same fashion for females (Williams & Van Dorn, 1999b; Williams, Van Dorn, Hawkins, Abbott, & Catalano, 1999). Although rates among females historically have been relatively flat when compared with rates among males (Chesney-Lind & Shelden, 1998), there have been increases in female rates of violence in recent years.

Youth Gangs

Counting the number of gangs, gang members, and gang crimes in the United States is difficult. There are estimates for each category, but no precise figures (Curry et al., 1996; Curry, Ball, & Fox, 1994; Miller, 1975, 1982). Curry and colleagues (1996) estimated that in 1992 there were 249,324 gang members, 4,881 gangs, 46,359 gang crimes, and slightly more than 1,000 gang homicides. By 1994, they estimated, gangs had nearly doubled in number to 8,652, membership had grown to approximately 380,000, and gang-related crimes increased to 437,066. Currently, there are approximately 23,388 youth gangs with a total of 664,906 members in all 50 states (Curry et al., 1996; OJJDP, 1997); 1,492 American cities reported having active youth gangs (OJJDP, 1997). Considering political and community images and the difficulty of determining the true numbers of youth gangs and members, these estimates are likely to be conservative.

Gangs exist in all ethnic groups. Although African American and Hispanic members dominate many gangs, there are also Caucasian and Asian gangs (Curry et al., 1994; Decker & Curry, 1999). Curry and colleagues (1996) assessed ethnicity of gang members, estimating that 48 percent were African American and 43 percent were Hispanic. These findings are supported by studies of gang migration, which report that 60 percent of gang migrants from southern California are African American (Maxson, Woods, & Klein, 1996).

Estimates of female gang membership tend to be less reliable. Curry and colleagues (1996), examining characteristics of gang-involved youths, estimated that females accounted for only a very small percentage (3.6 percent). Other studies have reported that females make up some 6 percent of all gang members in Los Angeles (Reiner, 1992) and 7 percent of suspected gang members in Hawaii (Chesney-Lind, Rockhill, Marker, & Reyes, 1994).

RISK FACTORS FOR VIOLENT DELINQUENCY AND GANG MEMBERSHIP

Knowledge of risk factors for delinquency, violence, and gang membership may be helpful in predicting the likelihood of an undesirable outcome (Hawkins, Abbott, Catalano, & Gillmore, 1991; Williams et al., 1997). Several comprehensive reviews of risk factors for delinquency, gangs, and violence have been published (Curry & Decker, 1998; Fraser, 1997; Klein, 1995; Loeber & Farrington, 1998). This section summarizes the literature on risk factors for delinquency, violence, and gang involvement across individual, family, school, peer, and community domains.

Individual-Level Risk Factors

Complications at birth seem to be related to the later development of violent behavior. Kandel and Mednick (1991) found that 80 percent of violent offenders experienced significant delivery complications, compared with 30 percent of property offenders and 47 percent of nonoffenders. An earlier study by Mednick and Kandel (1988) revealed interaction between an unstable home environment and delivery complications. This interaction may be more predictive of later violence than delivery complications alone (Mednick & Kandel, 1988). Prenatal trauma is also correlated with increased risk for hyperactivity, which itself is a risk factor for later adolescent delinquency and violence (Brennan, Mednick, & Kandel, 1991). The relationship of prenatal care, delivery complications, and violence should be further investigated.

Children with hyperactivity and impulsivity are at risk for delinquency, violence, and gang membership (Hill et al., 1996; Loeber, 1990; Williams et al., 1997). Children with attention deficit hyperactivity disorder (ADHD) are at particularly high risk for delinquent behavior. ADHD is also associated with the early onset of delinquency and is correlated with persistent disruptive behavior (Loeber, 1996). Hyperactivity and ADHD are considered to be individual characteristics that are not always identified in other siblings. Loney, Kramer, and Milich (1983) found that boys diagnosed as hyperactive were more violent than their male siblings.

Two symptoms of ADHD—problems concentrating and restlessness—are also predictive of violent behavior (Farrington, 1989). Concentration problems of boys ages 8 to 14 were significant predictors of self-reported violence and official arrests for violent offenses for males between ages 10 and 32 in a British study (Farrington, 1989). Concentration problems may best be understood, however, as influencing negative school outcomes—another predictor of delinquency.

Restlessness (for example, difficulty sitting still, talkativeness), as measured by teacher reports, is associated with later violence in adulthood (Farrington, 1989; Klinteberg, Anderson, Magnusson, & Stattin, 1993). Of boys experiencing difficulty with concentrating and with restlessness at age 13, 15 percent were arrested for violence by age 26, compared with 3 percent of nonrestless boys (Klinteberg et al., 1993).

Strong associations have been reported between risk-taking and sensation-seeking activities between the ages of 8 and 16 and concurrent or prospective delinquency and violence (Farrington, 1989; Maguin et al., 1995). The nature of risk taking independent of ADHD is not well understood, but risk taking with or without ADHD is a strong predictor of later delinquency and violence. Studies consistently reveal a positive relationship between (1) hyperactivity, attention problems, impulsivity, and risk taking and (2) later delinquency and violent behavior (Hawkins et al., 1998;

Williams & Van Dorn, 1999a, 1999b; Williams, Van Dorn, Hawkins, Abbott, & Catalano, 1999).

Extensive research has examined the relationship between childhood aggression and later delinquent and violent behavior (Farrington, 1991; Loeber, 1990, 1996; Loeber & Hay, 1996; McCord & Ensminger, 1995; Olweus, 1977; Stattin & Magnusson, 1989). In a longitudinal study in Sweden, two-thirds of boys were rated high on aggression by teachers at age 10, and 13 had criminal records for violent offenses by age 26 (Stattin & Magnusson, 1989). McCord and Ensminger (1995), evaluating a sample of African American youths, found that approximately half of the boys rated as aggressive by teachers were arrested for violent crimes by age 33, compared with about one-third of the boys the teachers rated as nonaggressive.

Investigations of the relationship between early female aggression and later violence have produced somewhat mixed results. McCord and Ensminger (1995) found a significant predictive relationship between aggression and violence among females in their study. However, another study of female antisocial behavior found no relationship between female aggression at age 10 and later arrests for violent offenses (Stattin & Magnusson, 1989).

Early onset of delinquency and violent behavior predicts chronic delinquency and an increased likelihood of violence (Farrington, 1991; Thornberry, Huizinga, & Loeber, 1995; Tolan & Thomas, 1995). Wolfgang, Figlio, and Sellin (1972) found in an oft-cited cohort study that the peak age of onset for delinquency was 16 years. Recent studies have found that youths are initiating delinquent activities early in the adolescent years and often before adolescence (Thornberry, 1996; Williams, Ayers, Abbott, & Hawkins, 1998). In the National Youth Survey, 60 percent of 11-year-olds reported participating in general delinquency (Elliott, Huizinga, & Menard, 1989). Early onset of delinquent behavior is also correlated with escalation to more serious delinquency (Loeber, Keenan, & Zhang, 1997). Most chronic and violent offenders exhibited delinquent behavior at an early age (Loeber, Farrington, Stouthamer-Loeber, Moffitt, & Caspi, 1998).

Thornberry (1998) found that depression, negative life events, and positive attitude toward drugs represented a significant risk for gang membership among youths in the Rochester Youth Study. All three risk factors were significant predictors for boys; only positive attitude toward drugs was significant for girls.

Family Risk Factors

Parental involvement in criminal behavior is predictive of later involvement in delinquency and violence (Baker & Mednick, 1984; Farrington, 1989; Rutter, 1985). In one study, parental arrests before a child's 10th birthday predicted self-reported and officially recorded involvement in violent acts

(Farrington, 1989). Alcohol and drug abuse by parents also places children at risk for early delinquent activities (Rutter, 1985; Williams, Ayers, et al., 1998). Marital conflict and family instability foster situations that reinforce aggressiveness and coercive behavior in children; such instability has also been moderately associated with gang involvement (Farrington, 1989, 1991; Hill et al., 1996; Loeber & Dishion, 1983; Patterson & Dishion, 1985).

Some studies posit that divorce and family instability are correlated with higher rates of delinquency (Williams et al., 1997; Williams, Stiffman, & O'Neal, 1998). Although little is known about the relationship between divorce and youth antisocial behaviors, it has been hypothesized that the transitions youths experience because of divorce become a risk factor, along with the increased likelihood that mother and child will fall into poverty (Williams et al., 1997). Divorce may be an outcome of marital conflict and family instability, indicating that the effect of divorce on delinquency and violence may be indirect. Parental attitudes supporting violent behavior are a risk factor for delinquency, violence, and gang involvement (Hill et al., 1996; Williams et al., 1997).

One of the most important and consistent risk factors for delinquency, violence, and gang involvement is child maltreatment. In prevalence and causal studies, maltreatment as a child has been implicated in later delinquency, and more specifically in violence (C. Smith & Thornberry, 1995; Widom, 1989; Zingraff, Leiter, Myers, & Johnson, 1993). Inconsistencies in discipline, harsh punishment, authoritarian parenting style, and parental abuse have been linked to severe conduct problems. These often persist through childhood and into adolescence (McCord, McCord, & Zola, 1959; Patterson & Stouthamer-Loeber, 1984; Robins, 1991).

Poor family management practices, lack of interaction between parent and child, and lack of bonding to family members are related to delinquency, violence, and gang involvement (Hawkins et al., 1998; Hill et al., 1996). Two of the strongest correlates of violence are poor parental supervision and lack of parental involvement in children's activities (Loeber & Stouthamer-Loeber, 1986). Parental failure to set clear rules, monitor children's behaviors, and use consistent rewards and praise at age 14 predicted self-reported violence at age 16 for Caucasians and African Americans in a study by Williams (1994).

School Risk Factors

Poor academic achievement is a consistent predictor of later involvement in delinquency, violence, and gangs (Hill et al., 1996; Loeber et al., 1991; Maguin & Loeber, 1996). However, there is a lack of consensus about the effect of academic failure on delinquency across ethnic groups and gender. Maguin and Loeber (1996) found that poor academic performance was a stronger predictor of delinquent behavior for Caucasians than for African Americans and for males compared with females. However, other studies have found that poor academic performance was more predictive of antisocial behaviors for females than for males (Denno, 1990). Early academic failure, like early onset of delinquent behavior, is a strong predictor of chronic and violent offending (Loeber et al., 1998). Low educational attainment in elementary school is predictive of later convictions for violence (Farrington, 1989). Low academic achievement starting at the fourth grade has been found to be a stable predictor of later delinquency in several studies (Hawkins, Arthur, & Catalano, 1995; Williams et al., 1997; Yoshikawa, 1994).

Lack of commitment to school is among the most consistent predictors of violence and gang involvement. Williams (1994) found that level of commitment to school was more significant in reducing later violence for African Americans and males than for Caucasians and females. Level of commitment to school becomes a more important risk factor as a youth progresses. For example, Maguin and colleagues (1995) found that low commitment to school at age 10 did not predict later self-reported violence at age 18, but that low commitment to school at ages 14 and 16 combined with low educational aspirations did predict violence at age 18. Youths who report low levels of school commitment, low educational aspiration, and overall school antisocial behavior are more likely to be in gangs (Hill et al., 1996). Yet the National Youth Survey found no relationship between school bonding and later violence (Elliott, 1994).

Low levels of bonding to school may be characteristic of youths who drop out of school. Whatever the reasons for failing to complete school, dropping out is a risk factor for delinquent and violent behavior. Farrington (1989) found that leaving school before age 15 was a significant predictor of self-reported violence and official arrests for violence.

Peer Risk Factors

The consistent findings about the impact of delinquent peers on delinquency are consistent (Ageton, 1983; Bjerregaard & Smith, 1993; Elliott, 1994; Farrington, 1989; Maguin et al., 1995). Results from one longitudinal study indicate that having delinquent siblings is also a risk factor for later violence and gang membership (Farrington, 1989; Hill et al., 1996; Maguin et al., 1995). Among boys in the Cambridge study who had delinquent siblings at age 10, 26 percent were convicted of a violent act, compared with only 10 percent of those without delinquent siblings (Farrington, 1989). Seattle Social Development Project results indicate that the impact of delinquent siblings is more significant in adolescence than in early childhood (Maguin et al., 1995). Delinquent peers also have a significant impact on youths who exhibit aggressive and violent behaviors early (Moffitt, 1993).

With regard to the effect of delinquent siblings on antisocial behavior in different ethnic groups and by gender, Williams (1994) found that females were negatively influenced more by delinquent siblings than were males, and Matsueda and Heimer (1997) reported that Caucasians were affected more by delinquent siblings than African Americans. Additional studies of these effects by ethnicity and gender are needed.

Gang membership appears to predict violence above and beyond peer associations (Battin, Hill, Abbott, Catalano, & Hawkins, 1998). Gang membership is also more predictive of increasingly serious and violent offending than non–gang membership (Huff, 1998). The Seattle Social Development Project found that gang membership at ages 14 and 16 predicted violent behavior at age 18 (Maguin et al., 1995).

Community Risk Factors

Several studies have assessed the effects of poverty within the community on delinquent behavior, violence, and gang formation (Elliott et al., 1989; Farrington, 1989; Hagedorn, 1988; Hill et al., 1996; Hogh & Wolf, 1983; D. R. Smith & Jarjoura, 1988). Communities with high concentrations of poverty have high rates of gang activity (Curry & Decker, 1998; Fagan, 1996). Farrington (1989) found that low family income predicted both self-reported violence and later criminal convictions: More than 23 percent of the boys from poor households were convicted for violent offenses, but fewer than 9 percent of the boys from nonpoor households were convicted for violent offenses.

Disorganized communities—communities with high levels of crime, drug selling, gangs, poor housing, physical deterioration, and population density—are predictive of more delinquent activities and violent acts by youths who grow up there (Maguin et al., 1995; Sampson & Laub, 1994). The Rochester Youth Study identified community disorganization as a specific risk for later gang involvement (Thornberry, 1998). Limited access to health care, social services, and good schools in neighborhoods characterized by social disorganization and poverty is associated with a variety of youth problems (Yoshikawa, 1994). Other risk factors in disorganized communities are the availability of drugs and norms favorable to drug use (Curry & Spergel, 1992; Hill, Hawkins, Catalano, Maguin, & Kosterman, 1995; Hill et al., 1996; Maguin et al., 1995).

Youths exposed to adults who have a history of criminal behaviors are more likely than other youths to participate in criminal behaviors and violence (Maguin et al., 1995). There is increased likelihood that youths exposed to violence and traumatic events will engage in violent acts (Garbarino, DuBrow, Kostelny, & Pardo, 1992; Paschall, 1996; Williams et al., 1998; Williams & Van Dorn, 1999a, 1999b). Chronic community violence or norms favorable to violence are detrimental to children's social and cognitive development (Garbarino et al., 1992). McCord and Ensminger (1995) found a relationship between retrospective accounts of exposure to racial prejudice and self-reported violent acts as adults.

In sum, risk factors for violence and gang activity have been identified in a variety of individual, social, and environmental contexts. Knowledge of these factors should be incorporated into prevention and treatment of violent conduct.

INTERVENTION WITH VIOLENT AND GANG-INVOLVED YOUTHS

Correlates and causal factors for delinquency, violent behaviors, and gang involvement are evident in all areas of a youth's environment. The challenge for practitioners is to understand how these risk factors manifest themselves in practice settings. The following case study highlights some of the challenges confronted by practitioners working with violent juvenile offenders and gang members.

LARRY'S STORY

Larry is a 17-year-old male currently detained at a medium security institution awaiting a sentencing hearing. Larry recently pleaded guilty to armed robbery, which occurred when he was a juvenile. The social worker was asked by the attorney to provide a social history to assist in making a sentencing recommendation.

Larry's parents never married; nor did they live together. Larry was raised by his mother. When he was three years old, he and his mother moved to another state to live with his mother's paramour. Larry reports that the paramour, Marvin Brown, was abusive toward his mother, and that his mother was heavily involved in drug use.

Larry's mother gave birth to her second son, Marvin Brown Jr., when Larry was four years old. She then separated from Mr. Brown and moved back to Larry's hometown with her two sons. She reunited with Larry's father for a short time and gave birth to a third son when Larry was five years old. Larry's third and youngest brother was born when Larry was nine years old.

Larry received his first court referral when he was nine. A year later he received a truancy referral after he was enrolled in his third elementary school because of the family's moves. Larry received five more referrals to the court during the next three years.

The family moved into a new home when Larry was 11 and remained there for the next few years. During this time Larry became involved in a local boy's club, participating in martial arts and football. The chief instructor at the boy's club recalled that Larry seemed to be very cautious about keeping out of trouble but seemed to have a lot going on at home. At this time Larry ceased all contact with his biological father. Larry reported that he and his father never had a close relationship, but his dad did visit him and his brother randomly.

Larry pleaded guilty to burglary when he was 14 years old. This was the first time the courts offered services to Larry. He was placed under official court supervision. Although Larry had missed more than 129 days of school during seventh grade, he was enrolled in the eighth grade. When he was 14 years old, Larry recalled witnessing a man being shot.

Three months after his burglary charge, Larry was detained, and he eventually pleaded guilty to tampering charges. He asked to be placed outside his family's home. Child welfare services had been involved with the family because of accusations that the children begged for food and ate out of trash cans. The home had been described as dilapidated and overcrowded, and the children were described as unkempt and with poor hygiene.

Larry was placed in long-term residential care and was discharged after a 12-month stay. He was concerned about returning to his home and his neighborhood, but stated that he did not really have any control over the situation. Larry enrolled in a new high school after discharge from the residential facility. The high school had no records of Larry's attendance or grades. It is unclear whether he ever attended high school. Larry received no court referrals for an entire year after being discharged from the residential care facility.

Certified to stand trial as an adult, Larry was transferred from the family court to the workhouse. It was learned that he may have been under the influence of heroin at the time of the robbery.

Larry's story illustrates the multiple risk factors affecting many youths in the juvenile and criminal justice systems. His case provides an excellent opportunity for practitioners to think about how to assess, identify, and treat such factors when working with chronic and serious violent juvenile offenders. Several issues can be extracted to assist practitioners working with youths involved in violent behaviors.

Assessment and intervention plans. Numerous influences in Larry's social environment would be considered risks for antisocial behavior. Instabilities within his home environment (for example, multiple moves, mother's multiple partners and possible drug use, estranged relationship with father) were evident before he entered the family court system. Such instability often makes it difficult for social workers to conduct adequate psychosocial and risk assessments. The course and escalation of Larry's antisocial activity indicate that assessment, early identification, and treatment are imperative.

Several developments in risk and protective factor assessment tools in recent years can be of use to practitioners (Catalano & Hawkins, 1996; Dahlberg, Toal, & Behrens, 1998; Howell, 1995), but regardless of the instrument used, it is necessary to assess and treat childhood problems early. In Larry's case, early comprehensive assessment might have allowed a practitioner to investigate possible child maltreatment, an event that is strongly correlated with many youth behavior problems (Smith & Thornberry, 1995; Widom, 1989; Zingraff et al., 1993). Here the Division of Family Services intervened with the family only after Larry had had numerous referrals to family court.

Larry's antisocial behavior as early as age 9, when he received his first court referral, reveals that he was no longer completely within the sphere of parental or school influence. Early antisocial behavior is a clear indicator of instability in the home environment and a lack of parental direction. Both these risk factors were evident in Larry's social history. The course of Larry's delinquent behaviors is consistent with research suggesting that early childhood intervention is critical to better adolescent outcomes (Loeber, 1996; McCord & Ensminger, 1995).

Another risk factor for Larry is his lack of bonding to school. It is apparent from his absences that Larry had lost interest in school. His school failure and lack of attachment to the school experience are likely associated with his criminal activity. It is not known whether Larry felt alienated in school. He did respond positively to the boy's club experience, indicating that prosocial opportunities provided a structure for achieving positive outcomes. The strengths assessed from the boy's club experience may be useful information.

Larry illustrates the complexity of working with delinquent and violent adolescents. The goals of all treatment approaches were to help Larry change his antisocial behaviors and to decrease future involvement in the juvenile justice system. Unfortunately, family court systems are overcrowded and effective interventions are difficult to implement. In Larry's case, it was only after multiple referrals and adjudication that the court provided any comprehensive service. As Larry's case suggests, treatment plans for violent youths must be multifaceted, addressing a wide range of risk factors.

PROMISING PREVENTION AND TREATMENT PROGRAMS

Intervention Approaches

The greater the number of risk factors present, the greater the probability of involvement in delinquent or violent behavior (Institute of Medicine, 1994; Williams et al., 1997). Therefore, prevention and treatment strategies should be comprehensive in their approach, emphasizing risk reduction to achieve positive outcomes.

Current violence prevention and treatment programs use three approaches. The first is *universal preventive interventions*. These target an entire population in which individual risk has not been previously identified (Institute of Medicine, 1994). Universal interventions are attractive because the cost per individual is low and there is no stigmatizing effect on individuals. Risk factors such as poverty, laws and norms favorable to delinquency and violence, poor family management practices, and inadequate parenting skills can be minimized with this approach. Parent and social-skills training can be effective even without targeting a specific population (Institute of Medicine, 1994). Programs and policies that decrease poverty, improve policing, develop more effective educational systems, and reduce handgun availability are considered universal precautions (Loftin, McDowell, & Wiersema, 1993; Loftin, McDowell, Wiersema, & Cottey, 1991).

Selective preventive interventions target populations whose risk of problem behavior is higher than average. Such programs use intervention to minimize risks and enhance or increase protective factors.

Indicated preventive interventions target high-risk individuals who are considered to have a predisposition for delinquency or violence, those whose symptoms appear early but who have not yet initiated delinquent or violent acts. These are referred to as early interventions.

Ten "blueprint" programs were identified by OJJDP as being effective in preventing violence; all were successful at several sites. (For further information about OJJDP's Blueprint Violence Prevention Project publications or training and technical assistance program, contact the Center for the Study of Violence, Institute of Behavioral Science, University of Colorado at Boulder, Campus Box 442, Boulder, CO 80309-0442.) The programs were the Midwestern Prevention Project (Pentz et al., 1989), Big Brothers/Big Sisters, Functional Family Therapy (FFT) (Barton, Alexander, Waldron, Turner, & Warburton, 1985), Quantum Opportunities (Taggart, 1995), Life Skills Training, Multisystemic Therapy (Henggeler & Borduin, 1990), Nurse Home Visitation (Olds, Henderson, Chamberlin, & Tatelbaum, 1986; Olds, Henderson, Phelps, Kitzman, & Hanks, 1993; Olds, Henderson, Tatelbaum, & Chamberlin, 1988), Treatment Foster Care (Chamberlin, 1996, 1998), Bullying Prevention Program (Olweus, 1991), and Promoting Alternative Thinking Strategies (PATHS) (Greenberg, Kusche, Cook, & Quamma, 1995).

Although prevention and intervention efforts for gangs have not received the same level of evaluation, several programs seem promising. They include Gang Resistance Education and Training (G.R.E.A.T.) (Esbensen & Osgood, 1997); Crisis Intervention Services Project (CRISP) (Spergel, 1986); Gang Violence Reduction Program (Spergel & Grossman, 1996, 1997); Communities That Care (Hawkins & Catalano, 1992); the Boston Gun Project (Kennedy, Piehl, & Braga, 1996); and Aggression Replacement Training (ART) (Goldstein & Glick, 1994). In this section we review effective and promising approaches to preventing violence and reducing youth gang problems.

Nurse Home Visitation Program

To prevent violence, it is essential to disrupt developmental pathways that lead to aggressive behavior. Many serious and chronic offenders show signs of aggressive and antisocial behavior as early as preschool years (Loeber, 1990; Loeber et al., 1993; Loeber & Hay, 1996). The Prenatal and Early Childhood Nurse Home Visitation Program can be either a universal or a selected preventive intervention for parents, infants, and toddlers. The program is designed to help low-income first-time parents reduce risks associated with early delinquent and violent behaviors. The program was implemented in Elmira, New York; Memphis, Tennessee; and Denver, Colorado, and was assessed in randomized clinical trials.

Risk factors addressed by this program include adverse maternal health-related behaviors during pregnancy and neuropsychological deficits in children, child maltreatment, and impaired maternal life course (Olds et al., 1986). In the program, nurses visit low-income first-time mothers during pregnancy and until the child is two years old. The nurses work to improve the mothers' health, parenting skills, educational achievement, and employment (Olds, Hill, & Rumsey, 1998). (For further information about the nurse home visitation program, contact the Kempe Prevention Research Center for Family and Child Health, 1825 Marion Street, Denver, CO 80218.)

Several rigorous evaluative studies have shown that the nurse home visitation program reduces risks for early antisocial behaviors and prevents child maltreatment, maternal substance abuse, and maternal criminal involvement—all problems associated with delinquency and violence (Olds et al., 1997; Olds, Henderson, et al., 1998). Program participation has been shown to decrease perinatal difficulties and child maltreatment referrals while increasing birthweight and parental employment (Greenwood, Model, Rydell, & Chiesa, 1996; Olds et al., 1986).

Initially it may be difficult to see how the Nurse Home Visitation Program applies to youth violence and gang involvement. The aim of the program is to strengthen family management, which in turn decreases the likelihood that children in these families will become violent or join gangs (Howell, 1997). Program evaluations have identified long-term positive effects. A 15-year follow-up of the Elmira and Memphis programs revealed that children affected by the intervention displayed relatively few serious delinquent and violent behaviors (Olds et al., 1997; Olds, Henderson, et al., 1998).

An evaluation by the RAND Corporation supports the cost-effectiveness of this approach (Greenwood et al., 1996). It estimates that by the time children from high-risk families who participated in the nurse home visitation program reach age 15, the cost savings are four times the original investment because of reductions in crime, welfare expenditures, and health care costs (Greenwood et al., 1996; Karoly et al., 1998). This strategy is currently being replicated in six high-crime urban neighborhoods (Olds, Henderson, et al., 1998).

Multisystemic Family Therapy

Multisystemic therapy (MST) addresses serious chronic delinquency and violent offending by incorporating the theoretical concepts of a socioecological perspective (Henggeler & Borduin, 1990). MST is a selected preventive intervention focused on delinquents who have two or more arrests or who are at imminent risk of incarceration (Borduin et al., 1995; Henggeler, Melton, & Smith, 1992, Henggeler, Melton, Smith, Schoenwald, & Hanley, 1993). MST is a promising treatment and rehabilitation program for youths exhibiting serious and chronic delinquent and violent behaviors. It also appears to have promise for working with gang members, even though it has not specifically targeted gang-involved youths.

MST incorporates a socioecological perspective by examining multiple systems across school, peer, family, and neighborhood domains (Borduin et al., 1995). To reduce antisocial behaviors in older youths, MST uses family therapy and parent management training that incorporates a present-focused, action-oriented framework to address intrapersonal and systemic factors associated with delinquent and violent behaviors. A single therapist operates across these systems. MST consists of brief, intensive treatment sessions in home or community. (For a complete review of the procedures and protocols for MST, see Henggeler & Borduin, 1990.)

MST is one of the first clinical interventions addressing serious and violent offending that has been subjected to randomized trials. Compared with other treatment interventions, such as behavioral parent training, individual outpatient therapy, and routine community-based and juvenile justice services, outcomes for MST have been positive (Santos, Henggeler, Burns, Arana, & Meisler, 1995). MST is especially important because it is one of the few interventions that addresses serious and chronic delinquent and violent behaviors (Henggeler & Borduin, 1990; Henggeler et al., 1992, 1993).

Numerous clinical trials have compared MST to eclectic, individual, and insight-oriented therapy (Borduin et al., 1995). Families randomly assigned to MST showed greater adaptability and increased family cohesiveness compared to those receiving other interventions (Henggeler et al., 1992). A one-year follow-up comparing youths receiving MST with youths receiving routine juvenile justice services indicated that MST adolescents were less likely to be rearrested and spent fewer days incarcerated (Henggeler et al., 1992). These outcomes were maintained in a follow-up assessment four years later (Borduin et al., 1995).

Gang Prevention, Intervention, and Suppression Programs

Determining the best course of action for dealing with street gangs is not easy. Although there is still much to be learned about the origins, activities, and formation of gangs, many efforts have been made to address the gang problem. Two principal types of programs have been those aimed primarily at prevention and intervention and those implemented within the criminal and juvenile justice system aimed primarily at suppression and social control. We review several promising strategies of each type.

Gang Violence Reduction Program. In the Little Village area of Chicago, the Gang Violence Reduction Program incorporates suppression, social intervention, opportunities, and community coordination and mobilization approaches (Spergel & Grossman, 1996, 1997). It has two strategies: (1) targeted control of violent youth gang offenders via increased probation, police supervision, and suppression and (2) a wide range of social services and opportunities for targeted youths. The latter gives youths legitimate options for transition from antisocial to more prosocial behaviors. The Gang Violence Reduction Program is a coordinated effort of the police department, the University of Chicago, and community organizations, including churches, youth service and job placement agencies, and citizen groups.

Preliminary evaluation has been positive. Spergel and Grossman (1996, 1997), using a quasi-experimental community comparison design, found that the intervention was associated with a reduction in gang violence. Gang-motivated violence in the communities where the program had been implemented did increase, but by only 32 percent compared with 77 percent in control communities (Spergel & Grossman, 1996, 1997). There was also a reduction in drug selling and property-related crimes in experimental communities. The Little Village project has clearly had a positive effect on gang violence.

Communities That Care. The Office of Juvenile Justice and Delinquency Prevention has released the *Guide for Implementing the Comprehensive Strategy for Serious, Violent, and Chronic Juvenile Offenders* (Howell, 1995), which describes prevention and intervention strategies using an approach called Communities That Care (CTC) (Hawkins & Catalano, 1992). CTC is a structured process addressing such major risk factors for gang involvement as social disorganization, family disorganization, academic failure, commitment to delinquent peers, and early antisocial behaviors (Bjerregaard & Smith, 1993; Curry & Spergel, 1992; Kosterman et al., 1996).

The premise behind CTC is to prioritize risk factors and develop programs to reduce them in a community. It is a comprehensive model of risk reduction based on the social development model of delinquency (Hawkins & Catalano, 1992). CTC encourages communities to develop interventions on the basis of identified risk and protective factors. It has not yet been evaluated.

School-based programs. Discouraging youths from joining gangs is the most cost-effective approach to reduce gang-related crime and violence. Two school-based gang prevention and intervention curricula have been developed. Broader Urban Involvement and Leadership Development (BUILD) and the Gang Resistance Education and Training Program (G.R.E.A.T.) have consistently shown positive results (Esbensen & Osgood, 1997; Thompson & Jason, 1988).

BUILD addresses gang violence, substance abuse, gang recruitment strategies, consequences, and values clarification (Brewer, Hawkins, Catalano, & Neckerman, 1995). An evaluation of BUILD suggested that at-risk children receiving the curriculum were less likely to join a gang than children in a nonequivalent comparison group (Thompson & Jason, 1988).

The major intent of the G.R.E.A.T. program is to discourage middle school students from joining gangs (Esbensen & Osgood, 1997). Law enforcement officers teach a nine-week curriculum addressing such topics as victimization, cultural sensitivity and prejudices, conflict resolution, drug use and selling, and goal setting (Esbensen & Osgood, 1997). A recent evaluation found lower levels of gang affiliation, more positive attitudes regarding law enforcement officers, and more prosocial involvement among G.R.E.A.T. participants compared with a comparison group of youths not receiving the intervention (Esbensen & Osgood, 1997).

The Boston Gun Project. A final strategy attempted by many communities to decrease gang activities, crime, and violence is suppression. The Boston Gun Project is one such program that has been effective in decreasing gang violence and juvenile homicides (Kennedy et al., 1996). Its design was informed by an analysis of the city's youth and gang violence problem and the illicit gun market. Community "hot spots" were mapped to identify gang territories and homicides and to provide better understanding of gang activities and behaviors. The program then used gun reduction techniques to disrupt the gun market (Kennedy et al., 1996). This program has not yet had a full-scale evaluation, but preliminary evaluations indicate that this may be a promising approach to reducing gang-related violence (Kennedy et al., 1996).

CONCLUSION

Although there is clearly an extensive knowledge base identifying prevalence, etiology, and prevention and treatment approaches for delinquency, youth violence, and gangs, conspicuous gaps in knowledge and considerable challenges for practice remain.

Many current interventions are untested or have produced mixed results. More rigorous design and methodology will be needed to determine their effectiveness. Interventions have seldom been replicated across sites or evaluated across race, ethnicity, and gender lines. Only now is a major effort being made to develop and evaluate a comprehensive strategy for addressing delinquency, gangs, and youth violence.

Prevention and intervention studies are needed that are useful to practitioners. The new wave of research may be more useful if it is developed and implemented in collaboration with practitioners; such a strategy may overcome common difficulties with sustaining prevention and intervention efforts.

Finally, reasons for the overrepresentation of African American males in juvenile gangs need to be further examined, as do factors explaining racial and gender differences in the prevalence of and participation in gang membership and violent behavior.

Our review discusses several programs that have been effective in preventing or reducing gang involvement and violence. Practitioners who work with at-risk children and troubled adolescents should use interventions of established effectiveness and begin comprehensive prevention and intervention efforts when clients are very young.

REFERENCES

Ageton, S. S. (1983). *Sexual assault among adolescents.* Lexington, MA: Lexington Books.

Baker, R. L., & Mednick, B. R. (1984). *Influences of human development: A longitudinal perspective.* Boston: Kluwer-Nijhoff.

Barton, C., Alexander, J. F., Waldron, H., Turner, C. W., & Warburton, J. (1985). Generalizing treatment effects of functional family therapy: Three replications. *American Journal of Family Therapy, 13,* 16–26.

Battin, S. R., Hill, K. G., Abbott, R. D., Catalano, R. F., & Hawkins, J. D. (1998). The contribution of gang membership to delinquency beyond delinquent friends. *Criminology, 36,* 93–115.

Bjerregaard, B., & Smith, C. (1993). Gender differences in gang participation, delinquency, and substance use. *Journal of Quantitative Criminology, 9,* 329–355.

Borduin, C. M., Mann, B. J., Cone, L. T., Henggeler, S. W., Fucci, B. R., Blaske, D. M., & Williams, R. A. (1995). Multisystemic treatment of serious juvenile offenders: Long-term prevention of criminality and violence. *Journal of Consulting and Clinical Psychology, 63,* 569–587.

Brennan, P., Mednick, S., & Kandel, E. (1991). Congenital determinants of violent and property offending. In D. Pepler & K. H. Rubin (Eds.), *The development and treatment of childhood aggression* (pp. 81–92). Hillsdale, NJ: Lawrence Erlbaum.

Brewer, D. D., Hawkins, J. D., Catalano, R. F., & Neckerman, H. J. (1995). Preventing serious, violent, and chronic offending: A review of evaluations of selected strategies in childhood, adolescence, and the community. In J. G. Howell, B. Krisberg, J. D. Hawkins, & J. Wilson (Eds.), *Sourcebook on serious, violent, and chronic juvenile offender* (pp. 61–141). Thousand Oaks, CA: Sage Publications.

Browning, K., & Loeber, R. (1999). *Highlights of findings from the Pittsburgh Youth Study: OJJDP Fact Sheet #5.* Washington, DC: U.S. Department of Justice, Office of Juvenile Justice and Delinquency Prevention.

Butts, J. A., Snyder, H. N., Finnegan, T. A., Aughenbaugh, A. L., Tierney, N. J., Sullivan, D. P., Poole, R. S., Sickmund, M. H., & Poe, E. C. (1994). *Juvenile court statistics—1991*. Pittsburgh: National Center for Juvenile Justice, Office of Juvenile Justice and Delinquency Prevention.

Catalano, R. F., & Hawkins, J. D. (1996). The social development model: A theory of antisocial behavior. In J. D. Hawkins (Ed.), *Delinquency and crime: Current theories* (pp. 149–197). New York: Cambridge University Press.

Chamberlin, P. (1996). Intensified foster-care: Multi-level treatment for adolescents with conduct disorders in out-of-home care. In E. D. Hibbs & P. S. Jensen (Eds.), *Psychosocial treatments for child and adolescent disorders: Empirically based strategies for clinical practice* (pp. 475–497). Washington, DC: American Psychological Association.

Chamberlin, P. (1998). *Treatment foster care*. Washington, DC: U.S. Department of Justice, Office of Justice Programs, Office of Juvenile Justice and Delinquency Prevention.

Chesney-Lind, M., Rockhill, A., Marker, N., & Reyes, H. (1994). Gangs and delinquency: Exploring police estimates of gang membership. *Crime, Law and Social Change, 21,* 210–228.

Chesney-Lind, M., & Shelden, R. G. (1998). *Girls, delinquency and juvenile justice*. New York: Wadsworth Publishing Company.

Curry, G. D., Ball, R. A., & Decker, S. H. (1996). Estimating the national scope of gang crime from law enforcement data. In C. R. Huff (Ed.), *Gangs in America* (pp. 21–36). Thousand Oaks, CA: Sage Publications.

Curry, G. D., Ball, R. A., & Fox, R. J. (1994). *Gang crime and law enforcement record-keeping* (Research in brief). Washington, DC: U.S. Department of Justice, National Institute of Justice.

Curry, G. D., & Decker, S. H. (1998). *Confronting gangs: Crime and community*. Los Angeles: Roxbury Publishing.

Curry, G. D., & Spergel, I. A. (1992). Gang involvement and delinquency among Hispanic and African American adolescent males. *Journal of Research in Crime and Delinquency, 29,* 273–291.

Dahlberg, L. L., Toal, S. B., & Behrens, C. B. (1998). *Measuring violence-related attitudes, beliefs, and behaviors among youths: A compendium of assessment tools*. Atlanta: Centers for Disease Control and Prevention, National Center for Injury Prevention and Control.

Decker, S. H., & Curry, G. D. (1999). Gang prevention and intervention with African American males. In L. E. Davis (Ed.), *Working with African American males: A guide to practice* (pp. 247–258). Thousand Oaks, CA: Sage Publications.

Denno, D. W. (1990). *Biology and violence: From birth to adulthood*. Cambridge, England: Cambridge University Press.

Elliott, D. S. (1994). Serious and violent offenders: Onset, developmental course, and termination (American Society of Criminology 1993 presidential address). *Criminology, 32,* 1–21.

Elliott, D. S., Huizinga, D., & Menard, S. (1989). *Multiple problem youth: Delinquency, substance use, and mental health problems*. New York: Springer.

Esbensen, F., & Osgood, D. W. (1997). *National evaluation of G.R.E.A.T.* (Research in brief). Washington, DC: U.S. Department of Justice, National Institute of Justice.

Fagan, J. (1996). Gangs, drugs, and neighborhood change. In C. R. Huff (Ed.), *Gangs in America* (2nd ed.) (pp. 39–74). Thousand Oaks, CA: Sage Publications.

Farrington, D. P. (1989). Early predictors of adolescent aggression and adult violence. *Violence and Victims, 4*, 79–100.

Farrington, D. P. (1991). Childhood aggression and adult violence: Early precursors and later-life outcomes. In D. Pepler & K. H. Rubin (Eds.), *The development and treatment of childhood aggression* (pp. 5–29). Hillsdale, NJ: Lawrence Erlbaum.

Federal Bureau of Investigation. (1993). *Crime in the United States 1992.* Washington, DC: U.S. Government Printing Office.

Fraser, M. W. (Ed.). (1997). *Risk and resilience in childhood. An ecological perspective.* Washington, DC: NASW Press.

Garbarino, J., DuBrow, N., Kostelny, K., & Pardo, C. (1992). *Children in danger: Coping with the consequences of community violence.* San Francisco: Jossey-Bass.

Goldstein, A. P., & Glick, B. (1994). *The prosocial gang: Implementing aggression replacement training.* Thousand Oaks, CA: Sage Publications.

Greenberg, M. T., Kusche, C.C.A., Cook, E. T., & Quamma, J. P. (1995). Promoting emotional competence in school-aged children: The effects of the PATHS curriculum. *Development and Psychopathology, 7*, 117–136.

Greenwood, P. W., Model, K. E., Rydell, C. P., & Chiesa, J. (1996). *Diverting children from a life of crime: Measuring costs and benefits.* Santa Monica, CA: Rand Corporation.

Hagedom, J. H. (1988). *People and folks: Gangs, crime, and the underclass in a rustbelt city.* Chicago: Lakeview Press.

Hawkins, J. D., Abbott, R., Catalano, R. F., & Gillmore, M. R. (1991). Assessing effectiveness of drug abuse prevention: Long-term effects and replication. In C. Leukefeld & W. Bukoski (Eds.), *Drug abuse prevention research: Methodological issues* (pp. 195–212), Washington, DC: U.S. Government Printing Office.

Hawkins, J. D., Arthur, M. W., & Catalano, R. F. (1995). Preventing substance abuse. In M. Tonry & D. P. Farrington (Eds.), *Building a safer society: Strategic approaches to crime prevention, Vol. 19: Crime and justice: A review of research* (pp. 343–427). Chicago: University of Chicago Press.

Hawkins, J. D., & Catalano, R. F. (1992). *Communities That Care: Action for drug abuse prevention.* San Francisco: Jossey-Bass.

Hawkins, J. D., Herrenkohl, T., Farrington, D. P., Brewer, D., Catalano, R. F., & Harachi, T. W. (1998). A review of predictors of youth violence. In R. Loeber & D. P. Farrington (Eds.), *Serious & violent juvenile offenders: Risk factors and successful interventions* (pp. 106–146). Thousand Oaks, CA: Sage Publications.

Henggeler, S. W., & Borduin, C. M. (1990). *Family therapy and beyond: A multisystemic approach to treating the behavior problems of children and adolescents.* Pacific Grove, CA: Brooks/Cole.

Henggeler, S. W., Melton, G. B., & Smith, L. A. (1992). Family preservation using multisystemic therapy: An effective alternative to incarcerating serious juvenile offenders. *Journal of Consulting and Clinical Psychology, 60*, 953–961.

Henggeler, S. W., Melton, G. B., Smith, L. A., Schoenwald, S. K., & Hanley, J. H. (1993). Family preservation using multisystemic treatment: Long-term follow-up to a clinical trial with serious juvenile offenders. *Journal of Child and Family Studies, 2*, 283–293.

Hill, K. G., Hawkins, J. D., Catalano, R. F., Kosterman, R., Abbott, R., & Edwards, T. (1996, November). *The longitudinal dynamics of gang membership and problem behavior: A replication and extension of the Denver and Rochester gang studies in Seattle.* Paper presented at the annual meeting of the American Society of Criminology, Chicago.

Hill, K. G., Hawkins, J. D., Catalano, R. F., Maguin, E., & Kosterman, R. (1995, November). *The role of gang membership in delinquency, substance use, and violent offending*. Paper presented at the annual meeting of the American Society of Criminology, Boston.

Hogh, E., & Wolf, P. (1983). Violent crime in a birth cohort: Copenhagen 1953–1977. In K. T. Van Dusen & S. A. Mednick (Eds.), *Prospective studies of crime and delinquency* (pp. 249–267). Boston: Kluwer-Nijhoff.

Howell, J. C. (Ed.). (1995). *Guide for implementing the comprehensive strategy for serious, violent, and chronic juvenile offenders*. Washington, DC: U.S. Department of Justice, Office of Juvenile Justice and Delinquency Prevention.

Howell, J. C. (1997). *Juvenile justice & youth violence*. Thousand Oaks, CA: Sage Publications.

Howell, J. C. (1998). Promising programs for youth gang violence prevention and intervention. In R. Loeber & D. P. Farrington (Eds.), *Serious & violent juvenile offenders: Risk factors and successful interventions* (pp. 284–312). Thousand Oaks, CA: Sage Publications.

Huff, C. R. (1998). *Comparing the criminal behavior of youth gangs and at-risk youths*. Washington, DC: U.S. Department of Justice, Office of Justice Programs.

Huizinga, D., Loeber, R., & Thornberry, T. (1993). *Urban delinquency and substance abuse*. Washington, DC: U.S. Department of Justice, Office of Juvenile Justice and Delinquency Prevention.

Institute of Medicine. (1994). *Reducing risks for mental disorders: Frontiers for preventive intervention research*. Washington, DC: National Academy Press.

Jankowski, M. (1991). *Islands in the street: Gangs and American urban society*. Berkeley, CA: University of California Press.

Kandel, E., & Mednick, S. A. (1991). Perinatal complications predict violent offending. *Criminology, 29*, 519–529.

Karoly, L. A., Everingham, S. S., Hoube, J., Kilburn, R., Rydell, C. P., Sanders, M., & Greenwood, P. W. (1998). *Investing in our children: What we know and don't know about the costs and benefits of early childhood interventions* (MR-898). Santa Monica, CA: RAND Corporation.

Kennedy, D. M., Piehl, A. M., & Braga, A. A. (1996). Youth violence in Boston: Gun markets, serious youth offenders, and a use-reduction strategy. *Law and Contemporary Problems* [Special issue], *59*, 147–196.

Klein, M. W. (1995). *The American street gang: Its prevalence and control*. New York: Oxford University Press.

Klinteberg, B. A., Anderson, T., Magnusson, D., & Stattin, H. (1993). Hyperactive behavior in childhood as related to subsequent alcohol problems and violent offending: A longitudinal study of male subjects. *Personality and Individual Differences, 15*, 381–388.

Kosterman, R., Hawkins, J. D., Hill, K. G., Abbott, R. D., Catalano, R. F., & Guo, J. (1996, November). *The developmental dynamics of gang initiation: When and why young people join gangs*. Paper presented at the annual meeting of the American Society of Criminology, Chicago.

Loeber, R. (1990). Development and risk factors of juvenile antisocial behavior and delinquency. *Clinical Psychology Review, 10*, 1–41.

Loeber, R. (1996). Developmental continuity, change, and pathways in male juvenile problem behaviors and delinquency. In J. D. Hawkins (Ed.), *Delinquency and crime: Current theories* (pp. 1–27). New York: Cambridge University Press.

Loeber, R., & Dishion, T. J. (1983). Early predictors of male delinquency: A review. *Psychological Bulletin, 94*, 68–99.

Loeber, R., & Farrington, D. P. (Eds.). (1998). *Serious & violent juvenile offenders: Risk factors and successful interventions.* Thousand Oaks, CA: Sage Publications.

Loeber, R., Farrington, D. P., Stouthamer-Loeber, M., Moffitt, T., & Caspi, A. (1998). The development of male offending: Key findings from the first decade of the Pittsburgh Youth Study. *Studies in Crime and Crime Prevention, 7*, 141–172.

Loeber, R., & Hay, D. F. (1996). Key issues in the development of aggression and violence from childhood to early adulthood. *Annual Review of Psychology, 48*, 371–410.

Loeber, R., Keenan, K., & Zhang, Q. (1997). Boys' experimentation and persistence in developmental pathways toward serious delinquency. *Journal of Child and Family Studies, 6*, 321–357.

Loeber, R., & Stouthamer-Loeber, M. (1986). Family factors as correlates and predictors of juvenile conduct problems and delinquency. In M. Tonry & N. Morris (Eds.), *Crime and justice: An annual review of research* (Vol. 7, pp. 219–339). Chicago: University of Chicago Press.

Loeber, R., Stouthamer-Loeber, M., Van Kammen, W. B., & Farrington, D. P. (1991). Initiation, escalation, and desistance in juvenile offending and their correlates. *Journal of Criminal Law and Criminology, 82*, 36–82.

Loeber, R., Wung, P., Keenan, K., Giroux, B., Stouthamer-Loeber, M., Van Kammen, W. B., & Maughan, B. (1993). Developmental pathways in disruptive child behavior. *Development and Psychopathology, 5*, 101–133.

Loftin, C., McDowell, D., & Wiersema, B. (1993). Evaluating effects of changes in gun laws. *American Journal of Preventive Medicine, 9* (Suppl.), 39–43.

Loftin, C., McDowell, D., Wiersema, B., & Cottey, T. J. (1991). Effects of restrictive licensing of handguns on homicide and suicide in the District of Columbia. *New England Journal of Medicine, 23*, 1615–1620.

Loney, J., Kramer, J., & Milich, R. (1983). The hyperkinetic child grows up: Predictors of symptoms, delinquency, and achievement at follow-up: Birth and childhood cohorts. In S. A. Mednick, M. Harway, & K. M. Finello (Eds.), *Handbook of longitudinal research* (Vol. 1, pp. 426–447). New York: Praeger.

Maguin, E., Hawkins, J. D., Catalano, R. F., Hill, K., Abbott, R., & Herrenkohl, T. (1995, November). *Risk factors measured at three ages for violence at age 17–18.* Paper presented at the American Society of Criminology, Boston.

Maguin, E., & Loeber, R. (1996). Academic performance and delinquency. In M. Tonry (Ed.), *Crime and justice: A review of research* (Vol. 20, pp. 145–264). Chicago: University of Chicago Press.

Maguire, K., Pastore, A. L., & Flanagan, T. J. (Eds.). (1993). *Sourcebook of criminal justice statistics 1992.* Washington, DC: U.S. Department of Justice, Bureau of Justice Statistics.

Matsueda, R. L., & Heimer, K. (1997). Race, family structure, and delinquency: A test of differential association and social control theories. *American Sociological Review, 52*, 826–840.

Maxson, C. L., Woods, M., & Klein, M. W. (1996). Street gang migration: How big a threat? *National Institute of Juvenile Justice Journal, 230,* 26–31.

McCord, J., & Ensminger, M. (1995, November). *Pathways from aggressive childhood to criminality.* Paper presented at the American Society of Criminology, Boston.

McCord, W., McCord, J., & Zola, I. K. (1959). *Origins of crime: A new evaluation of the Cambridge-Somerville Youth Study.* New York: Cambridge University Press.

Mednick, S. A., & Kandel, E. S. (1988). Congenital determinants of violence. *Bulletin of the American Academy of Psychiatry and the Law, 16,* 101–109.

Miller, W. B. (1975). *Violence by youth gangs and youth groups as a crime problem in major American cities.* Washington, DC: U.S. Government Printing Office.

Miller, W. B. (1982). *Crime by youth gangs and groups in the United States.* Washington, DC: U.S. Department of Justice, National Institute of Juvenile Justice and Delinquency Prevention.

Moffitt, T. E. (1993). Adolescence-limited and life-course-persistent antisocial behavior: A developmental taxonomy. *Psychological Review, 100,* 674–701.

Office of Juvenile Justice and Delinquency Prevention. (1997). *Highlights of the 1995 National Youth Gang Survey, Fact Sheet #63.* Washington, DC: U.S. Department of Justice.

Olds, D. L., Eckenrode, J., Henderson, C.C.R., Kitzman, H., Powers, J., Cole, R., Sidora, K., Morris, P., Pettitt, L., & Luckey, D. (1997). Long-term effects of home visitation on maternal life course and child abuse and neglect: 15-year follow-up of a randomized trial. *JAMA, 278,* 637–643.

Olds, D. L., Henderson, C.C.R., Chamberlin, R., & Tatelbaum, R. (1986). Preventing child abuse and neglect: A randomized trial of nurse home visitation. *Pediatrics, 78,* 78.

Olds, D. L., Henderson, C.C.R., Cole, R., Eckenrode, J., Kitzman, H., Luckey, D., Pettitt, L., Sidora, K., Morris, P., & Powers, J. (1998). Long-term effects of nurse home visitation on children's criminal and antisocial behavior: 15-year follow-up of a randomized trial. *JAMA, 280,* 1238–1244.

Olds, D. L., Henderson, C.C.R., Phelps, C. C., Kitzman, H., & Hanks, C. C. (1993). Effects of prenatal and infancy nurse home visitation on government spending. *Medical Care, 31,* 155–174.

Olds, D. L., Henderson, C.C.R., Tatelbaum, R., & Chamberlin, R. (1988). Improving the life course development of socially disadvantaged mothers: A randomized trial of nurse home visitation. *American Journal of Public Health, 78,* 1436–1445.

Olds, D., Hill, P., & Rumsey, E. (1998). Prenatal and early childhood nurse home visitation. *Juvenile Justice Bulletin.* Washington, DC: U.S. Department of Justice, Office of Juvenile Justice and Delinquency Prevention.

Olweus, D. (1977). Aggression and peer acceptance in adolescent boys: Two short-term longitudinal studies of rating. *Child Development, 48,* 1301–1313.

Olweus, D. (1991). Bully/victim problems among schoolchildren: Basic facts and effects of a school based intervention program. In D. J. Pepler & K. H. Rubin (Eds.), *The development and treatment of childhood aggression* (pp. 411–448). Hillsdale, NJ: Lawrence Erlbaum.

Paschall, M. J. (1996, June). *Exposure to violence and the onset of violent behavior and substance use among black male youth: An assessment of independent effects and psychosocial mediators.* Paper presented at the Society for Prevention Research, San Juan, Puerto Rico.

Patterson, G. R., & Dishion, T. J. (1985). Contributions of families and peers to delinquency. *Criminology, 23,* 63–77.

Patterson, G. R., & Stouthamer-Loeber, M. (1984). The correlation of family management practices and delinquency. *Child Development, 55,* 1299–1307.

Pentz, M. A., MacKinnon, D. P., Flay, B. R., Hansen, W. B., Johnson, C. A., & Dwyer, J. H. (1989). Primary prevention of chronic diseases in adolescence: Effects of the Midwestern Prevention Project on tobacco use. *American Journal of Epidemiology, 130,* 713–724.

Reiner, I. (1992). *Gangs, crime and violence in Los Angeles: Findings and proposals from the District Attorney's Office.* Arlington, VA: National Youth Gang Information Center.

Reiss, A. J., & Roth, J. A. (Eds.). (1993). *Understanding and preventing violence.* Washington, DC: National Academy Press.

Robins, L. N. (1991). Conduct disorder. *Journal of Child Psychology and Psychiatry and Allied Disciplines, 32,* 193–212.

Rutter, M. (1985). Resilience in the face of adversity: Protective factors and resistance to psychiatric disorder. *British Journal of Psychiatry, 147,* 598–611.

Sampson, R. J., & Laub, J. H. (1994). Urban poverty and the family context of delinquency: A new look at structure and process in a classic study. *Child Development, 65,* 523–540.

Sampson, R. J., & Lauritsen, J. (1994). Violent victimization and offending: Individual-, situational-, and community-level risk factors. In A. J. Reiss & J. A. Roth (Eds.), *Understanding and preventing violence, Vol. 3: Social influences* (pp. 1–115). Washington, DC: National Academy Press.

Santos, A. B., Henggeler, S. W., Burns, B. J., Arana, G. W., & Meisler, N. (1995). Research on field-based services: Models for reform in the delivery of mental health care to populations with complex clinical problems. *American Journal of Psychiatry, 152,* 1111–1123.

Sickmund, M., Snyder, H. N., and Poe-Yamagata, E. (1997). *Juvenile offenders and victims: 1997 update on violence.* Washington, DC: U.S. Department of Justice, Office of Juvenile Justice and Delinquency Prevention.

Smith, C., & Thornberry, T. P. (1995). The relationship between childhood maltreatment and adolescent involvement in delinquency. *Criminology, 33,* 451–481.

Smith, D. R., & Jarjoura, G. R. (1988). Social structure and criminal victimization. *Journal of Research in Crime and Delinquency, 25,* 27–52.

Spergel, I. (1986). The violent youth gang in Chicago: A local community approach. *Social Service Review, 60,* 94–131.

Spergel, I. (1990). Youth gangs: Continuity and change. In N. Morris & M. Tonry (Eds.), *Crime and justice: A review of research* (Vol. 12). Chicago: University of Chicago Press.

Spergel, I., & Grossman, S. F. (1996). *Evaluation of a gang violence reduction project: A comprehensive and integrated approach.* Chicago: University of Chicago, School of Social Service Administration.

Spergel, I., & Grossman, S. F. (1997). *Evaluation of Little Village Gang Violence Reduction Project.* Chicago: University of Chicago, School of Social Service Administration.

Stattin, H., & Magnusson, D. (1989). The role of early aggressive behavior in the frequency, seriousness, and types of later crime. *Journal of Consulting & Clinical Psychology, 57,* 710–718.

Taggart, R. (1995). *Quantum Opportunity Program.* Philadelphia: Opportunities Industrialization Centers of America.

Thompson, D. W., & Jason, L. A. (1988). Street gangs and preventive intervention. *Criminal Justice Behavior, 15,* 323–333.

Thornberry, T. P. (1996). *The contribution of gang members to the volume of delinquency.* Washington, DC: U.S. Department of Justice, Office of Juvenile Justice and Delinquency Prevention.

Thornberry, T. P. (1998). Membership in youth gangs and involvement in serious and violent offending. In R. Loeber & D. P. Farrington (Eds.), *Serious & violent juvenile offenders: Risk factors and successful interventions* (pp. 147–166). Thousand Oaks, CA: Sage Publications.

Thornberry, T. P., Huizinga, D., & Loeber, R. (1995). The prevention of serious delinquency and violence: Implications from the program of research on the causes and correlates of delinquency. In J. C. Howell, B. Krisberg, J. D. Hawkins, & J. J. Wilson (Eds.), *Sourcebook on serious, violent, and chronic juvenile offenders* (pp. 213–237). Thousand Oaks, CA: Sage Publications.

Tolan, P. H., & Thomas, P. (1995). The implications of age of onset for delinquency risk II: Longitudinal data. *Journal of Abnormal Child Psychology, 23,* 157–181.

U.S. Department of Justice, Federal Bureau of Investigation. (1965–93). *Uniform crime reports of the United States.* Washington, DC: U.S. Government Printing Office.

Widom, C. S. (1989). The cycle of violence. *Science, 244,* 160–166.

Williams, J. H. (1994). *Understanding substance use, delinquency involvement, and juvenile justice system involvement among African-American and European-American adolescents.* Unpublished doctoral dissertation, University of Washington, Seattle.

Williams, J. H., Ayers, C. D., Abbott, R., & Hawkins, J. D. (1998). *Understanding race and gender differences in adolescent delinquency and substance use initiation: Implications for the academic setting.* Unpublished manuscript.

Williams, J. H., Ayers, C. D., & Arthur, M. W. (1997). Risk and protective factors in the development of delinquency and conduct disorder. In M. W. Fraser (Ed.), *Risk and resilience in childhood: An ecological perspective* (pp. 140–170). Washington, DC: NASW Press.

Williams, J. H., Stiffman, A. R., & O'Neal, J. L. (1998). Environmental and behavioral factors associated with violence among urban African American youths. *Social Work Research, 22,* 3–13.

Williams, J. H., & Van Dorn, R. A. (1999a, January). *Predictors of male violence: An analysis of psychological, social, community, and family correlates across racial groups.* Paper presented at the Third Annual Conference, Society for Social Work and Research, Austin, TX.

Williams, J. H., & Van Dorn, R. A. (1999b, March). *Correlates contributing to involvement in violent behaviors among young adults.* Paper presented at the 45th Annual Program Meeting, Council on Social Work Education, San Francisco.

Williams, J. H., Van Dorn, R. A., Hawkins, J. D., Abbott, R., & Catalano, R. F. (1999). *Correlates contributing to involvement in violent behaviors among young adults.* Unpublished manuscript.

Wolfgang, M. E., Figlio, R. M., & Sellin, T. (1972). *Delinquency in a birth cohort.* Chicago: University of Chicago Press.

Yoshikawa, H. (1994). Prevention as cumulative protection: Effects of early family support and education on chronic delinquency and its risks. *Psychological Bulletin, 115,* 28–54.

Zimring, F. E. (1998). *American youth violence.* New York: Oxford University Press.

Zingraff, M. T., Leiter, J., Myers, K. A., & Johnson, M. C. (1993). Child maltreatment and youthful problem behavior. *Criminology, 31,* 173–202.

Part III

Future Directions

Chapter 9

Advancing Knowledge for Practice with Aggressive and Violent Youths

Jeffrey M. Jenson and Matthew O. Howard

S hootings at schools occurred in Littleton, Colorado, and Conyers, Georgia, while this book was being written. Public reaction was swift and strong. Congress passed legislation strengthening handgun controls. President Clinton initiated investigations of media violence and the influence of violent video games on youths. Parents and teachers began the slow process of reexamining their relationships with children and students. School officials and legislators questioned the wisdom of recent funding cuts in school-based mental health services. These national debates, local discussions, and policy actions were long overdue.

Youth violence may be more difficult to understand today than at any previous period of American history. As was noted in chapter 1 of this book, rates of violence among young people in the United States decreased during the latter half of the 1990s. These declines have been attributed to reductions in gang- and drug-related crime, a healthy economy, and to invigorated prevention and law enforcement (see, for example, Jenson & Howard, 1998).

Reductions in violent offending offer hope during a time when the nature of American youth violence is changing. Once common only in inner-city neighborhoods, violence has spread to rural and suburban neighborhoods and schools. New perpetrators and victims of youth violence do not fit the prevailing stereotypes of gang conflict on inner-city streets. Of course, all types of violence are deplorable. Yet recent acts of school violence have captured the nation's attention in an unprecedented fashion.

There are reasons for both optimism and concern about youth violence. Effective violence prevention programs have been identified in each chapter of this book. American schools, cities, and towns are trying out new prevention efforts every day, though many are yet to be rigorously evaluated. However, while great strides have been made in prevention, successful treatments for violent youths are sorely lacking. Further, little is known about the developmental processes that lead to persistent aggressive and violent behavior.

PRACTICE WITH HIGH-RISK AND VIOLENT YOUTHS

The authors of chapters in this book have identified a number of principles and strategies that are necessary to prevent and treat violent conduct. We begin with a discussion of clinical practice priorities and then note policy, research, and educational priorities.

Practice Priorities

Incorporation of what has been learned about the causes of youth violence.
Chapter 2 of this book reviewed individual, social, family, and community factors that increase the likelihood of violence among youths. Effective prevention and treatment programs address known risk factors for violence (Dryfoos, 1998). An emerging literature suggests that there are also factors that protect youths from violence (e.g., Fraser, 1997; J. D. Hawkins et al., 1998). In chapter 4 Jonson-Reid noted that most youths who are exposed to risk factors for violence never become violent. For some, resilience against violence is created through meaningful relationships with grandparents, mentors, or other adults. Activities in the church or community protect other high-risk youths (J. D. Hawkins et al., 1998). Unfortunately, little is currently known about the factors that moderate known risk factors for violence and increase the resiliency of youths. Additional research is needed to understand why many youths exposed to multiple risk factors never become violent.

Risk and protective factor frameworks provide useful summaries of the relationship between violence and individual, social, family, and community influences. Incorporating knowledge of such frameworks into practice is thus an important first step in preventing and treating youth violence. However, these models fail to specify the temporal order and developmental progression of such influences on violent behavior. Integrated theories explaining onset of, and sustained involvement in, youth violence are needed to inform developmentally appropriate practice approaches and interventions.

Few etiological explanations of youth violence specify the developmental processes that lead to violence. One exception is the work, both theoretical and applied, of Loeber and Hay (1994, 1997), who identified three pathways that lead to violence in boys: (1) *overt* behaviors such as bullying and fighting, (2) *covert* behaviors such as lying and burglary, and (3) *authority conflict,* represented by truancy and running away. The specification and onset of behaviors that are typical of youths on each of these paths may give practitioners clues about the nature and timing of intervention. For example, if bullying in the early grades increases the risk for violence during adolescence, early prevention efforts should work to reduce school-related bullying. Similarly, if aggressive boys are often in conflict with teachers or other adults, they may need cognitive training to improve their social and problem-solving skills.

The social development model, a theory frequently used to explain adolescent drug abuse, is also helpful in understanding the developmental processes that lead to violence (Catalano & Hawkins, 1998). An integration of social control (Hirschi, 1969) and social learning (Bandura, 1986) theories, this model posits that violence is the product of weak bonds to parents and teachers, limited prosocial opportunities, and inadequate social, behavioral, and cognitive skills. Catalano and Hawkins (1998) suggest that unskilled youths who fail to develop healthy bonds to parents or teachers and who lack opportunities to be successful at school or in the community are at elevated risk for violence during adolescence.

Theories developed by Loeber and Hay (1997) and Catalano and Hawkins (1998) are useful in practice because they provide guidelines for violence prevention and treatment activities, though additional study is necessary to understand how factors associated with violence interact. Practitioners should take into account lessons learned from empirically tested theories of youth violence as they select interventions for high-risk or violent youths.

Systematic assessments of aggression and violence in all high-risk and violent youths. In chapter 3 of this book, Macgowan identified instruments that are useful in assessing violence. He strongly encouraged practitioners to use assessment tools when intervening with high-risk or violent youths. Too often in youth service organizations, the assessment of propensity toward violence is sporadic when it should be routine. Though evaluation results do not guarantee accurate prediction of future violent acts, systematic, rigorous assessment does alert practitioners to potential warning signals. Culturally relevant assessment instruments should be used whenever possible.

Assessment must consider evidence of childhood maltreatment of adolescent perpetrators. Jonson-Reid stated in chapter 4 that maltreatment during childhood may lead to a repeating cycle of violence when child victims become adolescents and young adults. Other investigators (for example, Garbarino, 1999) have found that maltreatment increases the risk for acting out, aggression, and violence during adolescence.

The overlap of violence, substance abuse, and mental health problems also warrants consideration. In chapter 7 of this book, Moran and Jenson reviewed evidence supporting a reciprocal relationship between substance abuse and violence. Assessment of aggression and violence must look at indicators of substance abuse. Reliable instruments to assess adolescent substance abuse are readily available (Martin & Winters, 1998).

School violence in 1998 and 1999 precipitated an interest in understanding the relationship between mental health problems and aggression. Young perpetrators in Littleton, Colorado, and Conyers, Georgia, had experienced episodic depression (Cloud, 1999). Mental health problems were also evident among perpetrators of earlier school shootings in Springfield, Oregon; West Paducah, Kentucky; and Jonesboro, Arkansas (Bragg, 1998; Cloud, 1999).

The influence of mental health disorders on violent youth behavior is poorly understood. Several studies have reported a significant overlap between mental disorders, substance abuse, and delinquency among seriously and chronically delinquent youths (Huizinga & Jakob-Chien, 1998; Jenson & Potter, 1999; Timmons-Mitchell et al., 1997). However, the causal relationships between mental disorders and youth violence have seldom been studied. Collaborative investigations between practitioners and researchers are needed to develop reliable mental health assessment protocols.

Proven prevention programs in schools, families, and communities. The authors of chapters 4 through 8 identified promising programs for reducing the violence associated with child abuse; violence committed by girls, by substance-abusing youths, and by gang members; and violence in schools. These programs, often quite different in scope and purpose, share common elements. Successful prevention programs do the following:

- Use knowledge of theory in program design and implementation.
- Target known risk and protective factors.
- Involve parents, teachers, and the community in intervention.
- Use culturally relevant and gender-specific curricula and training materials.
- Adjust program content for developmental changes in adolescents.
- Engage youths in active participation by teaching appropriate skills and responses to deal with anger or frustration.
- Provide intensive services, followed by frequent booster sessions.

Practitioners and administrators adopting new prevention programs should be aware of these elements.

Development of effective treatment approaches for violent youths. Treating violent youths poses significant challenges for practitioners. Violent youths often have extensive criminal backgrounds and years in the juvenile justice system. Low motivation to change and inadequate parental support often render such conventional treatments as group therapy and counseling ineffective. As Williams and Van Dorn discussed in chapter 8, treatment programs for violent youths have yielded less positive findings than prevention programs. Although violent youths often show positive gains while in treatment, they fail to maintain the changes after treatment is terminated.

Several effective treatment programs were reviewed in this book. Effective treatments ensure frequent contact between youths and practitioners, acknowledge the need for long-term treatment, and use interdisciplinary approaches to treating violence. Multisystemic therapy (MST) represents one such treatment effort (Henggeler, Cunningham, Pickrel, Schoenwald, & Brondino, 1996). In MST social workers, juvenile justice staff, family therapists, substance abuse counselors, and other professionals work collaboratively to reduce violence and antisocial behavior among serious delinquents. MST has reduced violence in controlled studies of adjudicated youths (see, for example, Henggeler et al., 1996). Potter noted in chapter 5 of this book that MST is one of the few programs that has shown positive outcomes for aggressive girls.

Garbarino (1999) suggests that exposing violent offenders to calm and stable environments may be critical in rehabilitating adolescents. Youths who experience violence early in childhood often fail to develop trusting relationships with adults; emerging programs that instill empathy in order to reduce the tendency of perpetrators to depersonalize violence should be evaluated (Garbarino, 1999).

Culturally relevant and gender-specific interventions for high-risk and violent youths. Most violence prevention and treatment programs, being designed for Caucasian youths, fail to consider the unique needs of youths in other ethnic groups. Moran and Jenson described a promising program tailored to meet the developmental and social needs of American Indian youths in chapter 7. Potter made a strong case for gender-specific programs for girls in chapter 5. More efforts of this type are needed. To be effective, clinical strategies must be sensitive to ethnicity and gender. Policy directives necessary to implement effective prevention and treatment strategies are discussed next.

Policy Priorities

Effective interventions are based on policies that promote best practices with high-risk and violent youths. Here are some clear priorities.

A continuum of prevention, early intervention, and long-term treatment services for high-risk and violent youths. Policies to reduce violence must enhance program development across a continuum of prevention, early intervention, and treatment services. In chapters 7 and 8, the authors emphasize the importance of teaching young children appropriate ways to deal with anger and conflict. Components of effective prevention programs were described by Avi Astor and colleagues in chapter 6 and by Potter in chapter 5. Policymakers should place a high priority on funding effective violence prevention programs in family, school, and neighborhood settings.

There are many different developmental trajectories leading to violent behavior. Some youths display violent tendencies early in childhood; others become violent during their middle-school or high school years. Thus, a comprehensive approach to reducing youth violence must range from early interventions targeting middle-school children to long-term treatments for older adolescents. Rehabilitation of the nation's most violent youths requires a long-term commitment from law enforcement, juvenile justice, and professions such as social work.

Parent and community involvement in solutions to youth violence. Effective prevention and treatment efforts involve parents and community leaders. Public policies should encourage parents to be active partners in school- and community-based programs. Parent training programs, support groups, parent involvement in school, and parent-based organizations are among the promising strategies identified by authors in this book.

Efforts to involve community members in violence prevention and treatment are in their infancy. One promising community violence reduction program discussed by Moran and Jenson in chapter 7 is Communities That Care (J. D. Hawkins & Catalano, 1992). Communities That Care requires community leaders to systematically assess both risk and protective factors for youth violence in their towns and cities, and then to select programs that target the community's most prevalent risk and protective factors. The model is being evaluated in five states (personal communication with J. D. Hawkins, professor and director, Social Development Research Group, University of Washington, December 6, 1998).

Policies to protect youths from exposure to violence. The average young person in the United States is exposed each year to countless acts of violence on television and in motion pictures. Chapter 2 summarized studies that examined the relationship between exposure to violence on television and aggressive behavior. The evidence is clear: Viewing violence is associated with increased levels of aggression in adolescents. Policies are needed to help the entertainment industry regulate violence in television and films. Ironically, television has the potential to be one of the most effective ways to send positive messages about healthy development to American youths. Policymakers should explore the creation of a national television campaign against violence and stricter monitoring of violence in motion pictures.

Point-and-shoot video games are another source of media violence commonly experienced by young people. Anecdotal evidence (Garbarino, 1999) suggests that youths who play games in which they actually hold a gun and shoot "people" on screen experience decreased inhibition of violence. Further studies are needed to understand the relationship between exposure to violent video games and actual participation in aggressive behavior.

Reduction of youth access to handguns and other weapons. Comparative studies of youth violence indicate that availability of weapons contributes to high rates of youth violence in the United States (Zimring, 1998), yet restrictions on gun sales are hotly contested. Lobbying by organizations like the National Rifle Association (NRA) has made it difficult for antigun supporters to pass legislation requiring stricter regulation of handguns. A recent example of the NRA's opposition to gun control comes from Colorado. The NRA's 1999 national convention was scheduled for Denver less than two weeks after the fatal shootings at Columbine High School in nearby Littleton. Despite pleas to cancel the convention out of respect for the victims and their families, the NRA met as planned, though convention activities were cut back. The organization issued a statement expressing sympathy for the victims of the shootings but suggested that guns were not the source of the tragedy at Columbine High.

Gun control and the right to bear arms are issues of significant historical contention in the United States. Many citizens believe that any infringement on their right to purchase or carry a weapon is a constitutional violation. Others believe that it is only logical that a civilized country would limit the purchase of weapons. Garbarino (1999) summarizes this complicated relationship between guns and violence in the United States, observing that

> The relation between availability of guns and homicide leads to at least one important conclusion: It requires a highly controlled and healthy society to live with guns in its midst and not end up with people using those guns against other members of that society. The pervasive societal toxicity of American life, coupled with our strong individualist impulse, makes us a bad risk when it comes to widespread availability of guns. (p. 201)

Communities can reduce the number of handguns within their borders. The Boston Gun Project has been successful in enforcing legislation that restricts youth access to firearms and in educating adolescents about the consequences of using guns to settle disputes. In 1996 not a single person under 18 years old was killed by a handgun in Boston (Garbarino, 1999).

Increased funding for school-based mental health and social work services. During the 1990s mental health and social work services were reduced or eliminated in many American public schools. Recent school shootings reinforce the need for school-based counselors and supportive school services. The perpetrators in Littleton were isolated youths who became defiant toward their school and classmates. Counselors at the school, overwhelmed with student and teacher requests, were only vaguely familiar with their antisocial posturing.

No one is certain that additional mental health experts would have prevented the shootings at Columbine High School, but mental health specialists and social workers do provide important services to high-risk and troubled youths in school settings.

Research Priorities

Several authors have outlined research priorities for advancing knowledge of youth violence.

The developmental processes related to the onset of violence. In chapter 2 we called for studies examining factors associated with the onset of violence. We reiterate the need for such studies here. Violence is a complex behavior caused by individual, family, social, biological, and environmental factors. Longitudinal studies are needed to identify reciprocal influences on violence and to build accurate predictive models.

Comparative studies of the likelihood of violent behavior among different ethnic groups. Most etiological explanations of violence are based on studies of Caucasian youths. Many theories fail to consider the interaction of ethnicity with broader environmental or economic factors (D. F. Hawkins, Laub, & Lauritsen, 1998). Studies are needed to clarify the role of culture and ethnicity in youth violence.

Aggression and youth violence among girls and young women. Potter noted in chapter 5 that nearly all violence research has been conducted with males. Little is known about differences between boys and girls in causal factors for violence. Studies about how violence develops in girls are needed to inform prevention and treatment efforts with young women.

Longitudinal investigations of the effectiveness of violence prevention and treatment programs. Massive amounts of federal and state funding are allocated to violence prevention each year, yet funding sources rarely require programs to evaluate their long-term outcomes. Systematic evaluations of violence prevention and treatment programs should be routine, as should data collection to assess the impact of programs.

Elliott and associates at the Center for the Study and Prevention of Violence have demonstrated the utility of evaluating interventions to prevent or treat violence. Reviewing such programs across the United States, Elliott (1998) found 10 that reported positive long-term outcomes for youths. Several of these were described in chapters 7 and 8.

A national interdisciplinary social work research center to address youth violence. A national research center, similar to social work research centers funded by the National Institute of Mental Health (Austin, 1998), should be created to coordinate research on youth violence, especially studies examining the etiology, prevention, and treatment of violence; longitudinal assessments of the onset of violence; and applied studies of program effectiveness.

Educational Priorities

Social work's long-standing commitment to addressing the contextual factors related to individual and social problems is an asset to developing new knowledge about youth violence. Educational priorities that build on this strength include the following.

Social work graduate concentrations or specialized fields of study in youth violence. Schools of social work should explore ways for graduate students to develop advanced practice skills in working with violent youths. Specialized concentrations devoted to youth violence should be considered in the second year of graduate study. To maximize learning, practicum placements in youth service agencies or violence prevention programs should be integrated with course content. Council on Social Work Education (CSWE) accreditation standards currently require students to complete a variety of courses across the curriculum during two years of graduate study. Schools should explore how to meet such standards while allowing students the opportunity to take concentrated course work in such substantive areas as youth violence.

University and community partnerships that target youth violence. In some cities schools of social work and community agencies have formed partnerships to address youth violence. The University of Chicago's Little Village project, discussed by Williams and Van Dorn in chapter 8, is an excellent example of the promise of combining community and educational resources to prevent youth violence. In the Bridge Project, the Graduate School of Social Work at the University of Denver collaborates with the Denver Public Housing Authority to provide violence prevention services to high-risk youths and families. Graduate students on field placements in public housing projects work with families to reduce risk factors associated with violence. University of Denver faculty members participate in a school-sponsored learning center at the Bridge to coordinate student learning and field experiences. Similar partnerships are found in schools of social work at Case Western Reserve University, Washington University, and the University of North Carolina at Chapel Hill.

Practice, policy, research, and educational priorities to address youth violence are summarized in Table 9-1.

CONCLUSION

American society has changed significantly during the past several decades. Alterations in parenting practices and family life, technological advancements

Table 9-1. **Summary of Recommendations to Address Youth Violence**

Practice Priorities

• Incorporate causes of youth violence in practice
• Systematically assess violent behavior in child welfare, mental health, and juvenile justice settings
• Implement empirically supported prevention programs
• Develop innovative and effective treatment programs
• Emphasize culturally relevant and gender-specific interventions for violent youths

Policy Priorities

• Support a continuum of prevention, early intervention, and treatment services
• Encourage parent and community involvement in finding solutions to youth violence
• Enhance policies that protect youths from exposure to media violence
• Reduce access to handguns and other weapons
• Increase mental health and social work services in school settings

Research Priorities

• Conduct studies to examine the developmental processes associated with violence
• Investigate the processes that increase or decrease the likelihood of violence among different ethnic groups
• Examine violence among girls and young women
• Conduct longitudinal studies of the effectiveness of violence prevention and treatment programs
• Create a national interdisciplinary social work research center to address youth violence

Educational Priorities

• Offer concentrations or specialized fields of study in youth violence
• Develop university and community partnerships that target youth violence

---

that expose youths to a variety of antisocial influences, and the pressure to be successful in school and in the community create considerable stress for young people. Most adolescents find effective ways to cope with daily demands and become healthy adults. Others experience frustration as a result of peer rejection and low self-esteem. Sadly, violence is sometimes the product of that frustration.

History reminds us that solutions to youth violence, as for all human problems, will not be easy. There is little consensus among elected officials or the public at large about the most effective way to curb violence. While some officials favor get-tough policies and punitive approaches to handling violent offenders, others argue for more rehabilitative programs. There is equally little agreement on gun control or the role that educational institutions should play in addressing youth violence.

A balanced approach that includes prevention programs for high-risk youths and sanctions, accountability, and rehabilitation for violent offenders is likely to be most successful in reducing youth violence. Prevention must be a critical component of the nation's efforts to reduce the early onset of aggressive behavior. Early intervention to interrupt the progression from antisocial to violent behavior should be offered in the mental health, child welfare, substance abuse, and juvenile justice systems. Finally, long-term treatments are necessary for youths with extensive histories of violent conduct.

This book reveals that there are many promising strategies and programs to reduce and treat youth violence. There is also a tremendous resolve among Americans to reduce interpersonal, family, school, and community violence. Social work practitioners, educators, and researchers should lead the way in addressing this critical social problem. There is no time to waste.

REFERENCES

Austin, D. M. (1998). *A report on progress in the development of research resources in social work.* Washington, DC: Institute for the Advancement of Social Work Research.

Bandura, A. (1986). *Social foundations of thought and action: A social-cognitive view.* Englewood Cliffs, NJ: Prentice-Hall.

Bragg, R. (1998, March 26). Arkansas boys held as prosecutors weigh options. *New York Times,* p. A1.

Catalano, R. F., & Hawkins, J. D. (1998). The social development model: A theory of antisocial behavior. In J. D. Hawkins (Ed.), *Delinquency and crime: Current theories* (pp. 149–197). New York: Cambridge University Press.

Cloud, J. (1999, May 31). Just a routine school shooting. *Time,* 34–38.

Dryfoos, J. (1998). *Safe passage.* New York: Oxford University Press.

Elliott, D. S. (1998). *Blueprint programs for violence prevention.* Boulder, CO: University of Colorado, Center for the Study and Prevention of Violence

Fraser, M. W. (1997). *Risk and resilience in childhood. An ecological perspective.* Washington, DC: NASW Press.

Garbarino, J. (1999). *Lost boys: Why our sons turn violent and how we can save them.* New York: Free Press.

Hawkins, D. F., Laub, J. H., & Lauritsen, J. L. (1998). Race, ethnicity, and serious juvenile offending. In R. Loeber & D. P. Farrington (Eds.), *Serious & violent juvenile offenders: Risk factors and successful interventions* (pp. 30–46). Thousand Oaks, CA: Sage Publications.

Hawkins, J. D., Catalano, R. F. (1992). *Communities That Care: Action for drug abuse prevention.* San Francisco: Jossey-Bass.

Hawkins, J. D., Herrenkohl, T., Farrington, D. P., Brewer, D., Catalano, R. F., & Harachi, T. W. (1998). A review of predictors of youth violence. In R. Loeber & D. P. Farrington (Eds.), *Serious & violent juvenile offenders: Risk factors and successful interventions* (pp. 106–146). Thousand Oaks, CA: Sage Publications.

Henggeler, S. W., Cunningham, P. B., Pickrel, S. G., Schoenwald, S. K., & Brondino, M. J. (1996). Multisystemic therapy: An effective violence prevention approach for serious juvenile offenders. *Journal of Adolescence, 19,* 47–61.

Hirschi, T. (1969). *Causes of delinquency.* Berkeley: University of California Press.

Huizinga, D., & Jakob-Chien, C. (1998). The contemporaneous co-occurrence of serious and violent juvenile offending and other problem behaviors. In R. Loeber & D. P. Farrington (Eds.), *Serious & violent juvenile offenders: Risk factors and successful interventions* (pp. 47–67). Thousand Oaks, CA: Sage Publications.

Jenson, J. M., & Howard, M. O. (1998). Youth crime, public policy, and practice in the juvenile justice system: Recent trends and needed reforms. *Social Work, 43,* 324–334.

Jenson, J. M., & Potter, C. (1999). *The co-occurrence of mental health and delinquency among adjudicated youth.* Unpublished manuscript. Graduate School of Social Work, University of Denver.

Loeber, R., & Hay, D. F. (1994). Developmental approaches to aggression and conduct problems. In M. Rutter & D. F. Hay (Eds.), *Development through life: A handbook for clinicians* (pp. 485–515). Oxford, England: Blackwell Scientific.

Loeber, R., & Hay, D. F. (1997). Key issues in the development of aggression and violence from childhood to early adulthood. *Annual Review of Psychology, 48,* 371–410.

Martin, C. S., & Winters, K. C. (1998). Diagnosis and assessment of alcohol use disorders among adolescents. *Alcohol, Health, and Research World, 22,* 95–105.

Timmons-Mitchell, J., Brown, C., Schulz, S. C., Webster, S. E., Underwood, L. A., & Semple, W. E. (1997). Comparing the mental health needs of female and male incarcerated juvenile delinquents. *Behavioral Sciences and the Law, 15,* 195–202.

Zimring, F. E. (1998). *American youth violence.* New York: Oxford University Press.

Index

Note: Material presented in tables and figures is indicated by *t* or *f* after page numbers.

About the Editors

Jeffrey M. Jenson, PhD, is professor and director of research in the Graduate School of Social Work at the University of Denver. His research interests include the etiology, prevention, and treatment of juvenile delinquency, youth violence, and substance abuse. He has published widely on topics of delinquency and violence, juvenile justice policy, adolescent substance abuse, and social work education; recent articles appear in *Criminal Justice and Behavior, Addictive Behaviors, Social Work,* and *Research on Social Work Practice.* Dr. Jenson is consulting editor to *Social Work Research* and the *Journal of Social Work Education* and a member of the editorial board of *Research on Social Work Practice.* He is also co-principal investigator of a longitudinal study examining the co-occurrence of mental health problems and delinquency among youths in the juvenile justice system.

Matthew O. Howard, PhD, is assistant professor in the George Warren Brown School of Social Work at Washington University in St. Louis. He was formerly research assistant professor in the Department of Psychiatry and Behavioral Sciences at the University of Washington and research associate professor in the Department of Psychiatry at Oregon Health Sciences University. He has published more than 50 articles relating to substance use, antisocial personality disorder, and empirically based social work practice. His research interests

258 About the Editors

include cognitive processes in substance dependence, inhalant abuse, and the etiology and treatment of alcohol and drug dependence in persons with anti-social personality disorder. Dr. Howard is on the editorial boards of the *Journal of Studies on Alcohol* and *Research on Social Work Practice* and received the 1999 Excellence in Teaching Award at the George Warren Brown School of Social Work.

About the Contributors

Ron Avi Astor, PhD, is assistant professor of social work and education at the University of Michigan. His research focuses on school violence and children's moral reasoning about violence. Dr. Avi Astor's research has been funded by the Fulbright Foundation, the National Academy of Education, the Spencer Foundation, the National Institute of Mental Health, the H. F. Guggenheim Foundation, and the Israeli government. Currently, he is examining how children think about issues of poverty and violence and how culture influences children's understanding and acceptance of violence. Dr. Avi Astor has published articles about mapping school violence and the role of school social workers in preventing violence.

Melissa Jonson-Reid, PhD, is assistant professor at the George Warren Brown School of Social Work at Washington University in St. Louis. Her research interests include the consequences of childhood exposure to violence and outcomes of child welfare and public school social work services. Recent publications addressing these topics appear in *Children and Youth Services Review* and *Aggression and Violent Behavior.*

Mark J. Macgowan, PhD, is assistant professor of social work at North Carolina State University, Raleigh. His research has focused on measurement development and testing and on evaluations of interventions to reduce aggression and violence. Recent publications have appeared in *Violence and Victims,* the *Journal of Social Service Research,* and *Research on Social Work Practice.* He is licensed as a clinical social worker in Florida and North Carolina and has had many years of direct practice experience working with aggressive and violent youths in clinical and juvenile justice settings in Canada and the United States.

Heather Ann Meyer, EdM, is a doctoral candidate in the combined education and psychology program, University of Michigan. Her research focuses on how children understand the context of the school as it relates to school violence. Her most recent work explores how teachers think about issues of gender and school violence.

James R. Moran, PhD, is professor and director of the doctoral program in the Graduate School of Social Work at the University of Denver and research associate at the National Center for American Indian and Alaska Native Mental Health Research, University of Colorado Health Sciences Center. A member of the Little Shell Chippewa tribe, he grew up in Montana near the Flathead reservation. Dr. Moran's primary research interest is alcohol use among urban American Indians. He is principal investigator of a study funded by the National Institute on Alcohol Abuse and Alcoholism to develop and evaluate an alcohol prevention program for urban American Indian youths.

Ronald O'Neal Pitner, MSW, is a doctoral candidate in the joint social psychology and social work PhD program at the University of Michigan. His research focuses on the process of stereotyping and violence. He has also examined the effect of culture on interpersonal practice.

Cathryn C. Potter, PhD, is assistant professor in the Graduate School of Social Work, University of Denver, and co-principal investigator of the Mental Health, Substance Use and Delinquency among Incarcerated Youth study, coinvestigator of the Programming for Female Offenders study, and principal investigator of the Child Welfare Training and Research Project. Dr. Potter's interests lie in developing and evaluating interventions for youths and families with multiple problems, including those in the child welfare, mental health, and juvenile justice systems.

Richard A. Van Dorn, MSW, is a doctoral student in social work at the University of North Carolina–Chapel Hill. His current research interests are the identification of risk and protective factors for adolescent delinquent and violent behaviors, and predictors of transitions from nonviolent to violent offending in adolescents. He received awards for his research on the trajectory of adolescent offending behavior from the Melissa Institute for Violence Prevention and Treatment in Miami, Florida, and the George Warren Brown School of Social Work at Washington University in St. Louis.

Lorelei Atalie Vargas is a doctoral student in administration and policy at the University of Michigan School of Education. She also works as a consultant and counselor for a gang intervention program (Project GRACE) in Detroit. Her research focuses on the educational experiences of gang-involved youths. Her most recent research explored teachers' perceptions of students in their classrooms who were gang members.

James Herbert Williams, PhD, is assistant professor of social work at the George Warren Brown School of Social Work at Washington University in St. Louis. He is currently examining risk and protective factors for childhood and adolescent antisocial behavior, racial disproportionality in juvenile justice, comorbidity of mental illness and violence in African American youths, predictors of transitions in adolescent from nonviolent to violent offending, and barriers to service use in high crime communities. He is on the editorial board of the *Journal of Applied Social Sciences*. Recent publications have appeared in *Social Work Research*, the *Journal of Quantitative Criminology*, the *Journal of Black Psychology*, *Research on Social Work Practice*, and the *Journal of Gay and Lesbian Social Services*.